Hugh Archibald Clarke

Pronouncing Dictionary of Musical Terms

Giving the Meaning, Derivation, and Pronunciation of Italian, German, French, and other words

Hugh Archibald Clarke

Pronouncing Dictionary of Musical Terms
Giving the Meaning, Derivation, and Pronunciation of Italian, German, French, and other words

ISBN/EAN: 9783337236571

Printed in Europe, USA, Canada, Australia, Japan

Cover: Foto ©Andreas Hilbeck / pixelio.de

More available books at **www.hansebooks.com**

PRONOUNCING DICTIONARY OF MUSICAL TERMS

GIVING THE

MEANING, DERIVATION, AND PRONUNCIATION IN PHONETIC SPELLING OF ITALIAN, GERMAN, FRENCH, AND OTHER WORDS; THE NAMES WITH DATE OF BIRTH AND DEATH AND NATIONALITY OF THE LEADING MUSICIANS OF THE LAST TWO CENTURIES

ENGLISH VOCABULARY, WITH EQUIVALENTS IN ITALIAN, GERMAN, AND FRENCH

A LIST OF THE MOST CELEBRATED OPERAS, WITH THE COMPOSERS' NAMES

BY

H. A. CLARKE, Mus. Doc.

PROFESSOR OF MUSIC, UNIVERSITY OF PENNSYLVANIA

PHILADELPHIA
THEODORE PRESSER CO.
1712 CHESTNUT STREET

COPYRIGHT, 1896, BY THEO. PRESSER

PREFACE

This Dictionary has been undertaken with the object of putting into the hands of every student of music, in convenient shape, a work in which may be found the meanings, derivations, and pronunciations of the English, Italian, German, and French words used in musical works; also the names, nationality, and dates of birth and death of the leading musicians of the eighteenth and nineteenth centuries.

A feature of especial value is the list of English words with their Italian, German, and French equivalents. The author's design has been to produce a useful work. He has therefore omitted many Greek and Latin terms which are never met with, except in obsolete treatises; the admission of such words would only serve to swell the size of the volume, without, in the least degree, adding to its value.

H. A. CLARKE.

DIRECTIONS FOR PRONUNCIATION.

All Italian, French, and German words are written out phonetically, on the following system:

A as in *far*, represented by *ah*.

The Continental *e* has the sound of *a* in *fare;* it is represented by *eh*.

The Continental *i* has the sound of *e* in *deer;* it is represented by *ee*.

The following vowel sounds have no equivalents in English: French *e*, when not accented, something like the vowel sound in *love*. German *ö* (*o* modified, or *Umlaut*) has nearly the same sound. German *ü* is about half-way between the sound of *o* in *love* and *e* in *deer*. *O* and *u* have the same sound as in English, the *u* sound being represented by *oo*, as in *cool*. Italian *ae* has the sound of long *i* in English. German *ä* is the equivalent of *a* in *air*. German *eu* is sounded like *oi*, as in *toil*.

The following consonantal sounds have no English equivalents: German hard guttural *ach* and soft guttural *ag*. The French sound of *j* is represented by *zh* as nearly as possible. The French nasals *an, en, in, on*, can be represented but very unsatisfactorily in English only by adding a final *g*.

Whenever *ch* is found it is to be sounded like *ch* in *chair*. *C* always has this sound in Italian when followed by *i* or *e*. The Italian *ch*, on the contrary, always has the sound of *k*, or *c* hard, and is thus represented. The Italian *zz* has the sound of *ts* or *ds*, and is thus represented.

With this explanation of the phonetic system adopted to represent the foreign sounds, it is believed that the reader will find no difficulty in acquiring their proper pronunciation.

PRONOUNCING DICTIONARY OF MUSIC TERMS

A

A. The 6th of the normal major scale; the 1st of the normal minor scale; the standard by which the orchestra is tuned, given by the oboe.

A, A (It. and Fr.) (*ah*). At, in, by, for, with.

A battuta (*bat-too'-ta*). By the beat.

A bene placito (*beh-neh plah-chee'-to*). At pleasure, without regard to time.

Alla breve (*breh-veh*). Same as above; also a rhythm of two in the measure, indicated by ₵. Alla breve time resembles 2/4 time in having but one accent in each measure. It was originally written with a breve in the measure, thus:—

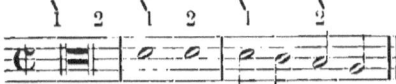

but as the breve is rarely used in modern music the whole note (semi-breve) is substituted with the direction: alla breve, *i. e.*, in the manner of music written with a breve in each measure. The following passage—written (1) alla breve, (2) 4/4, (3) 2/4—will exhibit the difference of accent between alla breve and 4/4 and its similarity to 2/4.

A or **Alla capella** (*cah-pel'-la*). In church style, *i. e.*, either without accompaniment or with the instruments in unison with the voices.

Abbott, Emma. Soprano; U. S. A. B. 1850; d. 1891.

A capriccio (*cah-pritch'-eo*). Capriciously; without regard to time in performance; without regard to form in construction.

A demi-jeu (*deh-mee-zheoo*). With half force or play. A direction to use half the power of the instrument, generally used of the organ.

A deux cordes (*doo-cord*). On two strings.

A deux mains (*doo-mang*). By or for two hands.

A deux temps (*doo-tahm*). In 2/4 time.

A la. In the manner of, as *a la chasse* (*shass*). Like a hunt; hunting song.

A mezza voce (It.) (*met-za vo-chee*). With half voice.

A piacere (*pee-ah-cheh'-reh*), or **Al piacer**, or **A piacimento** (*pee-ah-chee-men'-to*). At pleasure.

A poco a poco (It.). Little by little

A poco piu lento (It.). A little slower.

A poco piu mosso (It.). A little faster.

A punto (It.). Accurate, strict time.

A punto d'arco (It.). With the point of the bow.

A quatre mains (Fr.) (*katr-mang*). For four hands.

A quattro mani (It.) (*kwat-tro mah-nee*). For four hands.

A suo arbitrio (*soo-oh ar-bee'-tre-o*). At your will.

A tempo (*tem'-po*). In time. A direction to resume strict time after *Rall.* or *Rit.*, *q. v.*

A tempo giusto (*joos'-to*). In strict time.

A tempo rubato (*roo-bah'-to*). In stolen time, *i. e.*, retarding and hurrying the time irregularly.

A tres cordes (*tray*). On three strings.

Abbellimento (It.) (*ab-bel-lee-men'-to*). Embellishment.

Abbellitura (It.) (*ab-bellee-too'-ra*). Embellishment. Both are derived from—

Abbellire (*abbel-lee'-reh*). To ornament.

Abt, Franz (*apt, frants*). Song writer; Germany. B. 1819; d. 1885.

Abbreviation. A system frequently employed in music, by which a portion of a technical term is made to stand for the whole. The following is a list of the abbreviations in most common use; the explanation of each term may be found on reference to the words themselves in their proper places:—

Accel. Accel⁰	} Accelerando
Acc. Accom. Accomp.	} Accompaniment
Accres.	Accresciamento
Adg⁰ or ad⁶	Adagio
Ad l. Ad lib.	} Ad libitum
Affett⁰	Affettuoso
Affrett⁰	Affrettando
Ag⁰ Agit⁰	} Agitato
All⁰	Allegro
Allgtt⁰	Allegretto
All' ott. All' 8ᵛᵃ	} All' ottava
Al seg.	Al segno
And⁽ᵘ⁰⁾	Andantino
And⁽ᵗᵉ⁾	Andante
Anim⁰	Animato
Arc.	Coll arco, or arcato
Ard⁰	Ardito
Arp⁰	Arpeggio
A t. A tem. A temp.	} A tempo
Aug.	By Augmentation
B.	{ Bass (voice) / Bassoon / Contre bass
B. C.	Basso continuo
Brill.	Brillante
C. B.	Col basso
C. D.	Colla destra
C. S.	Colla sinistra
Cad.	Cadence
Cal.	Calando
Can.	Cantoris
Cant.	Canto
Cantab.	Cantabile
Cello	Violoncello
Cemb.	Cembalo
Ch.	Choir organ
Chal.	Chalameau
Clar.	Clarinet
Clar⁽ᵗᵗᵒ⁾	Clarinetto
Clar.	Clarino
Co. so.	Come sopra
Col C.	Col canto
Col ott⁽ᵃ⁾	Coll' ottava
Col. vo.	Colla voce
Con esp.	Con espressione
Cor.	Cornet or horn
Cres⁰ Cresc.	} Crescendo
C. S.	Colla sinistra
C. 8ᵛᵃ	Coll' ottava
C⁰ 1ᵐᵒ	Canto primo
Co. 1ᵐᵒ	Come primo
C⁽ᵗᵒ⁾	Concerto
D.	Destra, droite
D. C.	Da capo
Dec.	Decani
Decres.	Decrescendo
Delic.	Delicamente
Dest.	Destra
Diap.	Diapasons
Dim.	By diminution
Dim.	Diminuendo
Div.	Divisi
Dol.	Dolce
Dolcis.	Dolcissimo
Dopp. ped.	Doppio pedale
D. S.	Dal segno
Energ.	Energicamente
Espr. Espres.	} Espressivo
F. or for.	Forte
Fag.	Fagotto
Falset.	Falsetto
Ff. or Fff.	Fortissimo
Fl.	Flauto
F. O. F. Org.	} Full Organ
Forz. Fz.	} Forzando
G.	Gauche
G. O. G. Org. Gt.	} Great Organ
Gr.	Grand
Grand⁰	Grandioso
Graz⁰	Grazioso
Hauptw. Hptw. H. W.	} Hauptwerk
Haut.	Hautboy
H. C.	Haute contre
Intro.	Introduction
Inv.	Inversion
l..	Left
Leg.	Legato
Legg⁰	Leggiero
L. H.	Left Hand
Lo.	Loco
Luo.	Luogo
Lusing.	Lusingando
M. Main. Mano.	} Manual
Maest⁰	Maestoso
Magg.	Maggiore

Man.	Manuals
Manc.	} Mancando
Man^{do}	
Marc.	Marcato
M. D.	{ Mano diritta / Main droite / Mano destrâ
M. G.	Main gauche
M. M.	{ Maelzel's Metronome
M. M. ♩ = 92	{ The beat of a quarter-note is equal to the pulse of the pendulum of the Metronome said to be Maelzel's, with the weight set at 92.
M. P.	Mezzo piano
MS.	{ Manuscript or Mano sinistra
Men.	Meno
Mez.	Mezzo
Mf. or Mff.	Mezzo forte
Mod^{to}	Moderato
Mus. Bac.	Bachelor of Music
Mus. Doc.	Doctor of Music
M. V.	Mezzo voce
Ob.	Oboe, or Hautbois
Obb.	Obbligato
Oberst.	Oberstimme
Oberw.	} Oberwerk
Obw.	
Oh. Ped.	Ohne Pedal
Org.	Organ
8va	} Ottava
8^a	
8va alta	Ottava alta
8va bas.	Ottava bassa
P.	Piano
Ped.	Pedal
Perd.	Perdendosi
P. F.	Piu forte
Piang.	Piangendo
Pianiss.	Pianissimo
Pizz.	Pizzicato
P'mo.	} Pianissimo
PP.	
PPP.	} Pianississimo
PPPP.	
1ma	Prima (volta)
1mo	Primo
4^{tte}	Quartet
5^{tte}	Quintet
Rall.	Rallentando
Raddol.	Raddolcendo
Recit.	Recitative
Rf., rfz., or rinf.	Rinforzando
R. H.	Right Hand
Ritar.	Ritardando
Riten.	Ritenuto
S.	Senza
𝄢	A Sign
Scherz.	Scherzando
2da	Seconda (volta)
2do	Secondo
Seg.	Segue
Sem.	} Sempre
Semp.	
7^{tt}	Septet
6^{tt}	Sestet
Sfz.	Sforzando
Sinf.	Sinfonia
Smorz.	Smorzando
S. Int.	Senza interruzione
S. S.	} Sensa sordini
S. sord.	
Sos.	} Sostenuto
Sos^t	
Spir.	Spiritoso
S. T.	Senza tempo
Stacc.	Staccato
St. Diap.	Stopped Diapason
String.	Stringendo
Sw.	Swell Organ
Sym.	Symphony
T.	{ Tenor, tutti, tempo, tendre
T. C.	Tre corde
Tem.	Tempo
Tem. 1°	Tempo primo
Ten.	Tenuto
Timb.	Timballes
Timp.	Timpani
Tr.	Trillo
Trem.	Tremolando
3°	Trio
Tromb.	Trombi
Tromb.	Tromboni
T. S.	Tasto solo
U.	Una
U. C.	Una corde
Unis.	Unisoni
V.	Voce
V.	Volti
Va.	Viola
Var.	Variation
Vello	Violoncello
Viv.	Vivace
Vo.	
Vno.	} Violino
Viol°	
V. S.	Volti subito
Vⁿⁱ	} Violini
VV.	

There are other abbreviations employed in manuscript or printed music, the chief of which are as follows:—

In time, a dash with a figure above signifies the length of the pause in bars, e. g.:—

In notes, the trouble of writing a passage in full is saved by the use of abbreviations, e. g.:—

Written.

Played.

Written.

Played.

Written.

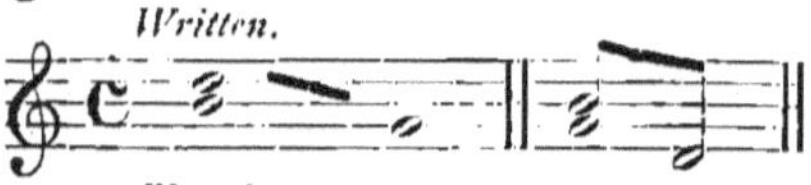

Played.

Written.

Played.

Repetition phrases are thus shortened:—

Abbreviations, by signs, of musical graces:—
The Turn.

Written.  *Sung.*

The back Turn,

Written.  *Sung.*

Passing shake,

Written.  *Sung.*

Beat,
Written. *Sung.*

Shake, *tr*
Sung.

Written. *Played.*

Written. *Played.*

Abgestossen (Ger.) (*ap-geh-stoss-en*) [from *abstossen*, to knock off]. Detached; staccato.

Absolute Music. Music independent of words, scenery, acting or "programme;" the highest class of instrumental music.

Accelerando (It.) (*at-chel-leh-ran-do*). Hastening the movement (tempo).

Accent. The stress which recurs at regular intervals of time. Its position is indicated by upright strokes called *bars*. The first note inside a bar is always accented. When the bars contain more than one group of notes, which happens in compound time, other accents of lesser force occur on the first note of each group; these are called *secondary* or *subordinate* accents, whilst that just inside the bar is termed the *primary* or *principal* accent. Other accents can be produced at any point by the use of the sign ⸺ or *sf*. The throwing of the accent on a normally unaccented portion of the bar is called *syncopation*. A proper grouping of accents will produce rhythm. It is considered a fault if an accented musical note falls on a short syllable.

Acciacatura (It.) (*at-cheea-ca-too'-ra*). A short grace note, written thus: takes the place in the harmony of the note it precedes; is played rapidly. [From **Acciaccare** (*at-chee-ac-ca'-reh*), to crush or jam together.]

Accidentals. All signs for raising or depressing letters that are not found in the signature.

Accolade (Fr.) (*ac-co-lahd'*). A brace enclosing two or more staves. [From Latin *ad*, to; *collum*, the neck.] To embrace.

Accompagnamento (It.) (*ac-com-pan-ya-men-to*), **Accompagnement** (Fr.) (*ac-com-pang-mongt*), **Accompaniment.** The separate part or parts that accompany a solo or

Accompaniment chorus; generally instrumental, but a vocal solo with vocal accompaniment is frequently met with.

Accompaniment ad libitum (Lat.). An accompaniment that may be omitted without injury to the musical effect.

Accompanist or Accompanyist. One who plays or sings an accompaniment to a solo.

Accoppiato (It.) (*ac-cop-pee-ah'-to*). Coupled or joined together.

Accord (Fr.). A chord; agreement in pitch. Mode of tuning a string instrument.

Accordatura (It.) (*ac-cor-da-too'-ra*). The mode of tuning string instruments, as violin, guitar, etc.

Accordion. A small, portable instrument with free reeds.

Achtel (Ger.). Eighth-note.

Achtel Pause (*pow-ze*). Eighth-rest.

Acoustics (*a-koos-tics*) [from Greek *akuo*, to hear]. The science of sound; that which treats of the cause, nature, and phenomena of sound as a branch of physical science.

Action. The mechanism by means of which the hammers of the piano and the valves and stops of the organ are controlled by the performer.

Acuta (Lat.). Acute. A mixture-stop in the organ.

Acute. Pitched high; the opposite of grave.

Adagietto (It.) (*a-da-jee-et'-to*). Diminutive of Adagio; not so slow as Adagio.

Adagio (It.) (*a-da'-jee-o*). Slowly; also a name given to a movement written in that time.

Adagio assai (*as-sah-e*), **Adagio di molto** (*dee mol-to*). Very slowly.

Adagio cantabile (*can-tah'-bee-leh*). Very slow and sustained, as if being sung.

Adagio patetico (*pa-tch'-tee-co*). Slow and with pathos.

Adagio pesante (*peh-san'-teh*). Slow and weighty.

Adagio sostenuto (*sos-teh-noo-to*). Slow and sustained.

Adagissimo (It.). Superlative of Adagio. More than usually slow; very slow indeed.

Addolorato (It.) (*ad-do-lo-rah'-to*). Sorrowful; dolorous.

Adirato (It.) (*ad-ee-rah'-to*). Angrily; irritated.

Adjunct Keys or Scales. Those a fifth above and fifth below the given key or scale. Related scales. The scales or keys of the dominant and subdominant.

Adjunct Notes. Short notes, not essential to the harmony, occurring on unaccented parts of a bar. [Cf. *Auxiliary Notes, Passing Notes.*]

Ad libitum (Lat.). At will. (1) In passages so marked, the time may be altered at the will of the performer. (2) Parts in a score that may be omitted.

A dur (Ger.) (*dure*). A major.

Æolian. The name of one of the Greek scales; also of one of the ecclesiastical scales. Identical with modern A minor without sharped seventh.

Æolian Harp. A shallow, oblong box with gut-strings set in motion by the wind, generally made to fit a window with the lower sash raised enough to admit it. The strings should be tuned in unison.

Äussere Stimmen (Ger.) (*ois-eh-reh stimmen*). The outer parts, as soprano and bass in a chorus, or violin and violoncello in a quartet.

Äusserst (Ger.). Very; extremely.

Äusserst rasch (*rash*). Very quick.

Added Sixth. A name given to the subdominant chord with the 6th over its fundamental added, thus: F A C D. This explanation of this combination is not now generally accepted.

Affabile (It.) (*af-fah'-bee-leh*). Pleasing; affably; agreeably.

Affannato (It.) (*af-fah-nah'-to*) [from *affanno*, anxiety]. Distressfully.

Affannosamente (It.) (*af-fah-no-sah-men'-teh*). Restlessly.

Affannoso (It.) (*af-fah-no-so*). Mournfully.

Affettuosamente (It.) (*af-fet-too-o-sa-men-teh*), **Affetuoso** (It.) (*af-fet-too-o-so*). Affectionately.

Affinity. Connected by relation. Relative keys.

Afflitto (It.) (*af-flit'-to*). Sadly; afflictedly.

Affrettando (It.) (*af-fret-tan'-do*), **Affrettate** (It.) (*af-fret-tah'-teh*), **Affrettore** (It.) (*af-fret-to'-reh*). Hastening the time.

Agevole (It.) (*a-jeh'-vo-leh*), **Agevolezza** (It.) (*a-jeh-vo-letz'-ah*). With lightness or agility.

Agilmente (It.) (*a-jil-men'-teh*), **Agilmento** (It.). In a lively, cheerful manner.

Agitamento (It.) (*a-jee-tah-men'-to*). Restlessness.

Agitato (It.) (*a-jee-tah'-to*). Agitated. To sing or play in an agitated, hurried manner.

Air. A tune, song, melody.

Adam, Adolph Charles. Opera and song writer; France. B. 1803; d. 1856.

Agramonte, Emilio (*ah-gra-mon-teh*). Vocal teacher; France. B. 1844.

Ais (Ger.) (*a-iss*). A sharp.

A la mesure (Fr.) (*meh-zoor*). In time. Same as *A tempo* and *A battuta*.

Alberti Bass. Broken chords arranged thus:—

So called from the name of its reputed inventor, Domenico Alberti.

Al' loco. At the place. Used after the direction to play 8th higher or lower.

Al piacere. See *A piacere*.

Al rigore di (or **del**) **tempo** (*ree-go-reh dee tempo*). In strict time.

Al scozzese (*scots-zeh-zeh*). In Scotch style.

Al segno (*sen-yo*). To the sign. A direction to return to the sign 𝄋. D'al segno, from the sign, is used with the same intention.

All' antico (*an'-tee-ko*). In ancient style.

All' ottava (*ot-tah-vah*). When *over* the notes play octave higher than written, when *under*, an octave lower. In orchestral scores it means that one instrument is to play in octaves with another.

All' unisono. At unison.

Alla (It.). Written Al. or All. before words beginning with a vowel. Like ; in the style of.

Alla breve. The value of one or two whole notes in the measure, with rhythm of two beats. Indicated by ₵. In modern music, chiefly used in rapid tempo. See *A capella*.

Alla caccia (It.) (*cat-chia*). In hunting style.

Alla camera (It.) (*ca'-meh-rah*). In chamber-music style.

Alla capella. In church style. See *A capella*.

Alla deritta. By degrees.

Alla hanacca (*ha-nak-ka*). In the manner of a hanacca.

Alla marcia (*mar'-chee-a*). In march style.

Alla mente (*men-teh*). Extemporaneous.

Alla militare (*mee-lee-tah-reh*). In military style.

Alla moderno. In modern style.

Alla Palestrina. In the style of Palestrina, *i. e.*, strict C. P. without instrumental accompaniment.

Alard, Delphin (*ah-lard, del-feen*). Violinist; France. B. 1815; d. 1888.

Alary, Guilio Eugenio Abrama (*ah-lah-ree, ju-lio eu-jeh-ne-o ah-bra-mah*). Composer; Italy. B. 1814.

Alla polacca. Like a polacca or polonaise.

Alla quinta. At the fifth.

Alla rovescio (*ro-veh'-shee-o*). By contrary motion or reverse motion, as when a phrase is imitated with the movement of the intervals inverted. Example:—

Alla siciliana (*see-chee-lee-ah'-nah*). In the style of a Siciliana, *q. v.*

Alla stretta. Like a stretto, *q. v.*

Alla turca. In Turkish style.

Alla zingaro. In Gypsy style.

Alla zoppa. Lamely; halting.

Allegramente (It.) (*al-leh-grah-men'-teh*). Joyfully.

Allegretto (It.) (*al-leh-gret'-to*). Diminutive of *Allegro*. (1) Slower than Allégro. (2) A movement in this time.

Allegrettino (It.) (*al-leh-gret-tee'-no*). Diminutive of *Allegretto*. (1) Not so fast as Allegretto. (2) A short Allegretto movement.

Allegro (It.) (*al-leh-gro*). (Lit., joyful.) Quick, lively. The word is occasionally employed to describe a whole movement of a quartet, sonata, or symphony. In music it is sometimes qualified as:—

Allegro agitato (It.) Quick and in an excited manner.
" assai " Literally, fast enough. A quicker motion than simple allegro.
" commodo or comodo " An easy, graceful allegro.
" con brio " Quickly and with spirit.
" con fuoco " Rapidly and with fire.
" con moto " With sustained joyfulness.
" con spirito " Joyfully and with spirit.
" di bravura " A movement full of executive difficulties intended to exhibit the capacity of the singer or player.
" di molto " Exceedingly quick.

Albani, Marie Louise Emma Cécilie (*al-bah-nee*). Soprano singer; Canada. B. 1850.

Alboni, Marietta (*al-bo-nee, mar-yet-ta*). Contralto; Italy. B. 1824; d. 1894.

Allegro furioso (It.) Rapidly and with fury.
" giusto " In quick but steady time.
" ma grazi-oso } " Lively and with graceful motion.
" ma non presto } " Rapidly, but not too fast.
" ma non tanto } " Quickly, but not too much so.
" ma non troppo } " Lively, but not too fast.
" moderato " Moderately quick.
" molto " Very quick.
" risoluto " Lively and with firmness and decision.
" veloce " Lively and with speed.
" vivace " Lively and brisk.
" vivo " Quick and lively.

Allemande (Fr.) (*almain, allemaigne*). A German dance (or some authorities say French), originally in duple time. Adopted as one of the movements in the Suite by Bach, Händel, and others, and written in $\frac{4}{4}$ time.

Allentamento (It.) (*al-len-tah-men-to*), Allentato (It.) (*al-len-tah-to*), Allentando (It.) (*al-len-tan-do*). Giving way; slackening the time.

Allmählig (Ger.) (*all-may-lig*). Gradually; by degrees.

Alpenhorn or Alphorn. A wooden horn slightly curved, 4 to 8 feet long, used by the Swiss herdsmen.

Alt (Ger.). The alto voice or part.

Alt-Clarinette. Alto clarionet. Its pitch is a 5th below the ordinary clarionet.

Alt-Geige. The viola.

Alt-Oboe. Oboe de caccia, *q. v.*

Alt-Posaune (*po-zow-neh*). Alto trombone.

Alterato (It.) (*al-teh-rah'-to*), Altéré (Fr.) (*al-teh-reh*). Changed; altered.

Altered. Said of intervals, the normal condition of which in a scale or chord is changed.

Alternativo (It.) (*al-ter-nah-tee'-vo*). An alternate. A part of a movement to be played alternately with others. This name is frequently given to the second trio of a Scherzo in chamber music when (as is unusual) a second trio is added.

Albrechtsberger, Johann Georg (*al-brechts-berger, yo-hann G.*). Composer and theorist; Germany. B. 1736; d. 1809.

Amati, Andreas (*a-mah-tee, A.*). Italy. B. 1520; d. 1577.

Amati, Antonio. Italy. B. 1550.

Altissimo (It.). The highest.

Alto (It.). High, loud. Originally applied to high male voices, now generally to the lowest female voice. Also applied to the viola (or tenor violin).

Alto Clef. The C clef on the third line, used for the viola, alto trombone, and (in Europe) for the alto voice.

Altra, Altre, Altri, Altro (It.) (masculine and feminine forms in the singular and plural). Other, others.

Amabile (It.) (*ah-mah'-bee-leh*). Amiably, sweetly, tenderly.

Amarevole (It.) (*ah-mah-reh'-vo-leh*). Sad, bitter.

Amateur (Fr.) (*a-mah-toor*). A lover of art. Generally applied to one who does not follow it professionally.

Ambrosian Chant. The system of church music introduced by Ambrose of Milan in the fourth century.

Ambrosian Hymn. A name given to the Te Deum on account of the belief—now known to be erroneous—that it was written by Ambrose of Milan.

Ame (Fr.) (*am*). Soul. The French name for the sound-post of instruments of the violin family.

American Organ. The English name for American reed organs, in which the air is drawn through instead of being forced through the reeds, as in the usual European system.

A moll (Ger.). A soft, *i. e.*, A minor.

Amorevole (It.) (*a-mor-eh'-vol-eh*), Amorevolmente (It.), Amorosamente (It.), Amoroso (It.). Lovingly; tenderly; amorously.

Amusement (Fr.) (*a-mooz-mong*). A light composition; a divertimento.

Anche (Fr.) (*onsh*). A reed of organ-pipe, or mouth-piece of oboe, clarionet, etc. Jeu-d'anche, reed - stop. Ancia (It.) (*an-chee-ah*). Italian form of the same word.

Anche (It.) (*an-keh*). Also; yet; still.

Anche piu moto. Still or yet faster.

Ancor (It.). Also; yet; still; used in the same way as Anche.

Ancora (It.). Again. Fr., *encore*.

Andächtig (Ger.) (*an-daych-tig*). Devoutly.

Amati, Geronimo (*jeh-ro'-nee-mo*). Italy. B. ——; d. 1635. Sons of Andreas.

Amati, Nicolo (*nee-co-lo*). Italy. B. 1596; d. 1684. Son of Geronimo. Violin makers of Cremona.

Ambros, August W. Historian and pianist; Germany. B. 1816; d. 1876.

Andamento (It.) (*an-da-men'-to*). Movement; the coda to a long fugue theme frequently dropped in the "working out."

Andante (It.) [from *audare*, to walk or go slowly]. A slow movement; quiet, peaceful tempo.

Andante affettuoso. Slow, with tenderness.

Andante cantabile (*can-tah'-bee-leh*). Slow and singing.

Andante con moto. Slow, but with a little motion.

Andante grazioso. Slow and graceful.

Andante maestoso. Slow and majestic.

Andante non troppo or **ma non troppo.** Slow, but not too slow.

Andante pastorale. Slow, in pastoral style.

Andante sostenuto (It.) (*sos-teh-noo'-to*). Slow, with smoothness.

Andantemente (It.). Like an Andante.

Andantino (It.) (*an-dan-tee'-no*). A diminutive of *Andante*. A little faster than Andante (some say slower, but the Italian dictionaries say faster).

Anelantemente (It.) (*ah-neh-lan-teh-men'-teh*). Ardently; eagerly.

Anfang (Ger.). Beginning.

Anfangsgründe (Ger.). Rudiments.

Anfangs-Ritornel (Ger.). Introductory symphony.

Angenehm (Ger.) (*an'-geh-nehm*). Pleasing; agreeable.

Anglaise (Fr.) (*on-glehs*), **Anglico** (It.) (*an'-glee-ko*). The English country dance.

Angel'ica (Lat.). The vox angelica.

Angel'ique (Fr.) (*on-jeh-leek*). Voix angélique, angel voice, name of an organstop. Also called Voix Celeste (Fr.) (*vo-a sel-lest*). Celestial voice.

Angosciosamente (It.) (*an-go-shee-o-sa-men'-teh*). **Angoscioso** (It.) (*an-go-shee-o'-so*). Painfully; with anguish.

Anhang (Ger.) [*auhängen*, to hang to]. Coda.

Anima (It.) (*ah'-nee-mah*), **Animato** (It.) (*ah-nee-mah'-to*), **Animando** (It.). Soul; spirit; life; lively with animation.

Animosamente (It.) (*ah-nee-mo-sah-men'-teh*), **Animosissimo** (It.) or **Animosissamente.** Very energetic; boldly.

Animoso (It.). Spiritedly; energetically.

Anlage (Ger.) (*an-lah'-geh*). The plan of a composition.

Anleitung (Ger.) (*an-ley'-toong*). Direction; guidance; preface.

Anmuth (Ger.) (*an-moot*). Sweetness; grace; charm.

Anmuthig (Ger.). Sweetly; gracefully.

Ansatz (Ger.). (1) Attack. (2) Position of mouth in singing. (3) Position of lips in blowing a wind instrument. See *Embouchure*.

Anschlag (Ger.). Touch, as applied to piano and other keyed instruments.

Anschwellen (Ger.) (*an-shvel-len*). To increase in loudness; crescendo.

Antecedent [Lat. *ante, cado*, to fall before]. The subject or theme proposed for imitation; the subject of a fugue. The reply or imitation is called the consequent.

Anthem, *ănthěme, *ăntěm, s. [In A. S. *antefen*, a hymn sung in alternate parts, an anthem; O. Fr., *anthame, antene, antienne, antevene;* Prov., *antifene, antifona;* Sp. and It., *antifona;* Low Lat., *antiphona;* from Gr. ἀντίφωνον (*antiphōnon*), an antiphon, an anthem; ἀντίφωνος (*antiphōnos*), sounding contrary, . . . responsive to; ἀντί (*anti*), opposite to, contrary to; φωνή (*phōnē*), a sound, a tone.]

*(1) Originally: A hymn sung "against" another hymn; in other words, a hymn in alternate parts, the one sung by one side of the choir, the other by the other.

"*Anthem*, a divine song sung alternately by two opposite choirs and choruses."—*Glossog. Nov.*, 2d ed. (1719).

(2) *Now:* A portion of Scripture or of the Liturgy, set to music, and sung or chanted.

There are three kinds of anthems: (1) A verse anthem, which in general has only one voice to a part; (2) a full anthem with verse, the latter performed by single voice, the former by all the choir; (3) a full anthem, performed by all the choir.

Anthropoglossa [Gr. *anthropos*, man; *glossa*, the tongue]. Like the human voice; the vox humana stop in the organ.

Anticipation [Lat. *ante*, before; *capio*, to take]. To introduce a note belonging to the next chord before leaving the preceding chord.

Antiphon [Gr. *anti*, against; *phoneo*, to sing]. A short sentence or anthem sung before and after the psalter for the day.

Antiphony. The responsive singing of two choirs generally placed on opposite sides of the chancel, one called the Decani, on the

---

Ambrose, St. Established the Ambrosian Chant; Gaul. B. 340; d. 398.

André (*an-dray*), Johann; Germany. B. 1741; d. 1799.

André, Johann Anton, son of preceding. B. 1775; d. 1842.

André, Johann Baptist, son of preceding. B. 1823; d. 1882.

André, Peter F. I., brother of last. B. 1808; d. 1880.

Archer, Frederick. Organist; England. B. 1838; d. 1901.

Dean's side of the chancel, the other the Cantoris, on the precentor's or leader's side. The verses of the psalms are sung by the choirs alternately, but the Gloria by the united choirs.

Anwachsend (Ger.) (*an-vach-sent*). Swelling; crescendo.

Aperto (It.) (*ah-pehr-to*). Open. Direction to use the damper ("loud") pedal.

Appassionata (It.) (*ap-pas-sion-ah'-tah*), **Appassionamento** (It.). With strong passion or emotion.

Appassionatamente (It.). Impassioned.

Appenato (It.) (*ap-peh-nah'-to*). Distressfully.

Applicatur (Ger.) (*ap-plee-ka-toor'*). The fingering of a musical instrument.

Appoggiando (It.) (*ap-pod-je-an'-do*). Leaning upon; suspended notes.

Appoggiato (It.). Retardations; syncopations.

Appoggiatura (It.) (*ap-pod-jea-too'-rah*). To lean against. An ornamental note foreign to the harmony, one degree above or below a member of the chord, always on an accent or on a beat. It takes half the value of the note it precedes, but if the note it precedes is dotted, it takes two-thirds of its value.

Written.

Rendered.

Written.

Rendered.

The modern practice is to write as rendered, thus avoiding any confusion between the appoggiatura and the acciaccatura.

Arcato (It.) (*ar-kah'-to*). With the bow; a direction to resume the bow after pizzicato.

Arco (It.). The bow.

Ardente (It.) (*ar-den-teh*). Ardent; fiery.

Ardente (Fr.) (*ar-dongt*). Ardently.

Ardito (It.) (*ar-dee-to*). Ardently; boldly.

Aretinian Syllables. *Ut, re, mi, fa, sol, la,* given by Guido Aretinus to the hexachord. *Ut* was changed to *do*, as being a better vowel for solemnization.

Arditi, Luigi (*ar-dee-tee, lu-ee-jee*). Conductor and composer; Italy. B. 1822; d. 1903.

Aria (It.) (*ah'-ree-ah*). Air; song. In form the aria consists of three members: Part I, a more or less elaborate melody in the tonic key. Part II, another melody in a related key. Part III, a repetition of the first melody to which a coda is generally added.

Aria buffa (It.) (*boof'-fah*). An aria with humorous words.

Aria concertante (It.) (*con-cher-tan'-teh*). An aria with obbligato accompaniment of instruments.

Aria di bravura (It.) (*dee-brah-voo'-rah*) or **d'abilita** (*d'ah-bee-lee-tah*). An aria with difficult, showy passages.

Aria fugato (It.) (*foo-gah'-to*). An aria with an accompaniment written in fugue style.

Aria parlante (It.) (*par-lan'-teh*). Literally a speaking aria, one in which the music is designed for declamatory effect. The aria parlante was the precursor of the recitative.

Arietta (It.) (*ah-ree-et'-ta*). A small aria, less elaborate than the aria.

Arioso (It.) (*ah-ree-o'-so*). A short melody at the end of or in the course of a recitation.

Armonia (It.) (*ar-mo'-nee-ah*). Harmony.

Armoniosamente (It.) (*ar-mo-nee-o-sa-men'-teh*), **Armonioso** (It.) (*ar-mo-nee-o'-so*). Harmonious; harmoniously.

Arpa (It.) (*ar'-pah*). Harp.

Arpège (Fr.) (*ar-pehzh'*), **Arpeggio** (It.) (*ar-ped-jeeo*). In harp style. In piano music a direction to play the notes of a chord in rapid succession from the lowest upward. Indicated by

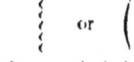

A reversed arpeggio is indicated by

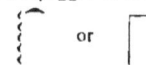

In old music the arpeggio is sometimes indicated thus:—

Arpeggiando (It.) (*ar-ped'-jee-an-do*). In harp style.

Arpeggiato (It.) (*ar-ped-jeea'-to*). Arpeggiated.

Arrangement (Fr.) (*ar-ranzh-mong*). A piece of music written for one or more instruments or voices adapted to other instruments or voices. Also called Transcription.

Ar'sis (Gk.). The unaccented or up-beat; the reverse of Thesis, the accented or down-beat.

Arne, Thomas Augustus. Composer; England. B. 1710; d. 1778.

Articolato (It.) (*ar-tik-ko-lah' to*). Articulated distinctly.

Artig (Ger.) (*ahr-teech*). Neat, pretty, unaffected.

As (Ger.). A flat. **As dur** (*doohr*), A flat major. **As moll**, A flat minor.

Assai (It.) (*as-sah'-ee*). Very, extremely, as Allegro assai, very fast. Adagio assai, very slow.

Assez (Fr.) (*as-seh*). Rather, as **Assez vite** (*veet*), rather quick, or quick enough.

Assoluto (masc.), **Assoluta** (fem.) (It.) (*as-so-loo'-to*). Absolute. Applied to the leading singers of an opera troupe, as Prima donna assoluta, first lady absolute; Prima uomo assoluto, first man absolute.

Attacca (It.) (*at-tak'-ka*). Attack. Begin the next movement with slight or with no pause.

Attacca subito (It.) (*soo-bee-to*). Attack quickly, without pause.

Attacco (It.), **Attaque** (Fr.) (*at-tak'*). The motive or theme of an imitation or short fugal subject.

Attaquer (Fr.) (*at-tak-keh*). Same as *Attacca*.

Attack. The manner of beginning a phrase or piece; refers generally to the promptness or firmness of the performer or performers.

Attendant Keys. The keys of the 4th and 5th above, and the relative minors of the principal key and these two major relations, as :— C F G
Rel. minors A D E

Aubade (Fr.) (*o-bad'*). Morning music; the opposite of *Serenade*, evening music.

Audace (Fr.) (*o-dass*). Bold, audacious.

Aufführung (Ger.) (*owf-fee-roonk*). Performance; representation of an opera.

Aufgeregt (Ger.) (*geh-rehgt*). With agitation.

Aufgeweckt (Ger.) (*geh-vekt*). With animation.

Aufhalten (Ger.) (*hol-ten*). To suspend (of dissonances). Also, to hold back or retard (of time).

Aufhaltung (Ger.) (*hol-toonk*). Suspension.

Auflösen (Ger.) (*leh-zen*). To let loose; resolve a dissonance.

Auflösungszeichen (Ger.) (*leh-soonks-tzeich-en*). Releasing sign; the ♮.

Artôt (*ar-to*), Alex. I. Violinist; Brussels. B. 1815; d. 1845.

Ascher, Joseph. Pianist. B. 1831; d. 1869.

Astorga, Emmanuele Baron D. Composer; Sicily. B. 1681; d. 1736.

Attwood, Thomas. Composer; England. B. 1765; d. 1838.

Auber, Daniel François Esprit (*o-behr, D. fran-*

Aufschlag (Ger.). Up-beat.

Aufschwung (Ger.) (*owf-shvoonk*). Soaring, elevation.

Aufstrich (Ger.). Up-bow.

Auftakt (Ger.). The unaccented part of the measure, or the fraction of a measure, at the beginning of a piece.

Augmentation. When the theme of a fugue or imitation is given in notes of double or quadruple the length of those in its original form.

Augmented. (1) Any interval greater than perfect or major. (2) A theme written in notes of greater value than in its original form.

Augmented Sixth Chord. Called also extreme sharp sixth; superfluous sixth; when formed thus, A♭ C F♯, the Italian sixth; thus, A♭ C D F♯, the French sixth; thus, A♭ C E♭ F♯, the German sixth.

Augmenter (Fr.) (*og-mong-teh*). To increase in force. Same as *Crescendo*.

Ausarbeitung (Ger.) (*ows'-ar-bye-toonk*). Development; the working out of a fugue or sonata, etc.

Ausdruck (Ger.) (*drook*). Expression.

Ausdrucksvoll (Ger.). With expression; literally, full of expression.

Ausführung (Ger.) (*fee-roonk*). Execution; manner of performance.

Ausweichung (Ger.) (*veich-oonk*). Literally, evasion; modulation; change of key.

Authentic. The Ambrosian scales. A melody that lies between the keynote and its octave is called authentic. One that lies between the fourth below and the fifth above the keynote is called plagal. These terms are only used in the ecclesiastical modes.

Authentic. The church scales beginning and ending on any given tonic (except B).

Authentic Cadence. Tonic preceded by dominant.

Autoharp. A modern instrument resembling a zither, of easy performance. The plectrum is drawn across all the strings at once, and those that it is not desired to sound are silenced by a series of dampers controlled by the left hand of the player.

Auxiliary Note. Grace note; appoggiatura.

Auxiliary Scales. Related scales.

soa es-pree). Opera composer; France. B. 1784; d. 1871.

Audran, Edmond (*o-drong*). France. B. 1842.

Auer (*our*), Leopold. Violinist; Germany. B. 1845.

Avison, Charles. Composer; England. B. 1710; d. 1770.

B

B. The seventh or leading tone of the natural major scale; in German, the note or key of B♭, B♮ being called H.

Baborak or **Baboracka.** A Bohemian dance.

Backfall. An ornament in harpsichord or lute music, written ♩ played ♪♩

Badinage (Fr.) (*bah-dee-naje*). Banter; raillery.

Bagatelle (Fr.) (*bah-gah-tell*). A trifle; a name frequently given to short pieces of music.

Bag-pipe. An instrument consisting of a leather bag into which air is forced either from a bellows or by the mouth of the player; furnished with from two to four pipes, one pipe with double reed pierced with holes upon which the melody is played, called in Scotland the chanter; the remaining pipes with single reeds, called drones, sound continuously the first and fifth of the scale or first fifth and octave.

Bajadere or **Bayadere** (*by-a dehr*). East Indian dancing girl.

Bakkia (*bak-kee-ah*). A Kamskatdale dance.

Balabile (It.) (*bah-lah-bee'-leh*). Any piece of music written for dancing purposes.

Ballad. A simple song, originally a song to accompany dancing; derived from the low Latin word *ballare*, to dance; in its French form, *ballade*, it is used by modern composers as a title for extended lyric compositions, as the ballades of Chopin.

Balladenmässig (Ger.) (*bal-la'-den-meh-sich*). In ballad style.

Ballad-opera. An opera made up of simple songs, and without recitative.

Balafo (*bah-lah-fo*). An African instrument resembling the xylophone; a South American variety is called the marimba.

Balalaika (Russ.) (*bah-lah-lye'-ka*). A Russian guitar with three or four strings, the body triangular.

Ballata (It.). A ballad.

Ballerina (It.) (*bal-leh-ree'-nah*). A female ballet dancer.

Ballet (Eng.), called also *Fa-la*. An old form of part song in simple counterpoint.

Ballet (Fr.) (*bal-leh*). A combination of music and dancing, designed to tell a story in pantomime.

Balletto (It.) (*bal-let'-to*). A ballet. Used as a name for a movement by Bach.

Ballo (It.). A dance; a ball.

Ballo in maschera (*mas-keh-rah*). Masked ball.

Band. (1) A company of instrumentalists. (2) The term is used to distinguish the various groups of instruments in the orchestra; as, string band, wood band, brass band. (3) The commonest use of the word is as applied to a company of players on brass instruments. (4) A band composed of wood and brass instruments is called a harmony band.

Band (Ger.) (*bont*). A volume; a part.

Banda (It.) (*ban-dah*). A band.

Bandola (*ban-do'-lah*). A variety of mandolin.

Bandora (Fr.) (*ban-do'-rah*), **Bandore** (Eng.), **Pandoura** (Gk.). An obsolete instrument of the guitar family.

Bandurria (Span.) (*ban-door-ree-ah*). A variety of guitar with wire strings.

Banger, Bania, Banja, Banjo. An instrument resembling a guitar, with a circular body, consisting of a broad hoop of wood covered with parchment, generally provided with live strings. The modern banjo is furnished with frets and with a screw mechanism to tighten the parchment.

Bar. A line drawn across the staff or staves to divide the music into portions of equal duration. The portion enclosed between two bars is called a measure. The almost universal custom of musicians, however, is to use *bar* in the sense of measure.

Barbaro (It.) (*bar'-bah-ro*). Savagely; ferocious.

Barbiton (Gk.). (1) A variety of lyre. (2) A string instrument resembling the violoncello (obsolete).

Barcarole, Barcarolle (Fr.) (*bar-ca-rol*), **Barcarola** (It.) (*bar-ca-ro-lah*), Barcaru-

---

Bach, Johann Sebastian. Composer; Germany. B. 1685; d. 1750.

Bach, Carl Philipp Emanuel. Inventor of the sonata; Germany. B. 1714; d. 1788.

Bach, Johann Christoph Friedrich. Organist; Germany. B. 1732; d. 1795.

Bach, Wilhelm Friedemann. Organist; Germany. B. 1710; d. 1784. Sons of J. S. Bach.

Baillot, Pierre Marie François de Sales (*bai-yo*). Violinist; France. B. 1771; d. 1842.

Balatka, Hans. Pianist and conductor; Germany. B. 1827.

Balfe, Michael William. Opera and song writer. B. 1808; d. 1870.

ola (It.) (*bar-ca-roo-o-la*). A boat-song; gondolier's song; vocal or instrumental compositions in the style of the Venetian gondoliers' songs.

Barem (Ger.) (*bah-rehm*). A soft organ-stop; closed pipes of eight- or sixteen-foot tone.

Bargaret (Fr.) (*bar-gah-reh*), **Barginet** (Fr.) (*bar-zhee-neh*), **Berginet** (Fr.) (*behr-zhee-neh*), **Bergiret** (*behr-zhee-reh*). A shepherd's song; pastoral song. From *berger* (Fr.), a shepherd.

Baribasso (It.). A deep bass voice.

Bariolage (Fr.) (*bah-ree-o-laje*). A medley; a series of cadenzas.

Baritenor. A low tenor.

Baritone. A brass instrument; a clarionet of low pitch; an obsolete variety of the viol family; the male voice ranging between bass and tenor (also written barytone); the F clef on the third line (not used now).

Barocco (It.), **Barock** (Ger.), **Baroque** (Fr.) (*ba-rok*). Irregular; whimsical; unusual.

Barquade, Barquarde (Fr.) (*bar-kad, bar-kard*). Same as *Barcarole*.

Barré (Fr.) (*bar-reh'*). In guitar playing, pressing the first finger of the left hand across all the strings; the finger acts as a temporary "nut," raising the pitch of the strings.

Barre (Fr.) (*bar*). Bar.

Barre de répétition. A double bar with repeat marks.

Bas dessus (Fr.) (*bah-des-soo'*). The mezzo-soprano voice.

Base. Old way of writing bass.

Bass, Basso (It.), **Basse** (Fr.), **Bass** (Ger.). Low; deep.

Basse chantante (Fr.) (*shan-tont*). Baritone voice.

Basse chiffrée (Fr.) (*shif-freh*). Figured bass.

Basse continué (Fr.). Same as *Figured Bass*.

Basse de cremone (Fr.) (*creh-mone*). Bassoon.

Basse d'harmonie (Fr.) (*d'ar-mo-nee*). The ophicleide.

Basse de hautbois (Fr.). The English horn.

Basse de viole (Fr.). Violoncello.

Basse de violon. The double bass.

Bargiel, Woldemar (*bar-geel, vol deh-mar*). Composer and pianist; Germany. B. 1828; d. 1897.

Bärman, Carl. Pianist and composer; Germany and U. S. B. 1839.

Barnby, Joseph. Composer; England. B. 1838; d. 1896.

Barnett, John. Composer. B. 1802; d. 1890.

Basse taille (Fr.) (*tah-ee*). Baritone voice.

Bass-bar. A strip of wood glued to the belly of instruments of the violin family under the lowest string.

Bass Clef. The F clef on the fourth line.

Bass-Flöte (Ger.) (*fla-teh*). A low-pitch flute.

Bass-Geige (Ger.). The violoncello.

Bass-Pommer (Ger.). An obsolete ancestor of the bassoon.

Bass-Posaune (Ger.) (*po-zow-neh*). Bass trombone.

Bass-Schlüssel (Ger.) (*schlis-sel*). Bass clef.

Bass-Stimme (Ger.) (*stim-meh*). Bass voice or part.

Bass Tuba. A brass instrument of low pitch.

Bass Viol. The largest viol of a set or "chest" of viols.

Bass Voice. The lowest male voice.

Basset Horn. A variety of the clarionet, ranging from F below bass staff to C above treble staff; rich quality of tone; a favorite of Mozart, who used it in several of his operas and in his Requiem Mass.

Basetto (It.). An eight- or sixteen-foot reed-stop in the organ; obsolete name for viola.

Basso (It.). The lowest part; a bass singer.

Basso buffo (It.). A comic bass singer.

Basso cantante (It.) (*can-tan'-teh*). A vocal or singing bass.

Basso concertante (It.) (*con-cher-tan'-teh*). The principal bass that accompanies solos and recitatives.

Basso continuo (It.). A figured bass.

Basso obbligato (It.) (*ob-blee-gah'-to*). An essential bass; one that may not be dispensed with.

Basso ostinato (It.) (*os-tee-nah'-to*). Literally, obstinate bass; a continuously repeated bass with constant variation of the upper parts; generally used as the foundation of that member of the suite called the Passacaglia.

Basso profundo (It.). A very deep, heavy bass voice.

Basso ripieno (It.) (*ree-pee-eh'-no*). A "filling up" bass. See *Ripieno*.

Bassoon, Basson (Fr.), **Fagotto** (It.), **Fagott** (Ger.). A wood wind instrument with double reed; the bass of the wind

---

Barnett, John Francis, nephew of above. Composer and pianist; England. B. 1837; d. 1898.

Bartholomew, Mrs. Ann. Organist and composer; England. B. 1811; d. 1891.

Bartlett, Homer N. Composer; U. S. A. B. 1846.

band; compass from B♭ below bass staff to B♭ in treble staff (two or three higher notes are possible).

Basson quinte (Fr.) (*kangt*). A bassoon a fifth higher than the preceding.

Bâton (Fr.). (1) The stick used by a conductor; also, figuratively, his method of conducting. (2) A pause of several measures, signified thus

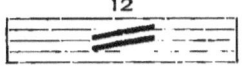

in modern music, viz.: one or two heavy diagonal lines with figures over to indicate the number of bars rest.

Batterie (Fr.) (*bat-teh-ree*). (1) The roll on the drum. (2) Repeated or broken chords played staccato. (3) Striking instead of plucking the strings of the guitar.

Battuta (It.) (*bat-too'-tah*). A measure or bar.

Bauerpfeife (Ger.) (*bower-pfifeh*). An 8-foot organ-stop of small scale.

Baxoncillo (Sp.) (*bah-hon-theel'-yo*). Open diapason.

Bayadere. See *Bajadere*.

Bayles (Sp.) (*bahl-yehs*). Comic dancing songs.

Bearings or Bearing Notes. The notes first tuned by an organ- or piano-tuner as a guide to the rest.

Beat. (1) The motion of the hand or baton by which the time (rate of movement) of a piece is regulated. (2) The equal parts into which a measure is divided. (3) The throbbing heard when two sounds not exactly in unison are heard together. (Beats are also produced by other intervals.)

Bebung (Ger.) (*beh-boonk*). Trembling; an effect obtained on the obsolete clavichord by rapidly vibrating the finger up and down without raising it from the key; the tremolo-stop in an organ.

Batiste, Antonio Edward (*ba-teest*). Organist and composer; France. B. 1820; d. 1876.

Beethoven, Ludwig van (*bay-to-fen*). Composer; Germany. B. 1770; d. 1827.

Bellini, Vincenzo (*bel-lee-nee, vin-chent-so*). Opera; Italy. B. 1802; d. 1835.

Benda, Georg. Composer; Bohemia. B. 1721; d. 1795.

Bendel, Franz. Pianist and composer; Bohemia. B. 1833; d. 1874.

Bendix, Otto. Composer and pianist; Copenhagen. B. 1850.

Benedict, Sir Julius. Composer and pianist; Germany. B. 1804; d. 1885.

Becken (Ger.). Cymbals.

Begeisterung (Ger.) (*be-geis'-te-roonk*). Spirit; excitement.

Begleitung (Ger.) (*be-glei'-toonk*). Accompaniment.

Bell. (1) A cup-shaped metal instrument. (2) The cup-shaped end of brass and some wood instruments.

Bell Diapason, Bell Gamba. Organ-stops with bell-shaped mouth.

Bellezza (It.) (*bel-let'-za*). Beauty of expression.

Bellicosamente (It.) (*bel-le-co-sa-men'-teh*). In a warlike manner; martially.

Belly. The upper side of instruments of the violin and guitar families.

Beklemmt (Ger.) (*beh-klemt'*). Anxious; oppressed.

Bémol (Fr.) (*beh-mol*). The sign ♭.

Ben (It.) (*behn*). Well; as, ben marcato, well marked.

Bene placito (It.) (*beh-neh pla-chee'-to*). At pleasure.

Béquarre or Bécarre (Fr.) (*beh-kar*). The sign ♮.

Berceuse (Fr.) (*behr-soos*). A cradle-song; lullaby.

Bergomask or Bergamask. A lively dance in triple time.

Bes (Ger.) (*behs*). B double flat.

Bestimmt (Ger.). With energy; con energia.

Bewegt (Ger.) (*beh-vehgt'*). Moved; with emotion; con moto.

Bewegung (Ger.) (*beh-veh'-goonk*). Motion.

Bien-chanté (Fr.) (*be-ang-shong-teh*). Literally, well sung; smoothly; cantabile.

Bifara (Lat.). An organ-stop; same as *l'ox angelica*; two pipes not in perfect unison.

Binary Form. A movement founded on two principal themes.

Bennett, Sir Wm. Sterndale. Composer and pianist; England. B. 1816; d. 1875.

Berg, Conrad M. Pianist; Alsace. B. 1785; d. 1852.

Beriot, Ch. Auguste de (*beh-ree-o*). Violinist; France. B. 1802; d. 1870.

Berlioz, Hector (*behr-lee-o*). Composer; France. B. 1803; d. 1869.

Bertini, Henry I. (*ber-tee-nee*). Pianist; England. B. 1798; d. 1876.

Best, Wm. Thomas. Organist; England. B. 1826; d. 1897.

Beyer, Ferdinand. Pianist; Germany. B. 1803; d. 1863.

Biletta, G. Emanuele (*bee-let-ta*). Composer; Italy. B. 1825.

Binary Measure. A measure with two beats.
Bind. A tie. The same sign, when over two or more notes on different degrees, is called a slur.
Bis (Lat.). Twice. When placed over a short passage, inclosed thus, Bis signifies that it is to be played twice.
Bit. A small piece of tube used to lengthen the trumpet or other brass instrument to alter the pitch.
Bizzarramente (It.) (*bid-zarra-mente*). **Bizzaria** (It.) (*bid-zarria*), **Bizzaro** (It.) (*bid-zarro*). Bizarre; fantastic; odd; droll.
Blanche (Fr.) (*blongsh*). A half-note; minim.
Blanche pointée (*poin-teh*). A dotted half-note.
Blase-Instrument (Ger.) (*blah-zeh*). Wind instrument.
Bob. A technical term in bell ringing.
Bocca (It.). The mouth. **Con bocca chiusa** (*kee-oo-sa*), with closed mouth; humming.
Bocca ridente (It.) (*ree-den'-teh*). Smiling mouth; the proper position of the mouth in singing.
Bocktriller (Ger.). A bad trill. (Literally, goat's bleat).
Bois (Fr.) (*bo-a*). Wood. **Les bois**, the wood wind.
Bolero (Sp.) (*bo-leh-ro*). Spanish dance in ¾-time; also called **Cachuca** (*ka-choo-ka*).
Bombard. An 8 or 16-foot reed-stop in the organ.
Bombardon. A large, deep-toned brass instrument.

Bird or **Byrd**, Wm. Composer; England. B. 1538; d. 1623.
Bishop, Anna. Soprano singer; England. B. 1810; d. 1884.
Bishop, Sir Henry Rowley, her husband. Composer, opera and song; England. B. 1785; d. 1855.
Bizet, "Georges" (*bee-zeh*). Opera; France. B. 1838; d. 1875.
Blahetka, Leopoldine (*blah-et-ka*). Pianist and composer; Austria. B. 1811; d. 1887.
Blangini, Giuseppe Marc. Mari Felice (*blan-jee-nee*). Tenor, composer, teacher; Italy. B. 1781; d. 1814.
Bloomfield-Zeisler, Fanny. Pianist; Austria. B. 1865.
Blumenthal, Jacob (*bloo-men-tall*). Song writer, pianist; Germany. B. 1829.
Boccherini, Luigi (*bok-keh-ree-nee*). Composer; Italy. B. 1740; d. 1805.
Boehm, Theobald (*behm*). Improved the flute; Bavaria. B. 1794; d. 1881.

Bouché (masc.), **Bouchée** (fem.) (Fr.) (*boo-sheh*). Closed. Applied to organ-stops with closed mouth.
Bouffe (Fr.) (*boof*). Comic.
Bourdon. (1) A closed organ-stop of 16 or 32-foot tone. (2) In France also 4 and 8-foot stops, analogous to the stop diapason, are so called. (3) A drone bass. (4) The largest bell of a chime.
Bourrée (Fr.) (*boor-reh*). A rapid dance in ¾ or ⅜ time, frequently used as one of the movements in a suite.
Bow. (1) The implement of wood and horse-hair by means of which the strings of the violin family of instruments are set in vibration. (2) The rim of a bell.
Bowing. (1) The art of managing the bow. (2) The signs indicating the way in which the bow is to be used.
Brabançonne (Fr.) (*bra-ban-sonn*). The Belgian national air.
Brace. The sign { used to join two or more staves.
Bransle (Fr.) or **Branle** (*brongl*), **Brawl.** An ancient French dance in ¾ time.
Bratche (Ger.) (*bratch-eh*). The viola. Corruption of the Italian **Braccia** (*brats-chia*), the arm-viol.
Bravo (masc.) (It.), **Brava** (fem.) (*bravah*), **Bravi** (plu.) (*bra-vee*). Literally, brave. Used to applaud performers, meaning "well done."
Bravura (It.) (*bra-roo'-rah*). Boldness; brilliancy. A composition designed to exhibit the powers of the performer.

Boieldieu, François Adrien (*boa-el-dee-oo*). Opera writer; France. B. 1775; d. 1834.
Boito, Arrigo (*bo-ee-to*). Composer, opera; Italy. B. 1842.
Bolck, Oscar. Pianist; Germany. B. 1839; d. 1888.
Bonewitz, J. H. Composer and pianist; Bavaria. B. 1839.
Bononcini or **Buononcini**, Giovanni Battista (*bo-non-chee-nee* or *bu-o-non-chee-nee*). Opera, Händel's rival; Italy. B. 1662; d. 1750.
Bordogni, Marco (*bor-done-yee*). Singer and teacher; Italy. B. 1788; d. 1856.
Bottesini, Giovanni (*bot-teh-se-nee*). Contrabassist, composer; Italy. B. 1821; d. 1890.
Bowman, E. M. Organist, theorist; U. S. A. B. 1848.
Brahms, Johannes. Composer and pianist; Germany. B. 1833; d. 1897.

Break. (1) The point at which the register of the voice changes. (2) The point at which the lower octave is resumed in compound organ-stops. (3) The point where the quality of the tone changes in wood instruments (of the clarionet family especially).

Breit (Ger.) (*bright*). Broad; stately.

Breve [from Lat. *brevis*, short]. Formerly the shortest note; now the longest, equal in value to two whole notes. Made ⊢ or ⊨

Bridge. A piece of wood resting on the sound-board or resonance box, upon which the strings of piano, violin, guitar, etc., rest.

Brillante (Fr.) (*bree-yant*), **Brillante** (It.) (*breel-lan-tch*). Brilliant.

Brindisi (It.) (*brin-dee'-zee*). Drinking song in ¾ or ⅜ time, so written as to resemble the Tyrolese Jodl.

Brio (It.) (*bree-o*). Fire; spirit.

Brioso (It.). Cheerfully; briskly; joyfully.

Bridge, John Frederick. Organist, composer; England. B. 1844.
Brinkerhoff, Clara M. Soprano. B. 1830.
Bristow, Frank L. Composer; U. S. A. B. 1844.
Bristow, George F. Composer; U. S. A. B. 1825.
Broadwood, John. Piano maker; England. B. 1742; d. 1812.
Bronsart, Hans von. Pianist, composer; Germany. B. 1830.
Bruch, Max. Composer; Germany. B. 1838.

Broken Cadence. An interrupted cadence.
Broken Chords. See *Arpeggio*.
Brumm-Stimmen (Ger.). Humming voices; con bocca chiusa.
Bruscamente (It.) (*broos-ka-men'-tch*). Roughly; strongly accented.
Brustwerk (Ger.) (*broost-vehrk*). The pipes in the organ belonging to the swell or choir organ.
Buca (It.), **Schall-Loch** (Ger.). The sound-hole of a guitar, mandolin, etc.
Buccolica (It.) (*buk-ko'-li-ka*), Bucolique (Fr.) (*boo-ko-leek*). In a rustic style.
Buffo (masc.), **Buffa** (fem.). A comic opera, or air, or singer.
Bugle. (1) A straight or curved hunting horn. (2) A keyed horn, generally made of copper. Chiefly used for military signals.
Burden. Old name for the refrain or chorus to a song.
Burletta (It.). A musical farce.
Busain. A 16-foot reed-organ stop.

Buck, Dudley. Composer, organist; U. S. A. B. 1839; d. 1900.
Bull, "Ole" Bornemann. Violinist; Norway. B. 1810; d. 1880.
Bülow, Hans von (*behl-o*). Pianist, composer; Germany. B. 1830; d. 1895.
Burchard, Carl. Pianist; Germany. B. 1820; d. 1896.
Burgmüller, Johann Friedrich (*boorg-meel-ler*). Pianist, composer; Germany. B. 1801; d. 1874.
Burmeister, Richard. Pianist; Germany. B. 1860.

C

C. The first note in the natural major scale. Middle C, the C lying between the fifth line of the bass staff and first line of the treble staff; the C clef 𝄢 or 𝄡 always signifies this C.

Cabaletta (It.). ("A little horse," so called from the rapid triplet accompaniment generally used with it.) A vocal rondo, the theme often repeated with elaborate variations.

Cabinet-d'orgue (Fr.) (*ca-bee-neh-d'org*). Organ case.

Cabinet Organ. A reed organ (American) in which the air is drawn instead of forced through the reeds.

Cabinet Piano. An old-style lofty upright piano.

Caccia (It.) (*cat'-chia*). Hunting chase.

Cachucha (Sp.) (*ca-choo'-cha*). The same as *Bolero*.

Cadence [from Lat. *cado*, to fall]. The end of a phrase, part, piece. The principal cadences are as follows: whole, or perfect, dominant to tonic; half, or imperfect, tonic to dominant; deceptive, dominant to subdominant or submediant.

Caccini, Guilio (*catch-ee-nee, julio*). Opera; Italy. B. 1558; d. 1640.

"Cafarelli," Gaetano Majorano (*ca-fa-rel-lee, gah eh-ta-no mah-yo-rah-no*). Sopranist; Italy. B. 1703; d. 1783.

Perfect.   *Plagal.*

Half.   *Deceptive.*

Plagal cadence, subdominant to tonic. In the perfect cadence the dominant is generally preceded by the 6-4 of the tonic; in the half cadence the 6-4 of the tonic before the dominant which is the final; half and deceptive cadences are used in the course of a piece; perfect and plagal at the end. The Phrygian cadence consists of the following chords :—

A long, brilliant, vocal or instrumental flourish introduced just before the close, or before the return of the principal theme, is also called a cadence (in Italian, cadenza).

Cadenz or **Kadenz** (Ger.). Cadence.

Cadenza (It.). A cadence. The Italian word is generally used when applied to the kind of passage described above.

Ça-ira (Fr.) (*sah-era*). That will do; lit., that will go. A revolutionary song in France.

Caisse (Fr.) (*case*). A drum.

Caisse claires (*clare*). Kettle drums. **Grosse Caisse**, large drum.

Caisse roulante. Side or snare drum.

Cal'amus (Lat.). A reed. From this are derived the words **Chalumeau** (Fr.) (*sha-loo-mo*), the first register of the clarionet, and **Shawm**, an obsolete reed instrument used in the Bible as the translation of a Hebrew instrument.

Calan'do (It.) [from *calare*, to go down or decrease]. Getting both slower and softer.

Calkin, James. Composer. B. 1786; d. 1862.

Calkin, James Baptiste, son of preceding. Pianist, composer; England. B. 1827; d. 1905.

Callcott, John Wall. Composer. B. 1766; d. 1821.

Calandrone (It.) [*calandra*, a lark]. A small reed instrument resembling the clarionet.

Cala'ta (It.). A lively dance in $\frac{2}{4}$ time.

Calcan'do (It.) [from *calcare*, to tread upon]. Hurrying the time.

Call. A military signal, given by drum or bugle.

Calma (It.). Calm, quiet.

Calma'to (It.). Calmed, quieted.

Calore (It.) (*kal'-o-reh*). Warmth, passion.

Caloro'so (It.). Warmly, passionately.

Cambiata (It.) (*camb-ya'-ta*) [from *cambiare*, to change]. **Nota cambiata**, changing note; a dissonant struck on the accent.

Camera (It.) (*ka'-meh-ra*). Chamber. **Musica di camera**. chamber music.

Camminan'do (It.) [from *camminare*, to travel or walk]. Walking, flowing. Same as *Andante*.

Campa'na (It.). A bell.

Campanello (It.) (*kam-pah-nel'-lo*). A small bell.

Campanet'ta (It.). Instrument consisting of a series of small bells tuned to the musical scale, played either with small hammers held in the hands, or by means of a keyboard.

Campanology. The art of making and using bells.

Canaries. A lively dance in $\frac{4}{4}$ time, of English origin.

Can'crizans [Lat. *cancer*, a crab]. A term applied to a canon in which the "follower" takes the theme backward.

Canon (Gk.). Law or rule. (1) The measurement of the ratios of intervals by means of the monochord. (2) A musical composition in which each voice imitates the theme given out by the leading voice; this imitation may be at any interval above or below, or may begin at any point of the theme. There are many varieties of the canon. The following are the most important, if any importance attaches to such dry productions: **Close Canon**, the entrance of the voices indicated by a sign; the parts not written out. **Open Canon**, the reverse of this; *i.e.*, written in full. **Finite Canon**, one with an ending. **Infinite Canon**, one without an ending.

There are also canons by augmentation, by diminution, by inversion, by retrogression (cancrizans), etc., etc.

Callcott, William Hutchings, son of preceding. Composer. B. 1807; d. 1882.

Campagnoli, Bartolomeo (*cam-pan-yo-lee*). Violinist; Italy. B. 1751; d. 1827.

Camporese, Violante (*cam-po-reh-seh*). Soprano; Italy. B. 1785; d. 1839.

Canonic Imitation. See *Canon*.
Cantabile (It.) (*can-tah'-bee-leh*) [from *cantare*, to sing]. In a singing style.
Cantan'do (It.). Singing.
Canta'ta. (1) A mixture of aria and recitative for one voice. (2) A short oratorio, or a secular work in oratorio form, sung without costume or action.
Cantatore (It.) (*can-ta-to'-reh*). A singer, male.
Cantatrice (It.) (*can-ta-tree'-cheh*). A singer, female.
Cantilena (Lat.). (1) A folk-song. (2) A solfeggio. (3) A smooth-flowing melody. (4) Anciently the Cantus firmus.
Canticle (Lat.). (1) A song of praise. **Cantico** (It.), **Cantique** (Fr.) (*kan-teek*), **Lobgesang** (Ger.) (*lope-ge-zang*). (2) The parts of Scripture—Te Deum and Benedicite Omnia Opera—that form the chief part of the musical service of the Protestant Episcopal Church.
Cantino (It.). See *Chanterelle*.
Canto (It.). The air; the melody; upper part.
Canto a capella (It.). Sacred music.
Canto fermo (It.). Cantus firmus.
Canto figura'to (It.). Florid melody; melody with variations.
Canto primo (It.). First soprano.
Canto recitativo (It.). Declamatory singing.
Canto ripieno (It.) (*ree-pe-eh'-no*). Additional soprano chorus parts.
Canto seconda (It.). Second soprano.
Cantor (Lat.), **Kantor** (Ger.). A precentor.
Cantore (It.). A singer; chorister.
Cantoris (Lat.). The side of a cathedral choir (the north) where the cantor sits is called the cantoris; the opposite side is called the decani side, where the dean sits.
Cantus (Lat.). Song.
Cantus ambrosia'nus (Lat.). Plain song.
Cantus mensura'bilis (Lat.). Measurable song; the name given to music when first written with notes of definite length.
Canzona (It.) (*cant-so'-na*). (1) A part song in popular style. (2) An instrumental composition in the old sonata form. (3) An indication of lively, rapid movement.
Canzonette (Fr.) (*can-so-net*), **Canzonetta** (It.), **Canzonet** (It.). A short part song.

Caradori, Allan Maria C. R. (*ca-ra-do-ree*). Soprano; Italy. B. 1800; d. 1865.
Carafa, Michael H. F. (*cah-rah-fah*). Composer; Italy. B. 1785; d. 1872.
Carey, Anna Louise. Contralto; U. S. A. B. 1846.

Capella (It.). Church. **Alla capella,** in church style.
Capellmeister (Ger.) (*ka-pel'-meis'-ter*). Master of the chapel; the head of the musical establishment of a noble or princely house.
Capellmeister-Musik (Ger.). Music made to order without inspiration is so called in Germany.
Capo (It.). Head; beginning. **Da capo,** from the beginning.
Capodastro (It.). Same as *Capo tasto*.
Capo tasto (It.). Head stop. A clamp which is screwed on the finger-board of the guitar, so as to "stop" all the strings, thus raising the pitch to any degree desired.
Capriccietto (It.) (*ca-pree-chee-et'-to*). A little caprice.
Caprice (Fr.) (*ca-prees'*), **Capriccio** (It.) (*ca-prit'-chio*). A whim; freak; composition without form. In German, Grille.
Caricato (It.) (*ca-ree-ca'-to*). Overloaded with display.
Carillon (Fr.) (*car-ee-yong*). (1) A set of bells played by hand or by machinery. (2) A mixture-stop in the organ.
Carilloneur (Fr.) (*ca-ree-yo-nure*). One who plays the carillon.
Carmagnole (Fr.) (*car-man-yole*). A wild song and dance of the French Revolution.
Carol. A song of praise, usually sung at Christmas and at Easter.
Carola (It.). See *Carmagnole*.
Carree' (Fr.). A breve.
Carressant (Fr.) (*ca-res-sawnt*), **Carrezzando** (It.) (*car-retz-zan'-ilo*), **Carrezzevole** (It.) (*car-retz-zeh'-vo-leh*). In a caressing manner.
Cassa grande (It.). The large drum.
Cassatio (It.) (*cas-sa-shio*). A suite; cassation.
Castanets, from *castagna* (It. *castanya*, a chestnut), **Castagnette** (It.) (*cas-tan-yet-teh*), **Castanettes** (Fr.) (*cas-tan-yet*), **Castañuelas** (Sp.) (*cas-tan-yu-eh-las*). Small wooden clappers used to mark the rhythm.
Catch. A species of canon so contrived that the meaning of the words is distorted.
Catena di trilli (It.) (*cat-teh-na dee trillee*). A chain or succession of trills.
Catgut. The usual name for gut-strings, made in reality from sheeps' intestines.

Carissimi, Giacomo (*cah-ris-see-mee*). Composer; Italy. B. 1582; d. 1671.
Carrēno, Theresa (*car-rehn-yo*). Pianist; U. S. A. B. 1853.
Catalani, Angelica (*cah-tah-lah-nee*). Soprano; Italy. B. 1783; d. 1849.

Catlings. The smallest lute strings.

Cattivo tempo (It.) (*cat-tee-vo*). The weak beat; literally, bad beat.

Cauda (Lat.). The tail or stem of a note.

Cavalet'ta (It.). See *Cabaletta*.

Cavalet'to (It., little horse). (1) Small bridge. (2) The break in the voice.

Cavatina (It.) (*cah-vah-tee'-nah*). A short air; a song without a repetition of the first member.

C Clef. See *Clef*.

Cebell. A theme consisting of alternate passages of high and low notes, upon which "divisions" or variations were played on the lute or viol.

Celere (It.) (*cheh'-leh-reh*). Quick; rapid.

Celerita (It.) (*che-leh'-ree-tah*), con. With speed.

Celeste (Fr.). Celestial. The soft pedal of the piano.

'Cello (It.) (*chel-lo*). Abbreviation of violoncello.

Cembalo (It.) (*chem'-ba-lo*). Harpsichord; piano.

Cembalist (It.) (*chem-ba-list*). A pianist.

Cembanella or **Cennamella** (It.). A flute or flageolet.

Cercar la nota (It.) (*cher-car la no-ta*). To slur or slide from one note to the next. Same as *Portamento*.

Ces (Ger.) (*tsehs*). C♭.

Chacona (Sp.) (*cha-co'-na*), **Ciaconna** (It.) (*chea-con'-na*), **Chaconne** (Fr.) (*sha-con*). A slow dance in ¾ time, written on a ground bass of eight measures, sometimes introduced in the suite.

Chair Organ. Choir organ.

Chalameau (*shah-lah-mo*) or **Chalumeau** (Fr.). See *Calamus*.

Chamber Music. Vocal or instrumental music suitable for performance in small rooms. Generally applied now to sonatas, trios, quartets, etc., for instruments.

Change of Voice. (1) Passing from one register to another. (2) The change from the child's to the adult's voice in boys. Generally occurs between fourteen and seventeen years of age.

Changes. The various melodies produced by the various ways in which a chime is rung.

Change Ringing. The art of ringing chimes.

Changing Chord. A chord struck with a bass that is not a member of the chord.

Changing Notes (nota cambiata, It.). Dissonant notes struck on the beat or accent; appoggiaturas.

Chanson (Fr.) (*shan-song*). A song, a part song; formerly a part song resembling a madrigal.

Chansonnette (Fr.) (*shan-son-net*). A little song.

Chant. A form of composition in which reciting notes alternate with phrases sung in time. There are two forms of chant, Anglican and Gregorian. The Anglican chant may be single, *i. e.*, with the reciting notes and two inflections (phrases in time) or double, that is, the length of two single chants. The Gregorian chant consists of: (1) The intonation. (2) The dominant or reciting note. (3) The mediation (analogous to the inflection, but not in strict time). (4) The dominant again. (5) Ending or cadence. The chant was undoubtedly first sung to metrical words, therefore was as rhythmic as a modern melody. This rhythmic character has been lost by adapting prose words to it.

Chant (Fr.) (*shawnt*). Song; melody; tune; vocal part.

Chantant (Fr.) (*shong-tawnt*). Singing. Café chantant, a café where singing is part of the entertainment.

Chanter. (1) A singing priest. (2) The melody pipe of the bagpipe.

Chanterelle (Fr.) (*shong-ta-rell*). The highest string of the violin, viola, and violoncello; also of the guitar and lute.

Chanteur (Fr.) (*shong-ture*). A singer (male).

Chanteuse (Fr.) (*shong-toose*). A singer (female).

Chant pastoral (Fr.). Shepherd's song.

Characters. The signs used in written music.

Characterstimme (Ger.). Lit., character voice; any solo-stop on the organ.

Characterstücke (Ger.) (*ka-rak'-ter-stee-ke*). Character pieces; descriptive music, as the pastoral symphony.

Chasse, à la (Fr.) (*a la shass*). In the hunting style.

Chef d'attaque (Fr.) (*shef d'at-tak*). The chorus leader, or leading instrument of any division of the orchestra.

Chef d'oeuvre (Fr.) (*shef d'oevr*). Masterwork.

Chef d'orchestre (Fr.) (*shef d'or-kestr*). Conductor of the orchestra; leader.

Chest of Viols. A "chest" containing two trebles, two tenors, and two basses. Called also "consort of viols."

Chadwick, Geo. W. Composer; U. S. A. B. 1854.

Chaminade, Mlle. C. (*shah-mee-nad*). Pianist, composer; France. B. 1860.

Chest Tone. The lowest register of the voice—male or female.

Chevalet (Fr.) (*she-va-lch*). Bridge of string instruments.

Chiara (It.) (*ke-ah-rah*). Clear, pure.

Chiaramente (It.) (*ke-ah-rah-men'-teh*). Clearly, distinctly.

Chiarezza (It.) (*ke-ah-ret'-za*), con. With clearness.

Chiarina (It.) (*ke-ah-ree'-na*). Clarion.

Chiave (It.) (*ke-ah'-veh*). Key or clef.

Chica (Sp.) (*chee-ka*). Old Spanish dance. The original of Giga, Jigue, and Jig.

Chiesa (It.) (*ke-eh'-sa*). Church. **Concerto da chiesa,** a church concert. **Sonata da chiesa,** a church sonata.

Chime. A set of bells, generally five to ten. To chime; to play a set of bells by striking them with hammers or by swinging their clappers. **Chime Ringing** is to swing the bells themselves.

Chirogymnast, Chiroplast. Obsolete machines for strengthening the fingers of pianists and keeping them in position.

Chitarra (It.) (*kit-tah'-rah*). Guitar.

Choeur (Fr.) (*koor*). Chorus, choir.

Choir. (1) A company of church singers. (2) The part of the church appropriated to the singers. In English churches (Anglican) the choir is divided into two parts, called the decani, or choir on the dean's side, and cantori, or choir on the cantor's side. When chanting, they generally sing antiphonally, joining in the "gloria." In anthems the words decani and cantoris are printed to indicate which side is to sing a given part.

Choir Organ. One of the divisions of the organ, the manual for which is generally the lowest. Was originally called chair organ; called in France *prestant*.

Chor (Ger.) (*kore*). Chorus, choir; a number of instruments of the same kind.

Choragus (Gk.). (1) Leader of a chorus. (2) A musical official at Oxford College, England.

Choral. (1) For a chorus. (2) An old form of psalm-tune.

Choral Service. A service of which singing is the most prominent part.

Chord, Akkord (Ger.), **Accord** (Fr.), **Accord** (It.). A combination of three or more sounds—common or perfect chord, or triad. Consists of any sound with its third and fifth; it is called major when the interval from one (or root) to three contains two whole tones; minor, when it contains a tone and a half; diminished, if there are three whole tones from one to five; augmented, if there are four whole tones from one to five. A chord is inverted when its root is not at the bass; chords with more than three letters are dissonant chords, called chords of the seventh if they contain four letters, chords of ninth if they contain five letters, etc., etc. Chords bear the name of the degree of the scale upon which they are written: First, tonic; second, supertonic; third, mediant; fourth, subdominant; fifth, dominant; sixth, submediant; seventh, leading note or diminished chord.

Chorister. A chorus- or choir-singer; a precentor.

Chorus. (1) A company of singers. (2) The refrain of a song. (3) A composition for a company of singers. (4) The mixture-stops in an organ.

Chromatic, Chromatisch (Ger.), **Chromatique** (Fr.), **Cromatico** (It.). (1) Sounds foreign to the key. (2) A scale, consisting of half-tones. Chromatic chord, one including foreign sounds. Foreign to the key; chromatic interval, one not found in the major scale; chromatic half-tone, changing the pitch without changing the letter, as C, C♯.

Church Modes. The scales derived from the Greek, in which Gregorian music or plain songs are written.

Cimbal. A dulcimer; harpsichord.

Cimbali (It.) (*chim-ba-lee*). Cymbals.

Cimbalo (It.) (*chim'-ba-lo*). See *Cembalo*. Also a tambourine.

Cimbel (Ger.) (*tsim-bel*). A mixture-stop in the organ.

Cink (Ger.) (*tsink*), **Cinq** (Fr.) (*sank*). A small reed-stop in the organ.

Cinque pace (Fr.) (*sank pace*). An old French dance. In old English, sink a pace.

Circular Canon. One which ends a half-tone higher than it begins, consequently will, if repeated often enough, go through all the keys.

Chappell, Wm. Historian; England. B. 1809; d. 1888.

Cherubini, Maria Luigi C. S. (*keh-roo-bee-nee*). Composer and theorist; Italy. B. 1760; d. 1842.

Chevé, Emile J. M. (*sheh-veh*). Inventor of simplified system of music; France. B. 1804; d. 1864.

Chickering, Jonas. Piano maker; U. S. A. B. 1798; d. 1853.

Chopin, Frederick F. (*sho-pang*). Composer and pianist; Poland. B. 1809; d. 1849.

Chorley, Henry F. Critic; England. B. 1808; d. 1872.

Chwatal, Franz X. (*shvah'-tal*). Composer; Bohemia. B. 1808; d. 1879.

Circulus (Lat.). A circle; the old sign for what was called perfect time, three beats in the measure; for imperfect time, two beats in the measure, the circle was broken in half, thus, C. It is from this the sign for common time is derived; it is not as is generally supposed the letter C.

Cis (Ger.) (*tsis*). C sharp.

Cithara (Gk.). An ancient lute.

Citoli. Old name for the dulcimer.

Civetteria (It.) (*chee-vet-tee'-rea*), con. With coquetry.

Clairon (Fr.). Clarion.

Clangtint. A term introduced by Tyndal to designate the quality of sounds (translation of Ger. *Klangfarbe*); means much the same thing as the French word *timbre*.

Claque bois (Fr.) (*clack boa*). The xylophone; in German, Strohfiedel; straw fiddle. Italian, Organo di legno. Graduated strips of hard wood laid on supports made of straw, played by striking with small hammers held in the hands.

Clarabella. An eight-foot soft organ-stop.

Clarabel Flute. The same stop when of four-foot tone.

Clarichord. An old variety of the harpsichord.

Clarinet or **Clarionet** (a little clarion). A wind instrument with a beating reed, invented in 1654 by Denner. The compass of the clarinet is from E third space bass to the second C above the treble (the highest octave is rarely used). Clarinets are made in several keys; those used in the orchestra are in C, B♭ and A; the B♭ clarinet sounds a whole tone lower than the written notes, the A clarinet a minor third lower; alto and bass clarinets are also used, the former in F and E♭, the latter an octave below the ordinary clarinet. The clarinet has four well-marked registers: the first, or chalumeau, extends from the lowest note to the octave above; second to B♭ in treble staff; third to C above treble staff; fourth the rest of the compass.

Clarinetto (It.), **Klarinette** (Ger.), **Clarinette** (Fr.). The clarinet.

Clarino (It.) (*clah-ree-no*). Clarion or trumpet; an organ-stop; four-foot reed.

Claviatur or **Klaviatur** (Ger.) (*kla-fee-a-toor'*). Keyboard.

Clavicembalo (It.) (*cla-vee-chem'-ba-lo*). keyed dulcimer; the harpsichord.

Clavichord. An instrument resembling a square piano. The strings were vibrated by forcing wedge-shaped pieces of brass called tangents against them. By depressing the keys, the tangent acted both as a means of vibrating the string and as a bridge. When the finger was raised, the string was damped by a piece of woolen cloth wrapped round it, between the tangent and the pin-block. The chief interest in this obsolete instrument is the fact that it was the favorite of J. S. Bach.

Claviçon (Fr.) (*cla-vee-soong*) [from Lat. *clavis*, a key]. The harpsichord.

Clavicytherium. A variety of harpsichord.

Clavier or **Klavier** (Ger.) (*klah-feer'*). (1) Keyboard. (2) Used as a name for the pianoforte.

Clavier (Fr.) (*klah-vee-eh*). An organ manual.

Clavierauszug (Ger.) (*klah-feer-ows-tsoog*). A pianoforte score or edition.

Clef [from Lat. *clavis*, a key]. A sign placed on the staff to indicate the names and pitch of the sounds. Three clefs are used in modern music: (1) The treble or G clef, also called violin clef; this is now always placed on the second line. (2) The C clef:—

this clef, when on first line, is called soprano clef; on second line, mezzo-soprano clef; on third line, alto clef, also viola or alto trombone clef; on fourth line, tenor clef; used also for upper notes of violoncello and bassoon. The C clef always signifies middle C; that is, C that lies between the fifth line bass staff and first line treble staff. Bass or F clef, placed on the fourth line, occasionally on the third, when it is called the baritone clef; used for bass voices and all bass instruments.

Cloche (Fr.) (*closh*). A bell.

Clochette (Fr.) (*closhet'*). A small bell.

Close Harmony. When the sounds forming the chords are drawn together as much as possible.

No. 1, close harmony; No. 2, open harmony.

Cimarosa, Dominico (*chee-mah-ro-sah*). Composer; Italy. B. 1749; d. 1801.

Clapisson, Antonie L. (*clah-pee-song*). Composer and pianist; Italy. B. 1808; d. 1866.

Clarke, Hugh A. Theorist and composer; Canada. B. 1839.

Clay, Frederick. Composer; England. B. 1840; d. 1889.

Coda (It.). "Tail." A passage added after the development of a fugue is finished, or after the "form" of a sonata, rondo, or any other composition has been completed, to produce a more satisfactory close.

Codetta (It.). A short coda.

Cogli stromenti (It.) (*col-yee stro-men'-tee*). With the instruments.

Coi (*coee*), **Col, Coll', Colla, Colle, Collo** (It.). With the.

Col arco. With the bow. Used after the direction "pizzicato."

Col basso. With the bass.

Col canto. With the melody.

Col legno (It.) (*col-lane-yo*). With the wood; a direction to strike the strings of the violin with the back of the bow.

Colla parte. With the principal part.

Colla voce. With the voice. In score writing, to save the labor of re-writing a part which is to be played by two or more instruments. It is usual to write the part for one instrument, for instance, the violin, and write the words *col violino* on the staff appropriated to the other instrument.

Colophony. Rosin.

Colorato (It.) (*co-lo-rah'-to*). Florid.

Coloratura (It.) (*co-lo-rah-too'-rah*). Florid passages in vocalization.

Come (It.) (*coh-meh*). As; like.

Come prima (It.) (*coh'-meh pree'-mah*). As at first.

Comes (Lat.) (*co mes*). The answer to the subject, dux of a fugue. *Dux* means leader; *comes*, follower.

Comma. The difference between a major and a minor tone.

Commodamen'te, Commodet'ta (It.). Quietly; leisurely; without hurry.

Commodo (It.) (*com-mo'-do*). At a convenient rate of motion.

Common Chord. The combination of any sound (called the root) with its major or minor 3d and perfect 5th.

Common Metre, or Ballad Metre. A stanza, consisting of alternate lines of four and three iambuses; as,

How blest is he who ne'er consents
By ill advice to walk.

Common Time. Two beats, or any multiple of two beats, in the measure. The signs $\frac{2}{4}$, C, ₵, $\frac{4}{4}$ ($\frac{3}{2}$, ?, $\frac{4}{2}$ rare) indicate simple common time; $\frac{6}{4}$, $\frac{6}{8}$, $\frac{12}{4}$, $\frac{12}{8}$ indicate compound common time, $\frac{6}{8}$ being compounded from two measures of $\frac{3}{8}$; $\frac{6}{4}$ from two measures of $\frac{3}{4}$; and $\frac{12}{8}$ from four measures of $\frac{3}{8}$ time.

Compass. The complete series of sounds that may be produced by a voice or instrument.

Compiacevole (It.) (*com-pea-chch'-vo-leh*). Agreeable; pleasing; charming.

Complement. The interval which being added to another, will make an octave. A complementary interval is found by inverting any given interval that is less than an octave.

Composer, Componista (It.), **Componist or Komponist** (Ger.). One who composes music.

Composition. The sounds that make up the series of a mixture- or other compound organ-stop.

Composition Pedal or Knob. A mechanism worked by the foot or by pressing a button with the finger, which throws on or off certain combinations of stops in the organ.

Compound Intervals. Intervals greater than the octave.

Compound Times. Those formed by adding together several measures of simple time. $\frac{6}{4}$, $\frac{6}{8}$, $\frac{12}{4}$, $\frac{12}{8}$ are compound common, having an even number of beats; $\frac{9}{4}$, $\frac{9}{8}$ are compound triple, having an odd number of beats.

Con (It.). With.

Concert. Any musical performance other than dramatic.

Concertante (It.) (*con-cher-tan'-tch*). A composition in which two or more parts are of equal importance.

Concerted Music. Music for several voices or instruments, or for voices and instruments combined.

Concertina. A small free-reed instrument somewhat like the accordion, but far superior.

Concertmeister (Ger.). Concert master; the leader or conductor of the orchestra.

Concerto (It.) (*con-cher'-to*), **Conzert** (Ger.), **Concert** (Fr.) (*con-sehr*). A composition designed to display the capabilities of one instrument accompanied by others.

Concert spirituel (Fr.) (*con-sehr spiri-too-el*). An association in Paris for the performance of sacred music, vocal and instrumental, founded 1725.

Concertstück (Ger.) (*steck*). Concert piece; concerto.

Concitato (It.) (*con-chee-tah' to*). Agitated.

Concone, Giuseppe (*con-co-neh, jew-sep-peh*). Teacher and composer; Italy. B. 1810; d. 1861.

C'ementi, Muzio (*cleh-men-tee, mootsio*). Composer and pianist; Italy. B. 1752; d. 1832.

Concord. Agreeing. Literally, chording with.

Concordant. (1) Agreeing with. (2, Fr.) The baritone voice.

Conductor. The director or leader of a chorus or orchestra.

Cone Gamba. An organ-stop with bell-shaped top.

Conjunct (Lat., *con-junctus*). Joined together. Adjacent sounds in the scale.

Conjunct Motion. Moving by steps.

Consecutive. Two or more of the same intervals in succession.

Consecutive Fifths. Two voices or parts moving together a fifth apart.

Consecutive Octaves. Two voices or parts moving together an octave apart. Consecutive fifths and octaves are forbidden by the laws of composition, but the prohibition is frequently disregarded by the best writers.

Consequent. The answer to a fugue subject; comes.

Consolante (It.) (*con-so-lan'-teh*). Soothing.

Consonance. Literally, sounding together. Those intervals that enter into the composition of the common chord and its inversions, viz., major and minor 3d and 6th, perfect 4th and 5th, and octave. The major and minor 3d and 6th are called imperfect consonances, being equally consonant whether major or minor. The perfect 4th, 5th, and 8th are called perfect because any alteration of them produces a dissonance; *i. e.*, an interval that requires resolution. N. B.—This definition of consonance applies only to the modern tempered scale.

Con sordini (It.) (*sor-dee'-nee*). With the mute. (1) In piano music, with soft pedal. (2) Instruments of the violin family: a direction to fasten on the bridge a small implement of wood or metal which has the effect of deadening the tone. (3) Brass instruments: a direction to place a cone-shaped piece of wood covered with leather in the bell, which has the same effect.

Consort. A chest of viols.

Contra (It.). Against; in compound words, means an octave below, as contra-bass, contra-fagotto.

Contra danza (It.). Country dance.

Contralto (It.). The lowest female voice, usually called alto.

Contraposaune. A 16 or 32-foot reed-organ stop.

Converse, C. C. Composer; U. S. A. B. 1832.

Corelli, Arcangelo (*cor-rel-lee*). Violinist; Italy. B. 1653; d. 1713.

Contrapuntal. Belonging to counterpoint.

Contrapuntist. One skilled in counterpoint, or who writes on the subject of counterpoint.

Contratenor. The highest male voice.

Contra violone (It.) (*vee-o-lo'-neh*), **Contra basse** (Fr.). Double bass.

Countertenor. The developed falsetto. See *Alto.*

Convict of Music. An institution for musical instruction. [Lat., *convictus*, an associate, from *convivere*, to live together.]

Cor (Fr.). A horn.

Cor Anglais (*ong-lay*). English horn; a variety of the hautboy, sounding a fifth lower.

Corale (It.) (*co-rah'-leh*). A choral.

Coranto (It.), **Courante** (Fr.). An old dance in triple time, used as a movement in the suite.

Corda (It.). String. **Una corda, Due corde, Tre corde** or **Tutte corde,** one string, two strings, three strings, all the strings, are directions for the use of the pedal in Grand *p. f.* that shifts the action so as to strike one, two, or all of the strings allotted to each key.

Cornamusa (It.) (*corna-moo-sa*), **Cornemuse** (Fr.) (*corn-moos*). Bagpipe.

Cornet, Cornetto (It.), **Zinke** (Ger.). (1) Originally a coarse-toned instrument of the haut-boy family. (2) A compound stop in the organ. (3) **Cornet-a-piston,** a brass instrument of the trumpet family. (4) Echo cornet, a compound organ-stop with small scale pipes, usually in the swell.

Corno (It.). Horn; the French horn, or Waldhorn (Ger.). The horn of the orchestra.

Corno alto. High horn. **Corno basso,** low horn.

Corno di basetto. Basset horn.

Corno di caccia. Hunting horn.

Corno Inglese. Cor Anglais.

Cornopean. Same as *Cornet* (brass); a reed-stop on the organ, 8-foot tone.

Coro (It.). Chorus.

Corona (It.). "Crown;" a pause.

Corrente (It.) (*cor-ren'-teh*). Coranto.

Cottillion (Fr., Cottillon, *co-tee-yon'*). A dance with numerous figures, originally rather lively, now much the same as the Quadrille.

Couched Harp. The spinet.

Corri, Domenico (*cor-ree*). Composer; Italy. B. 1746; d. 1825.

Costa, Sir Michael. Composer and conductor; Italy. B. 1810; d. 1884.

Count. The beats in the measure are called counts, from the practice of counting the time.

Counterpoint [from Latin *contra-punctus*, against the point]. Notes were originally called points, hence when another set of points were added above or below the points of the theme, they were called counterpoints. In modern use counterpoint may be defined as the art of making two or more parts move together with such freedom that they seem to be independent, each one with a design of its own.

Counter-subject. A theme employed in conjunction with the principal theme in a fugue.

Coup d'archet (Fr.) (*coo d'ar-shay*). A stroke of the bow.

Coupler. A mechanism in the organ, by means of which the keys of two manuals are joined so that the depression of the keys of one causes the depression of the corresponding keys of the other. **Pedal Coupler** joins pedal keys to one of the manuals. **Octave Coupler** causes the octave above or below each key struck to sound either on the same or on another manual.

Couplet (Fr.) (*coo-play*). Stanza; ballad.

Couplet (Eng.). A pair of rhyming lines. Two notes played in the time of three of the same denomination.

Cracovienne (Fr.). Polacca.

Cremona. (1) A town in Italy celebrated for its violin makers. (2) A violin made in Cremona. (3) A soft 8 ft. reed organ stop (corrupted from *Krummhorn*).

Couperin, Armand Louis. Organist. B. 1600; d. 1665.

Couperin, François (*koo-peh-rang*). Called le Grand. Composer and improver of system of fingering; France. B. 1668; d. 1733.

Cowen, Frederick H. Composer; England. B. 1852.

Cramer, John Baptist (*crah-mer*). Pianist and composer; Germany. B. 1771; d. 1858.

Crescentini, Girolamo (*creshen-tee'-nee*). Sopranist and composer; Italy. B. 1766; d. 1846.

Cristofori, Bartolomeo di F. (*cris-to-fo-ree*). Inventor of the piano; Italy. B. 1651; d. 1731.

Crescendo (It.) (*cray-shen-do*). Abbreviation, *cres.*, sign: ⸺⸺ to increase in loudness [from It. *crescere*, to increase].

Crescendozug (Ger., hybrid of It. and Ger.). The swell box of the organ.

Croche (Fr.) (*crosh*). An eighth-note.

Crotchet. A quarter-note.

Crowd, Crouth, Crood, Crooth. An ancient string instrument played with a bow. Of celtic origin.

Crush Note. Appoggiatura.

Cue. The last notes of one voice or instrument, written in the part of another as a guide to come in.

Cuivre (Fr.). Brass. **Faire cuivrer** (*fare koo-e-vreh*), a direction to produce a rattling metallic note on the horn by inserting the hand partway in the bell.

Cuvette (Fr.) (*koo-vet'*). The pedal of a harp.

Cyclical Forms. Forms of composition in which one or more themes return in prescribed order, as sonata, rondo, etc.

Cymbals (*Becken*, Ger., *Piatti*, It.). (1) Discs of metal clashed together or struck with drumsticks, used in the orchestra and in military music. (2) A shrill compound stop in the organ.

Czakan (*cha-kan*). A cane flute.

Czardas (*char-dash*). A Hungarian dance with sudden alterations of tempo.

Czimbel (*chim-bel*). A dulcimer strung with wire strings; a national instrument in Hungary.

Czimken (*chim-ken*). A Polish dance.

Crivelli, Domenico (*cree-vel-lee*). Teacher of singing; Italy. B. 1794; d. 1856.

Cross, Michael H. Composer, organist; U. S. A. B. 1833.

Crouch, Frederick N. Ballad writer; England. B. 1808; d. 1896.

Cui (*coo-ee*), Cesar A. Pianist; Poland. B. 1835.

Curschmann, Karl F. (*koorsch-man*). Composer; Germany. B. 1805; d. 1841.

Curwen, Rev. John. Inventor of Curwen's system; England. B. 1816; d. 1880.

Cusins, Sir Wm. G. Pianist, composer. B. 1833; d. 1893.

Cuzzoni, Francesca (*coolzo-nee*). Soprano; Italy. B. 1700; d. 1770.

Czerny, Karl (*chur-neh*). Composer and pianist; Austria. B. 1791; d. 1857.

D

D. Second letter in the natural scale; the third string of the violin; second string of viola and 'cello; abbreviation of Da or Dal; from D. C., da capo, D. S., dal segno.

Da (It.). From.

Da ballo (It.). In dance style.

Da camera (It.). Chamber music.

Da capo (It.). From the beginning; abbreviated D. C.

Da capo al fine. From the beginning to the word fine (*fee-neh*), the end, or a double bar with ⌒ over it.

Da capo al segno (It.) (*sehn-yo*). From beginning to the sign 𝄋

D. C. al 𝄋 e poi la coda. From the beginning to the sign, then the coda.

D. C. senza replica (It.) (*sehntza reh'-pleccah*). From the beginning without repeating the parts.

D. C. senza repetitione (*rch-peh-tee-shee-o-neh*) means the same as above.

Da capella (It.). Church music.

Daina or Dainos. A Lithuanian love-song.

Damper. A mechanism in the piano to stop the vibration of the strings when the finger is raised from the key.

Damper Pedal. The miscalled loud pedal, a mechanism controlled by the foot for raising all the dampers at once from the strings.

Danse. A piece of music meant to accompany rhythmical movements of the body.

Darabookka. An Arabian drum.

Dash. (1) A line drawn through a figure (𝄖) in figured bass signifies the note must be raised chromatically. (2) A short stroke over a note, signifying it is to be played staccato.

Daumen (Ger.) (*dow-men*). The thumb.

D dur (Ger.). D major.

Début (Fr.) (*deh-boo*). A first appearance.

Decani (Lat.). (1) The dean's side in a cathedral. (2) That part of a choir that occupies the dean's side.

Deceptive Cadence. One in which the dominant chord is not followed by the tonic.

Decima (Lat.). An organ-stop pitched an octave above the tierce.

Deciso (It.) (*deh-chee'-so*). Decided; energetically.

Declamando (It.) (*deh-cla-man'-do*). In declamatory style.

Declamation. The correct enunciation of the words in singing, and their rhetorical accent.

Decres. Abbreviation of **Decrescendo** (It.) (*deh-creh-shen'-do*). To decrease in volume of sound. Sign : >

Decuplet. A group of ten notes played in the time of eight of the same denomination.

Defective. The diminished 5th is sometimes so called.

Degree. From one letter to the next, a degree may be a half-tone, minor second; whole tone, major second; tone and a half, augmented second.

Del, Della, Delli, Dello (It.). Of the.

Deliberatamente (It). Deliberately.

Deliberato (It.) (*deh-lee-beh-rah'-to*), con. With deliberation.

Delicatamente (It.). Delicately; gently.

Delicatezza (It.) (*deh-lee-cah-tetza*), con. With delicacy.

Delicatissimo (It.). Exceedingly delicate.

Delicato (It.) (*deh-lee-cah-to*). Delicate.

Délie (Fr.) (*deh-lee-a*). The reverse of legato. Literally, not tied.

Delirio (It.) (*deh-lee-reeo*), con. With frenzy.

Demi-baton (Fr.) (*deh-mee-bah-tong*). A rest of two measures.

Dalayrac, Nicolas (*dah-leh-rak*). France. B. 1753; d. 1809.

D'Albert, Ch. L. N. Writer of band music; Germany. B. 1809; d. 1886 in London.

D'Albert, Eugene, his son. Pianist; Scotland. B. 1864.

Damoreau, Laura C. M. (*dah-mo-ro*), known as **Cinti Damoreau** (*chin-tee*). Singer. B. 1801; d. 1863.

Damrosch, Leopold. Violinist; Posen. B. 1832; d. 1885.

Damrosch, Walter, his son. Composer, conductor; Germany. B. 1862.

Damrosch, Frank. Conductor, educator; Germany. B. 1859.

Dancla, Jean Ch. Violinist; France. B. 1818; d. 1895.

David, Felicien C. (*dah-veed*). Composer; France. B. 1810; d. 1876.

David, Ferdinand (*dah-veed*). Violinist; Germany. B. 1810; d. 1873.

Day, Alfred. Theorist; England. B. 1810; d. 1849.

De Koven, R. Composer; U. S. A. B. 1859.

Delibes, Leo (*deh-leeb*). Operas; France. B. 1836; d. 1891.

Demi-croche (Fr.) (*crosh*). A sixteenth-note.

Demi-jeu (Fr.) (*zheu*). Half play; a direction in organ playing to use half the power of the instrument.

Demi-pause (Fr.). A half-rest.

Demi-semi-quaver. Thirty-second note.

Demi-soupir (Fr.) (*soo-pee*). Eighth-rest.

Derivative. Any chord of which the root is not at the bass; an inverted chord.

Des (Ger.). D flat.

Descant or **Discant.** (1) The earliest attempts at adding other parts to a cantus were called descant. (2) The highest part (soprano) in vocal music.

Des dur (Ger.). D♭ major.

Desiderio (It.) (*deh-see-deé-rio*). Longing.

Des moll (Ger.). D♭ minor.

Dessus (Fr.) (*des-soo*). The soprano part in vocal music.

Destinto (It.) (*deh-stin-to*). Distinct.

Desto (It.). Sprightly; briskly.

Destra (It.). Right. **Mano destra**, the right hand. **Mano sinistra**, the left hand. **Colla destra**, with the right. A direction in piano music.

Détaché (Fr.) (*deh-tash-ch*). Detached; staccato.

Determinato (It.). Resolutely; with determination.

Detto (It.). The same. **Il detto voce**, the same voice.

Development. [In German, *Durchführung*.] (1) The technical name of that part of a sonata form which precedes the return of the principal theme. In the development both the themes are used in fragments mixed with new matter, the object being to present the musical thought in every possible aspect. (2) The working out of a fugue.

Devoto (It.). Devout.

Devozione (It.) (*deh-vot-see-o'-neh*), con. With devotion.

Di (It.) (*dee*). By, with, of, for. **Di bravura**, with bravura. Literally, with bravery.

Diana (It.), **Diane** (Fr.). A morning serenade; aubade.

Diapason (Gr.). (1) An octave. (2) An organ-stop of 8-foot pitch, open or closed (stopped). (3) The standard pitch, A = 435 vibrations per second, not yet universally adopted.

Diatonic. (1) The major and minor scales. Strictly speaking, the modern harmonic minor is not purely diatonic, owing to the presence of the augmented 2d between 6 and 7. (2) Diatonic chords, melody, progressive modulation, are those in which no note foreign to the scale in which they are written appears. [From Gr. *dia teino*, to stretch; referring to the string of the canon or monochord.]

Di colto (It.). Suddenly.

Diecetto (It.) (*dee-chetto*). A composition for ten instruments.

Dièse (Fr.) (*dee-ehs*). A sharp.

Difficile (It.) (*dif-fee'-chee-leh*), **Difficile** (Fr.) (*dif-fi-seel*). Difficult.

Di gala (It.). Merrily.

Diluendo (It.) [*diluere*, to dilute]. Wasting away; decrescendo.

Diminished. (1) Intervals less than minor or perfect. (2) A chord with diminished 5th, as on the 7th of the scale or the 2d of the minor scale. (3) Diminished 7th chord, a chord composed of three superimposed minor thirds, as B D F A♭

Diminuendo (It.). Same as *Decrescendo*.

Diminution. In canon and fugue, when the answer (comes) is given in notes of half (or less) the value of those in the subject (dux).

Di molto (It.). Very much. **Allegro di molto**, very fast.

Direct. (1) A sign 🎵 placed at the end of a staff to indicate what is the first note on the next page. (2) In MS. music it indicates that the measure is completed on the next line.

Direct Motion. Both (or all) parts ascending or descending together.

Dis (Ger.). D sharp.

Discant. See *Descant*.

Discord. Cacophony; noise. Used incorrectly for dissonance. Dissonance is musical, but discord never is.

Disinvolto (It.). Free; naturally; easily.

Disjunct Motion. Moving by skips.

Dis moll (Ger.). D♯ minor.

Disperato (It.), **Con disperazione** (*dis-peh-ratz-ee-o'-neh*). Desparingly; with desperation.

Dispersed Harmony. When the members of the chords are separated widely.

Disposition. (1) Of a chord, the order in which its members are arranged. (2) Of a score, the order in which the instruments

---

De Reszke, Eduard (*rets-kay*). Baritone; Poland. B. 1855.

De Reszke, Jean (*rets-kay*), his brother. Tenor. B. 1852.

Devrient, Ed. P. (*deh'-vree-ong*). Basso; Germany. B. 1801; d. 1877.

Devrient, Mme. W. Schroeder. Soprano. B. 1804; d. 1860.

are arranged on the page. (3) Of an orchestra, the positions assigned to the different instruments.

Dissonance. An interval, one or both of whose members must move in a certain way to satisfy the ear. All augmented and diminished intervals, seconds, sevenths, and ninths, are dissonances.

Ditty. A short simple air, originally with words that contained a moral.

Divertimento (It.) (*dee-ver-tee-men'-to*), **Divertissement** (Fr.) (*dee-vehr-tiss-mong*). (1) A pleasing, light entertainment. (2) A composition or arrangement for the piano; this is the most usual meaning. (3) A suite or set with a number of movements for instruments, called also a serenata.

Divisi (It.). Divided; a direction that the string instruments must divide into two masses or more, as may be indicated by the composer.

Divisions. An old name for elaborate variations.

Divoto (It.). See *Devoto*.

D moll (Ger.). D minor.

Do. (1) The first note in the natural scale in Italy; this syllable was substituted for *ut*, the first of the Guidonian syllables; *ut* is still retained in France. (2) In the "movable do" system of singing, the keynote of every scale is called *do*.

Dodecuplet. A group of twelve notes played in the time of eight of the same denomination.

Doigter (Fr.) (*doy-teh*). See *Fingering*.

Dolcan, Dulciana. Soft eight-foot open organ-stop.

Dolce. A stop of same character as dulciana, but softer.

Dolce (It.) (*dol-cheh*). Sweet.

Dolcemente, con dolcezza (It.) (*dol-chet-zah*). With sweetness.

Dolciano, Dolcino (It.), **Dulcan** (Ger.). Dulciana stop.

Dolcissimo (It.) (*dole-chis-see-mo*). As sweet as possible.

Dolente (It.). Afflicted.

Dolentimente (It.). Mournfully; afflictedly.

Dolzflöte (Ger.) (*dolts-fla-teh*). (1) The old German flute with six holes and one key. (2) A soft eight-foot organ-stop.

Diabelli, Anton (*dee-a-bel'-lee*). Composer; Germany. B. 1781; d. 1858.

Döhler, Theo. (*deh-ler*). Pianist; Italy. B. 1814; d. 1856.

Donizetti, Gaetano (*do-nee-tzet'-tee, gah-e-*

Domchor (Ger.) (*dome-kor*). Cathedral choir.

Dominant. (1) The fifth note in the scale. (2) The reciting note in Gregorian chants.

Dominant Chord. The major triad on the fifth of the major or minor scale.

Dominant Key. The usual key in which the second theme of a sonata or rondo in major mode is written.

Dominant Seventh. The seventh over the root added to the dominant chord.

Dopo (It.). After.

Doppio (It.) (*dop'-pee-o*). Double, as *doppio movemento*, double movement, *i. e.*, twice as fast.

Dorian. A Greek or ecclesiastical mode, D to D.

Dot. (1) A dot after a note or rest increases its duration one-half; a second dot increases the duration one-half of the first dot

(2) A dot over a note signifies that it is to be played or sung staccato. (3) Dots combined with slur

in music for bow instruments signify the notes are to be played with one motion of the bow with a slight stop after each note; in piano music, to raise the arm with stiff wrist after each note or chord and let it fall lightly from the elbow on the next. (4) Dots over a note thus signify that the note is to be repeated by sub-division into as many notes as there are dots.

Double. (1) An old name for *variation*. (2) An octave below the standard pitch, as double bass, double diapason, double bassoon.

Double (Fr.) (*doobl*). A variation on a minuet; in Italian, *alternativo*.

Double Bar. Two single bars placed close together signifying: (1) The end of a part or piece. (2) A change of key or of time signature. (3) In hymn-tunes the end of a line.

Double Bass. The violone [It., *vee-o-lo-neh*, Fr., *contrabasse*]. The largest of the

---

tah'-no). Composer; Italy. B. 1797; d. 1848.

Donzelli, Domenico (*doud-sel'-lee*). Tenor; Italy. B. 1790; d. 1873.

Dorn, Heinrich L. E. Composer, pianist; Germany. B. 1804; d. 1892.

violin family. Two kinds are in use, one with three strings tuned:

one with four strings tuned:

The pitch is an octave below the written notes.

Double Bassoon. A bassoon of 16-foot pitch.

Double Bourdon. An organ-stop of 32-foot tone.

Double Chant. See *Chant*.

Double Counterpoint. A counterpoint so contrived that it may be placed either above or below the theme, without producing any forbidden intervals. A double counterpoint is said to be at the octave when, if written above the theme, it may be moved down an octave; at the 10th, if it may be moved down a tenth; at the 12th, if it may be moved down a twelfth. Double counterpoint may also be at the 9th and 11th, but the former are much more used.

Double Croche (Fr.) (*doobl crosh*). A sixteenth-note.

Double Diapason. An organ-stop of 16-foot tone.

Double Drum. A drum struck at both ends.

Double Flat, ♭♭, depresses a letter a whole tone.

Double Main (*mang*). Octave-coupler in the organ.

Double Sharp, ×, raises a letter a whole tone.

Double Stop. In violin music, playing simultaneously on two strings.

Double Tongueing. Playing repeated staccato notes on the flute, cornet, etc., by a movement of the point of the tongue against the roof of the mouth.

Double Touche (*toosh*). A contrivance for regulating the depth of the descent of the keys of the harmonium.

Doublette (Fr.) (*doo-blet*). A two-foot organ-stop, the 15th, or a compound stop of two ranks.

Doucement (Fr.) (*doos-mong*). Sweetly, softly.

Doux (Fr.) (*doo*). Sweet, soft.

Dowland, John. Madrigalist and lutenist. B. 1562; d. 1626.

Dragonetti, D. (*drah-go-net'-tee*). Double bass player; Italy. B. 1755; d. 1846.

Down Beat. The first beat in the measure; the principal accent in the measure.

Down Bow. In instruments of the violin family, the motion of the bow from the nut to the point. The sign is ⊓ or ∧. In French the word *tirez* (*tee-reh*), draw.

Doxology [from Greek *doxa*, praise; *lego*, to proclaim]. A short ascription of praise to the Trinity, metrical or otherwise.

Drammatico (It.), **Drammaticamente** (It.) Dramatic; in dramatic style.

Drängend (Ger.) (*draynt'-gent*). Hurrying, accelerating.

Dritta (It.). The right hand.

Droit or Droite (Fr.) (*droa*). Right hand.

Drone. The pipe that sounds one note continuously in the bagpipe.

Drum. An instrument of percussion, the body hollow, made of wood or metal, one or both ends being covered with vellum or parchment drawn tight by braces. Three kinds of drum are used in modern music: (1) The kettle drum; this is the only one that may be tuned to definite pitch; a pair are generally used in the orchestra, tuned usually to the 1st and 5th of the key. (2) The snare drum or side drum, with parchment at both ends; that at one end is crossed by several thick gut-strings that rattle when the drum is struck on the other end by the pair of drumsticks. (3) The long drum, double drum, *grosse caisse*, used chiefly in military music; struck on both ends.

Drum Slade. A drummer.

Due (It.) (*doo-eh*). Two. **A due,** by two; that is, divide, when marked over a string part in the orchestra; but when over a wind instrument part it means that both of the pair are to play the notes.

Due corde (It.). Two strings. In violin music, means that the note is to be played on the open string and as a stopped note simultaneously. The only notes that may be so played on the violin are:—

sometimes signified by writing them as above.

Duet, Duo (Fr.), **Duetto** (It.). A composition for two voices or instruments or for two performers on the piano or organ.

Duettino (It.) (*doo-et-tee'-no*). A little duet.

Dulciana. A soft, open, 8-foot organ-stop; flue pipes; in some foreign organs, a soft reed-stop.

Dressel, Otto (*dreh-zel*). Pianist; Germany. B. 1826; d. 1890.

Dreyschock, Alex. (*dry-shock*). Pianist; Germany. B. 1818; d. 1869.

Dulcimer. (1) An instrument consisting of an oblong or square box strung with wire strings, struck by small hammers held in the hands of the performer. (2) A small toy instrument, in which strips of glass or metal are used instead of wire strings, played in the same way.

Duolo (It.) (*doo-o'-lo*), **con doloroso** (It.), **con dolore** (It.) (*do-lo'-reh*). Plaintively; mournfully.

Duple. Double. **Duple Time,** two beats in the measure.

Dur (Ger.) (*duhr*). Literally, hard; major.

Dur (Fr.). Hard; coarse; rough.

Duramente (It.) (*doo-ra-men'-teh*). Roughly.

Durchführung (Ger.) (*doorch'-fee-roonk*). The working out; development of a sonata or fugue. See *Development*.

Durchkomponirt (Ger.) (*doorch'-kom-po-neert*). Composed through. Applied to a song that has a separate setting for each stanza.

Durezza (It.) (*doo-retz-a*), **con.** With sternness.

Dur-moll Tonart (Ger.). Major-minor scale or mode; a diatonic scale with major 3d and minor 6th.

Duro (It.), **Durate** (It.). Harshly.

Düster (Ger.) (*dees-teh?*). Gloomy; mournful; sad.

Dux (Lat.). Leader; the theme of a fugue.

Dulcken, Ferdinand Q. (*dool-ken*). Composer, pianist; Germany. B. 1837.

Dulcken, Marie Louise. Pianist; Germany. B. 1811; d. 1850.

Duschek or **Dussek,** Franz. Composer; Hungary. B. 1736; d. 1799.

Duschek or **Dussek,** Johann L. Pianist. B. 1761; d. 1812.

Dussek, Sophia, wife of last. Pianist, singer, harpist; Scotland. B. 1775; d. 18—.

Duvernoy, Jean B. (*doo-ver-noy*). Pianist, teacher; France. B. 1802; d. 1880.

Dvorak, Anton (*tfor-shak*). Composer; Bohemia. B. 1841; d. 1904.

Dwight, J. S. Critic; U. S. A. B. 1813; d. 1893.

Dykes, Rev. J. B. Hymn writer; England. B. 1823; d. 1876.

E

E. (1) The third of the natural major scale, fifth of the natural minor. (2) The first or highest string (chanterelle) of the violin. (3) The fourth or lowest string of the double bass.

E (It.) (*eh*). And; when the word that follows begins with a vowel, **ed** (*ehd*).

Ebollimento or **Ebollizione** (It.) (*eh-bol-litz-ee-o'-neh*). Boiling over; sudden expression of passion.

Ecclesiastical Modes. The scales called also Ambrosian and Gregorian, in which plain song and plain chant are written. They differ from the modern diatonic in the position of the half-tones; their position depends upon the initial note of the scale.

Echelle (Fr.) (*eh-shel*). A scale.

Echo Organ. A set of pipes in old organs enclosed in a box.

Eclat (Fr.) (*eh-claw*). Fire; spirit.

Eclogue or **Eglogue** (Fr.) [from Greek ἐκλογή, to select]. A pastoral; a poem in which shepherds and shepherdesses are the actors.

Ecole (Fr.) (*eh-cole*). A school or style of music.

Ecossais (Fr.) (*ek-cos-seh*) or **Ecossaise** (*ek-cos-saze*). (1) In the Scotch style. (2) A lively dance.

Eguale (It.) (*eh-gwah-leh*). Equal; steady.

Egualmente. Equally; steadily.

Einfach (Ger.). Simple. **Einfachheit,** simplicity in construction.

Einfalt (Ger.). Simplicity in manner. **Mit Einfalt,** in a simple, natural manner.

Einleitung (Ger.) (*ein-lei-toonk*). Leading in; introductory.

Einschlafen (Ger.). Diminish in power and movement.

Eis (Ger.) (*eh-is*). E sharp.

Eisteddfod (Welsh) (*ice-steth'-fod*). In modern usage a musical contest for prizes.

Eleganza (It.) (*eh-lee-gantza*), **con.** With grace.

Elegy. A mournful poem commemorating the dead.

Elevato (It.) (*eh-leh-vah'-to*). Elevated; exalted.

Eberl, Anton (*eh'-berl*). Composer, pianist; Austria. B. 1766; d. 1817.

Eddy, Hiram Clarence. Organist; U. S. A. B. 1851.

Eligiac. In the style of an elegy.
Embellishment. The ornaments of melody, as trill, turn, mordent, etc.
Embouchure (Fr.) (*om-boo-shoor*). (1) The mouth-piece of a wind instrument. (2) The position and management of the mouth and lips of the player.
E moll (Ger.). E minor.
Empater les sons (Fr.) (*om-pahteh leh song*). Literally, to strike the sounds together; to sing extremely legato.
Empfindung (Ger.) (*emp-fin-doonk*). Emotion; passion.
Emporté (Fr.) (*om-por-teh*), **Empressé** (Fr.) (*om-pres-seh*). Hurried; eager; passionate.
Encore (Fr.) (*ong-core*), **Ancora** (It.). Again; a demand for the re-appearance of a performer; the piece sung or played on the re-appearance of the performer.
Energia (It.) (*eh-nur-jea*), con. With energy.
Energico, Energicamente, Energisch (Ger.). Energetic; forcibly.
Enfatico (It.) (*en-fa'-tee-ko*). Emphatic; decided.
Enfasi (It.) (*en-fah'-see*), con. With emphasis.
Engelstimme (Ger.). Angel voice; a soft organ-stop; vox angelica.
Enharmonic. In modern music, a change of the letter without changing the pitch, as, C♯, D♭.
Enharmonic Modulation. A modulation in which the above change takes place, as,

Ensemble (Fr.) (*ong-sombl*). Altogether. (1) The union of all the performers. (2) The effect produced by this union. (3) The manner in which a composition for many performers is "put together."
Entr'acte (Fr.) (*on-trakt*). Between the acts; music performed between the acts of a drama.
Entrata (It.), **Entrée** (Fr.). Entry; introduction, prelude; the first movement of a serenata.

Eichberg, Julius. Composer; Germany. B. 1824; d. 1893.
Elson, Louis C. Critic, historian; U. S. A. B. 1848.
Elvey, Sir George J. Organist, composer; England. B. 1816; d. 1893.
Elvey, Stephen, brother of preceding. B. 1805; d. 1860.

Entschlossen (Ger.) (*ent-shlos-sen*). Resolute; resolutely.
Entusiasmo (It.) (*ehn-too'-see-as-mo*), con. With enthusiasm.
Eolian or Æolian. (1) One of the Greek and ecclesiastical scales. (2) A species of harp played on by the wind.
Epicede (Fr.), **Epecedio** (It.) (*ep-ee-che-dee-o*). A funeral dirge.
Epinette (Fr.). A spinet.
Episode. The parts of a fugue that intervene between the repetitions of the main theme.
Epithalamium. A wedding song.
E poi (It.). And then; after.
Equabile (It.) (*eh-qua-bee-leh*). Equal; steady.
Equabilmente. Equally; steadily.
Equal Voices. A composition is said to be for equal voices when written for men's only or women's only. When male and female voices are combined the music is said to be for mixed voices.
Equisono (It.). Equal sounding; unison.
Equivocal Chords. Dissonant chords that are common to two or more keys, or that may be enharmonically substituted for each other, as the diminished 5th chord, diminished 7th chord, and augmented 6th chord.
Ergriffen (Ger.). Affected; moved.
Ergriffenheit. Emotion.
Erhaben (Ger.). Lofty; sublime.
Erhabenheit. Sublimity.
Ermattet (Ger.). Exhausted.
Ernst (Ger.). Earnest; serious.
Eroica (It.) (*eh-ro'-ee-ka*). Heroic.
Erotic. Amatory. [Gr. *Eros*, Cupid.]
Ersterbend (Ger.). Dying away; morendo.
Es (Ger.). E flat.
Es dur (Ger.). E flat major.
Es-es (Ger.). E double flat.
Es moll (Ger.). E flat minor.
Espagnuolo (It.) (*ehs-pan-yu-olo*). In Spanish style.
Espirando (It.). Dying away.
Espressione (It.) (*ehs-pres-see-o-neh*), con. With expression.

Emerick, Albert G. Organist; U. S. A. B. 1817.
Emory, Stephen. Theorist; U. S. A. B. 1841; d. 1893.
Epstein, Abraham, b. 1855; **Epstein, Marcus,** b. 1857, brothers. Four-hand pianists; U. S. A.
Erard, Sebastian. Piano maker; Paris. B. 1752; d. 1831.

Espressivo (It.). Expressive.

Essential Dissonances. Those that are added to the dominant chord. Auxiliary notes of all kinds are non-essential dissonances.

Essential Harmony. The harmony independent of all melodic ornaments, etc.

Estinguendo (It.) (*es-tin-guen-do*). As soft as possible.

Estinto (It.). Dying away; extinguishing.

Estravaganza (It.) (*es-trah-vah-gantza*). A fanciful composition; a burlesque.

Étoffé (Fr.). Full; sonorous.

Etouffée (Fr.). Stifled; damped.

Étude (Fr.) (*eh-tood*). A study, lesson.

Etwas (Ger.) (*et-vos*). Somewhat; as, **etwas langsam**, somewhat slow.

Euphonium. A large brass instrument of the saxhorn family, used in military bands; a free reed-stop in the organ, sixteen-foot pitch.

Euphony [Gr., *eu*, good; *phone*, sound]. Well-sounding; agreeable.

Exercise. (1) A study designed to overcome some special difficulty or strengthen special muscles. (2) A lesson in harmony, counterpoint, or composition. (3) A composition written as a thesis for the obtaining of a degree.

Ernst, H. W. Violinist, composer; Germany. B. 1814; d. 1865.

Exposition. The giving out of the subject and answer by all the voices in turn at the opening of a fugue.

Expression. The performance of music in such a manner as to bring out all its emotional and intellectual content. Intelligent, appreciative performance.

Expression (Fr.). The name of a harmonium stop.

Extempore (Lat.) (*ex-tem'-po-reh*). The gift of playing music composed as it is played.

Extemporize. To play unpremeditated music.

Extended Harmony. Reverse of close harmony, *q. v.*

Extension. (1) Violin playing, to reach with the fourth or first finger beyond the "position" in which the hand may be. (2) In piano music, spreading the hand beyond the "five-finger" position.

Extraneous Modulation. A modulation to a distant or non-related key.

Extreme. The outside parts, as bass and soprano.

Extreme. Used by many writers on harmony in the sense of augmented; as, extreme 2d or 5th or 6th.

Essipoff, Annette. Pianist; Russia. B. 1850.

F

F. The fourth or subdominant of the natural major or minor scale.

Fa. The fourth of the syllables adopted by Guido, called the Aretinian syllables. In "Movable Do" system the fourth of any scale.

Fa bemol (Fr.). F flat.

Fa burden, Falso bordone (It.), **Faux bourdon** (Fr.). (1) An ancient species of harmonization, consisting of thirds or sixths added to the cantus. (2) A drone bass like a bagpipe.

Facile (Fr.) (*fa-seel*), **Facile** (It.) (*fah-chee-leh*). Easy.

Facilment (Fr.) (*fa-seel-mong*), **Facilmente** (It.) (*fa-cheel-men-teh*). Easily; fluently.

Facilité (Fr.). Made easy; an easy version of a difficult passage.

Facture (Fr.) (*fak-toor*), **Fattura** (It.) (*fat-too-rah*). Literally, the making. The construction of a piece of music; the scale of organ-pipes.

Fa dièse (Fr.) (*dee-ehs*). F sharp.

Fagotto (It.), **Fagott** (Ger.). Bassoon (so called from its resemblance to a fagot or bundle of sticks). A double-reed instrument of great utility in the orchestra. Compass, three octaves (and over) from B♭ below the bass staff.

Fagottone (It.) (*fag-got-to'-neh*). Double bassoon.

Faible (Fr.) (*faybl*). Weak. **Temps faible**, weak beat.

False Cadence. A deceptive cadence.

False Fifth. A name for the diminished fifth.

False Relation. When a note sounded by one voice is given in the next chord, altered by ♯, ♭, or ♮, by another voice, thus:—

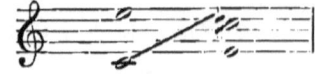

Falsetto (It.). The highest register of the voice.

Fandango (Sp.). A rapid dance in triple time.

Fanfare (Fr.), **Fanfara** (It.). A brilliant trumpet call or flourish; a brass band.

Fantasia (It.), **Fantasie** (Ger.), **Fantaisie** (Fr.). A composition that is not in any of the regular forms; often used of pianoforte arrangements of themes from operas.

Fantasia, Free. The name sometimes given to that part of a sonata that comes after the double bar; the Durchführung or development.

Fantasiren (Ger.) (*fan-ta-see-ren*). To improvise.

Fantastico (It), **Fantastique** (Fr.). Fantastic; grotesque.

Farandola (It.), **Farandole** or **Farandoule** (Fr.). A rapid dance in $^6_8$ time, Southern France and Italy.

Fascia (It.) (*fashiah*). A tie.

F Clef. See *Clef*.

F dur (Ger.). F major.

Feierlich (Ger.). Festal; pompously; grandly; solemnly.

Feld (Ger.). Field; open air.

Feldmusik. Military music.

Feldton. The key of E♭, often used for military band music.

Fermata (It.) [from *fermare*, to stay]. A pause. ⌒ A cessation of accompaniment and time, while a soloist executes a cadenza.

Fermato, Fermamente (It.). Firmly; decidedly.

Feroce (It.) (*feh-ro'-cheh*). Wild; fierce.

Ferocita (It.) (*feh-ro'-chee-tah*), con. With ferocity.

Fertig (Ger.). Quick; ready; nimble.

Fertigkeit. Dexterity; technical skill.

Fervente (It.) (*fer-ven'-teh*). Fervent; vehement.

Fes (Ger.). F flat.

Fest (Ger.). Festival.

Fest (Ger.). Fast; fixed.

Fester Gesang. Canto firmo.

Festgesang. Festival song.

Festivo (It.) (*fes-tee'-vo*). Festive; solemn.

Festivamen'te (It.). Festively; solemnly.

Festivita (It.) (*fes-tee'-vee-ta*), con. With joyfulness.

Faelten, Carl. Pianist; Germany. B. 1846.
Farinelli, Carlo B. (*fah-ree-nel-lee*). Sopranist; Italy. B. 1705; d. 1782.
Faure, J. B. (*fore*). Baritone and composer; France. B. 1830.
Favarger, René (*fa-var-zheh*). Pianist; France. B. 1815; d. 1868.

Festo'so (It.). Gay; joyful.
Feuer (Ger.) (*foy-ehr*). Fire.
Feuerig (Ger.). Fiery.
F-holes. The openings in the belly of instruments of the violin family; so called from their shape, *f*.
Fiacco (It.) (*fee-ak'-ko*). Weak; faint.
Fiasco (It.). A failure; breakdown. Literally, "a flask."
Fiato (It.). Breath.
Fiddle. This word and "violin" both come from the same root—the Low Latin word *vitula*.
Fidicen (Lat.). A harp or lute player. [From Lat. *fides*, a string, and *cano*, to sing.]
Fidicinal. A general term for string instruments.
Fiedel (Ger.). Fiddle.
Fieramente (It.). Proudly; fiercely.
Fiero (It.) (*fee-eh-ro*), **Fier** (Fr.) (*fee-eh*). proud; fierce.
Fife, Fifre (Fr.), **Piffero** (It.), **Querpfeife** (Ger.) (*kvehr-pfei-feh*). A small flute without keys, an octave higher than the flute, used in conjunction with drums for military purposes.
Fifteenth. An organ-stop of 2-foot pitch; open; metal.
Fifth. (1) An interval which includes five letters. (2) The dominant of the key.
Figure. (1) A form of accompaniment maintained without change. (2) A repeated melodic phrase. (3) Sequence.
Figured Bass, Basso figurato (It.), **Basse chiffre** (Fr.). A bass with figures over it (or under it) to indicate the chord each note is to bear. Invented as a species of musical short-hand it has been retained as a means of teaching harmony, although its warmest advocates admit its inadequacy to the indication of modern harmony.
Filar la voce (It.) (*fee-lar-la-vocheh*), **Filer la voix** (Fr.) (*fee-leh-la-voa*). To sustain a sound with even tone. Literally, to spin like a thread.
Fin (Fr.) (*fang*), **Fine** (It.) (*fee-neh*). End.
Finale (It.) (*fee-nah-leh*). Final. The last movement of a sonata or symphony or of the act of an opera.

Fesca, F. E. Composer; Germany. B. 1789; d. 1826.
Fétis, F. J. (*feh-tees*). Essayist, composer; France. B. 1784; d. 1871.
Field, John. Pianist; Ireland. B. 1782; d. 1837.
Fillmore, J. C. Pianist, essayist; U. S. A. B. 1843; d. 1898.

Fingerboard. The upper side of the neck of string instruments, generally a thin strip of ebony against which the strings are pressed by the fingers of the left hand.

Fingering. The art of using the fingers systematically when playing an instrument; the marks or figures that indicate what fingers are to be used.

Fingersetzung (Ger.). Fingering.

Finto (It.). A feint; applied to a deceptive cadence.

Fioretto (It.) (*fee-o-ret-to*). An ornament.

Fiorito (It.) (*fee-o-ree-to*). Florid.

Fiorituri (It.) (*fee-o-ree-too-ree*). Embellishments; florid passages.

Fis (Ger.). F sharp. **Fisfis or Fisis,** F double sharp.

Fis dur. F sharp major.

Fis moll. F sharp minor.

Fixed Do. *Do* used as the name of C; movable *do* is *do* used as the keynote of any scale.

Flageolet. A small pipe blown at the end; an organ-stop of 2-foot pitch.

Flageolet Tones. The harmonic sounds produced by touching lightly the strings of violin, etc.

Flat. The sign of depression (♭) lowers the letter a half-tone.

Flautando, flautato (It.). Flute-like; in violin playing, a direction to produce flageolet tones.

Flautino (It.). (*flau-tee-no*). A small flute; a piccolo.

Flue Stops. Organ stops, the pipes of which are constructed on the same principle as the whistle or flageolet.

Flute, Flauto (It.) (*flau-to*), **Flöte** (Ger.) (*flateh*). (1) One of the most important of orchestral instruments; a cylindrical tube blown at a hole in the side called the embouchure. The modern flute, constructed on the Boehm system, is very much superior to the older instrument in both tone and tune. Its compass is from

(2) An organ-stop of 8 or 4-foot pitch; in French organs a general name for flue stops.

There are many varieties of the flute, the major part of which are now either obsolete or used as names for organ-stops, as flauto traverso, transvere or German flute; flute d'amour, a soft-toned organ-stop; flute harmonique, an overblown flute, the pipe of which is twice the length necessary to produce the sound it is made to give.

F moll. F minor.

Foco (It.). Fire. **Con foco or fuoco,** with fire.

Focoso. Fiery; ardently.

Foglietto (It.) (*fol-yet'-to*). The part used by the leader of the violins in the orchestra, containing cues, etc., of the other instruments, sometimes used by the conductor in place of a score.

Fois (Fr.) (*foa*). Time; as, **première fois,** first time.

Folia (Sp.), **Follia** (It.). A Spanish dance. Elaborate variations are called Follias de España, in French, Folies de'Espagne, meaning "follies of Spain" (a pun on the word folia), which has become a proverbial expression for trifles.

Fonds d'orgue (Fr.) (*fond-dorg*). The 8-foot flue-stops of the organ. The foundation stops.

Foot. (1) A poetic measure or meter. (2) A drone bass. (3) The unit used in determining the pitch of organ pipes, the standard being 8-foot C,

the lowest note on the manuals of the modern organ. An open pipe must be eight feet long to produce this sound, if closed it must be four feet long. Applied to other instruments it signifies that their pitch corresponds with that of the organ diapasons, that is, it is the same as the written note. All the violin family are of 8-foot pitch, except the double bass, which is of 16-foot pitch, that is, the notes sound an octave lower than written. The flute, hautboy, clarionet, and bassoon are also of 8-foot pitch. Of brass instruments, the cornets, trumpets, and trombones are of 8-foot pitch. The high horn in C is 8-foot, but the low horn in C is 16 foot pitch.

Forlana (It.), **Fourlane** (Fr.) (*foor-lan*). A dance somewhat similiar to the tarantella.

Finck, H. T. Essayist. B. 1854.

Fioravanti, V. (*fee-o-rah-van-tee*). Composer; Italy. B. 1770; d. 1837.

Flotow, F. F. A. Opera composer; Germany. B. 1812; d. 1883.

Foerster, Adolph M. Composer; U. S. A. B. 1854.

Foote, Arthur. Composer; U. S. A. B. 1853.

Forkel, Johann N. Organist; Germany. B. 1749; d. 1818.

Formes, Karl (*for-mehs*). Basso; Germany. B. 1810; d. 1889.

Form. The number, order, and key relation of the several themes that are combined to make an extended composition, such as the sonata, rondo, symphony, concerto, etc. The lyric or dance form is the germ from which all varieties of instrumental music have been developed. The simplest form of lyric melody may be thus divided: Motive, two measures; Section, two motives; Phrase, two sections; Sentence, two phrases; Period, two sentences, making sixteen measures in all. The lyric form may be extended indefinitely by the addition of new periods in related keys. One of the most usual is the addition of a new period in the key of the dominant, subdominant, or relative minor, followed by a repetition of the first period. This is called the Aria Form. It was formerly largely used in vocal music, and is now one of the most usual forms for the lighter class of piano music. The following outlines of sonata and rondo forms give their main characteristics. The sonata form is the form of the symphony, and of the trio, quartet, etc., for string instruments, or for piano with strings, or other instruments. The same is the case with the rondo; this form is frequently used for the final movement.

Outline of Sonata Form in Major Key.

FIRST HALF.

| 1st Theme. | 2d Theme. |
| Tonic key. | Dominant key. |

SECOND HALF.

| | 1st Theme. | 2d Theme. |
| Development. | Tonic key. | Tonic key. |

Sonata in Minor Key.

FIRST HALF.

| 1st Theme. | 2d Theme. |
| Tonic. | Relative major. |

SECOND HALF.

| | 1st Theme. | 2d Theme. |
| Development. | Tonic. | Parallel major. |

Frequent deviations may be found from the foregoing schemes. The intervals between the themes are filled with transition passages or modulations so constructed as to heighten the effect of the theme that follows; codas are frequently added after both appearances of the second theme.

Modern Rondo Form, Major Key.

FIRST HALF.

| 1st Theme. | 2d Theme. | 1st Theme. |
| Tonic. | Dominant. | Tonic. |

SECOND HALF.

3d Theme.	1st Theme.	2d Theme.	Coda.
Sub-dom.	Tonic.	Tonic.	Made
Rel. minor.			from 1st
Parallel minor.			theme or all the themes.

For an example of this kind see Beethoven's No. 2 Sonata of the three dedicated to Haydn, last movement.

Same Form of Rondo in Minor Key.

FIRST HALF.

| 1st Theme. | 2d Theme. | 1st Theme. |
| Tonic. | Relative major. | Tonic. |

SECOND HALF.

| 3d Theme. | 1st Theme. | 2d Theme. | Coda. |
| Sub-dom. and relative major. | Tonic. | Tonic Minor. major. | |

See last movement of Sonata Pathetique — Beethoven.

Forte (It.) (*for-teh*). Loud. **Fort** (Fr.), **Stark** (Ger.). **Meno forte**, less loud. **Mezzo forte** (M. F.), half loud. **Piu forte**, louder. **Poco forte**, a little loud; rather loud. **Sempre forte**, always loud. **Forte stop**, a mechanism worked by the feet or the knee, or a draw-stop, by means of which the whole power of the harmonium, organ, etc., may be put on at once.

Forte possibile (It.) (*pos-see'-bee-leh*), **Fortissimo** (It.). Loud as possible.

Fortemente (It.). Loudly; forcibly.

Forza (It.) (*fortza*), **con**. With force.

Forzando (It.) (*fortzando*). Forcing the sound; emphasizing a certain note, indicated by $<$, $\wedge$, fz, sfz.

Forzato (It.) (*fortzato*), **Sforzando**, **Sforzato**. All have the same meaning as *Forzando*.

Fourniture (Fr.). A mixture-stop in the organ.

Fourth. (1) An interval embracing four letters. (2) The subdominant of the scale.

Française (Fr.) (*frong-says*). A dance in triple time.

Francamente (It.) (*frank-a-men'-teh*). Frankly; boldly.

Franchezza (It.) (*fran-ket'-za*), **Franchise** (Fr.) (*frong-shees*). Freedom; confidence.

Freddamente (It.). Frigidly; coldly.

Fredezza (It.) (*freh-det'-za*), **con**. With coldness.

Foster, Stephen. Song writer; U. S. A. B. 1826; d. 1864.

Franchomme, A. (*fransh-om*). 'Cellist; France. B. 1808; d. 1884.

Franz, Robert (*frants*). Composer; Germany. B. 1815; d. 1892.

Frescobaldi, G. (*fres-co-bal-dee*). Composer, organist; Italy. B. 1583; d. 1644.

Free Fugue. One that does not conform to strict rules.

Free Parts. Parts added to a canon or fugue that take no part in its development.

Free Reed. See *Reed*.

Free Style. The reverse of strict contrapuntal style.

French Horn. See *Horn*.

French Sixth. The augmented 6th with augmented 4th and major 3d.

French Violin Clef. The G clef on the first line (obsolete).

Frets. Pieces of wood, metal, or ivory, set across the fingerboard of some string instruments, raised slightly above its surfaces, to regulate the pitch of the sounds; the finger is pressed on the string behind the fret, which then acts as a bridge.

Fretta (It.). con. With haste; hurry.

Frisch (Ger.). Fresh; lively.

Fröhlich (Ger.). Gay; cheerful.

Frottola (It.). A comic ballad.

Fuga, Fugue (It.), **Fuge** (Ger.) (*foo-geh*). [From Lat., *fuga*, flight.] The parts seeming to fly one after another; the highest development of counterpoint; a composition developed from one or two (sometimes three) short themes, according to the laws of imitation. The chief elements of a fugue are: (1) Subject, or theme. (2) Answer, imitation of theme at 5th above or below. (3) Counter-subject, an additional theme which accompanies the main theme. (4) Episodes; these connect the various repetitions of the theme together. (5) Organ point, generally used before the stretto. (6) Stretto, a drawing together of the subject and answer; the stretto is often written on an organ point.

(7) Coda, the free ending after the development is completed. Although all these things enter into the fugue, it is not necessary that every fugue should include all of them. There are many varieties of fugue, now happily relegated to the limbo of musical antiquities. The most important are the Real fugue, in which the subject and answer are identical, and the Tonal fugue, in which an alteration must be made in the theme to prevent its going out of the key. In the tonal fugue the subject moves from the tonic to the dominant, or the reverse. The answer must move from dominant to tonic, or the reverse.

Fugara. An open, metal pipe organ-stop, generally of 4-foot tone.

Fugato. In fugue style. **Aria fugato,** a song with fugue-like accompaniment.

Fughetto (It.). A slightly developed fugue.

Full Cadence. Perfect cadence. See *Cadence*.

Fundamental. The generator or root of a chord.

Fundamental Bass. The roots of the harmonics on which a piece is constructed.

Fundamental Position. A chord with its root at the bass.

Funèbre (Fr.) (*foo-nebr*), **Funerale** (It.) (*foo-neh-rah'-leh*). Funereal; dirge-like.

Fuoco (It.) (*foo-o'-ko*). Fire. **Con fuoco,** with fire.

Furia (It.) (*foo'-re-ah*), con. With fury.

Furibundo (It.), **Furioso** (It.). Furiously; savagely.

Furlano (It.). See *Forlana*.

Furniture. A mixture-stop in the organ.

Furore (It.) (*foo-ro'-reh*), con. With fury; passion.

Fusée (Fr.) (*foo-seh'*). A slide from one sound to another.

Froberger, J. J. (*fro-behr-gehr*). Organist; Germany. B. 1615; d. 1667.

Fry, Wm. H. Composer; U. S. A. B. 1815; d. 1854.

Fuchs or **Fux,** J. J. (*fooks*). Theorist. B. 1660; d. 1741.

Fumagalli, Adolfo (*foo-mah-gal'-lee*). Pianist, composer; Italy. B. 1828; d. 1856.

G

G. (1) The fifth or dominant of the natural major scale. (2) The fourth or lowest string of the violin. (3) The third string of the viola and violoncello; the first string of the double bass. (4) The letter represented by the G or treble clef. (5) Abbreviation for Gauche (Fr.) (*gawsh*), left.

Gagliarda (It.) (*gal-yar-dah*), **Gailliarde** (Fr.) (*gah-yard*). A favorite dance in ¾ time resembling the minuet.

Gai (Fr.) (*gay*), **Gaja** (It.) (*gayah*), **Gaiment** (Fr.) (*gay-mong*), **Gajamente** (It.) (*gay-a-men-teh*). Gay; merry; gaily; merrily.

Gala (It.) (*gah-lah*), **di gala.** Finely; bravely. Literally, in fine array.

Galamment (Fr.) (*gal-lah-mong*), **Galantemente** (It.) (*galant-eh-men-teh*). Gracefully; freely; gallantly.

Galant (Ger.) (*gah-lant'*), **Galante** (Fr.) (*gah-longt*), **Galante** (It.) (*gah-lan-teh*). Free; gallant; graceful.

Galliard. See *Gagliarda*.

Galop (Fr.) (*gah-lo*), **Galopade** (Fr.) (*galopahd*), **Galopp** (Ger.). A rapid, lively dance in $\frac{2}{4}$ time.

Gamba (It.) [the leg]. (1) See *Viol di gamba*. (2) An organ-stop of eight-foot pitch; in German, **Gambenstimme**.

Gamma. The Greek letter g, Γ; in ancient music the letter G, first line bass staff; in the hexachord system this sound was called *gamma ut*, from whence comes gamut, a scale.

Gamme (Fr.) (*gahm*). A scale; gamut.

Gang (Ger.). Passage.

Ganz (Ger.) (*gants*). Whole. **Ganze Note**, whole note.

Garbo (It.). Gracefulness; refinement.

Gassenhauer (Ger.) (*gas-sen-how-er*). Lit., running the streets. An old dance in $\frac{3}{4}$ time.

Gauche (Fr.) (*gawsh*). Left. **Main gauche**, left hand.

Gavot (Fr.) (*gah-vo*), **Gavotte** (*gah-vot*), **Gavotta** (It.). An old dance in ₵ time; lively, yet dignified. Frequently introduced in the suite.

G Clef. 𝄞 See *Clef*.

Gedeckt (Ger.) [from *decken*, to close]. Closed; the stopped diapason.

Gedehnt (Ger.). Slow; stately.

Gedicht (Ger.). Poem.

Gade, Niels W. (*gah-deh*). Composer; Denmark. B. 1817; d. 1890.

Gadsby, H. R. Composer; England. B. 1842.

Galelei, Vincenzo (*gah-lee-leh-ee*, *vin-chent-zo*). Essayist and composer; Italy. B. 1535; d. 16—.

Galin, Pierre (*gah-long*). Inventor of numerical notation; France. B. 1786; d. 1821.

Galluppi, Baldessaro (*gah-loop-pee*). Composer; Italy. B. 1706; d. 1785.

Gänsbacher, J. B. (*gehns-bach-er*). Composer; Germany. B. 1778; d. 1844.

Ganz, Wilhelm (*gahnts*). Composer; Germany. B. 1830.

Garcia, Manuel (*gar-chee-ah*). Teacher of singing, inventor of laryngoscope; Spain. B. 1805; d 1900.

Gefallen (Ger.) (*geh-fal-len*). Pleasure. **Nach Gefallen**, at will. See *Bene placito* and **A piacere**.

Gefühl (Ger.) (*geh-feel*). Feeling. **Mit Gefühl**, with feeling.

Gegensatz (Ger.) (*geh-gen-sats*). The second theme in a sonata. Lit., the against or contrary theme; **Hauptsatz** being the chief or principal theme.

Gehalten (Ger.) (*geh-hal-ten*). Held; sustained; tenuto.

Gehend (Ger.) (*geh-end*). Going; andante. **Etwas gehend** (con moto), with motion.

Geige (Ger.). Fiddle; violin.

Geigenprincipal. An organ-stop of 8- or 4-foot pitch.

Geist (Ger.). Spirit; mind; genius.

Geistlich (Ger.). Sacred; spiritual.

Gelassen (Ger.). Tranquil; calm.

Gemächlich (Ger.) (*geh-mehch-lich*). Easy; convenient.

Gemächlich commodo. Not too fast.

Gemässigt (Ger.) (*geh-mehs-sicht*). Moderate. Lit., measured.

Gemshorn. An 8- or 4-foot organ-stop with horn-like tone.

Gemüth (Ger.) (*geh-meet'*). Heart; soul; feeling.

Gemüthlich (Ger.). Feelingly; heartily.

Generator. Root; fundamental of a chord.

Genere (It.) (*je'-neh-reh*), **Genre** (Fr.) (*zhongr*). Style; class; mode.

Generoso (It.) (*jeh-neh-ro'-so*). Freely; frankly.

Gentille (Fr.) (*zhong-til*), **Gentile** (It.) (*jen-tee-leh*). Graceful; delicate. **Con gentilezza** (It.) (*jen-tee-letza*), with grace; nobility.

Garcia, Malibran Maria F., his sister. Soprano; Spain. B. 1808; d. 1836.

Gaul, Alfred R. England. B. 1837.

Gavanies, Pierre (*gah-van-yeh*). Violinist; France. B. 1726; d. 1800.

Gazzaniga, Mme. (*gatz-ah-nee-gah*). Soprano; Italy.

Gelinek, Joseph (Abbé) (*geh-lee-nek*). Composer; Austria. B. 1758; d. 1825.

Geminiani, F. (*geh-mee-nee-ah-nee*). Violinist, composer; Italy. B. 1680; d. 1762.

Genée, R. (*zheh-neh*). Composer; Dantzig. B. 1824; d. 1896.

Gevaërt, François A. (*geh-rehrt*). Organ writer; Netherlands. B. 1828.

Gerke, Anton (*gur-keh*). Teacher; Germany. B. 1814; d. 1870.

German Flute. See *Flute.*
German Sixth. See *Augmented Sixth.*
Ges (Ger.). G flat.
Gesang (Ger.) (*geh-zong'*). Singing [from *singen*, to sing]; song; melody; air.
Gesangverein (Ger.). Singing society.
Geschmack (Ger.). Taste. **Mit Geschmack**, with taste. **Geschmackvoll**, tasteful.
Geschwind (Ger.) (*geh-shvint'*). Fast; presto.
Gesteigert (Ger.). Raised; exalted in volume; louder; crescendo.
Getragen (Ger.) (*geh-tra-gen*). Sustained. [*Tragen*, to bear up.] Sostenuto.
Gezogen (Ger.) (*geh-tso-gen*) [from *ziehen*, to draw]. Prolonged; sustained.
Ghazel or **Gazel.** A short Persian poem, used by Hiller as a name for short pianoforte pieces, in which a simple theme constantly occurs.
Ghiribizzo (It.) (*gee-ree-bitz'-o*). Whim; grotesque.
Giga (It.). Jig; a rapid dance in $\frac{6}{8}$ time, used as the final movement in the suite, where it is often developed in fugue form.
Giochevole (It.) (*jee-o-keh'-vo-leh*), **Giocondosa** (It.) (*jee-o-kon-do-sah*), **Giocoso** (It.) (*jee-o-co-so*), **Giocondezza** (It.) (*jee-o-con-detza*). Joyful; merry; sportive; happy; mirthful.
Gioja (It.) (*jeo-ya*), con. With joy.
Giojante (It.) (*jeo-yan-teh*), **Giojosamente** (It.) (*jeo-yos-a-men-teh*), **Giojoso** (It.) (*jeo-yo-so*). Joyous; mirthfully.
Gioviale (It.) (*jeo-ve-ah'-leh*). Jovial.

Giovialita (It.) (*jeo-vee-ah-lee-tah*), con. With joviality.
Gis (Ger.) (*ghiss*). G sharp.
Giubilio (It.) (*jew-bee-leo*). Jubilation.
Giubilioso (It.) (*jew-bee-lee-oso*). Jubilant.
Giustezza (It.) (*jews-tet'-za*), con. With exactness.
Giusto (It.) (*jewsto*). Strict; exact.
Glee. A composition for three or more voices without accompaniment. The glee differs from the madrigal, its predecessor, in being constructed more on the harmonic than the contrapuntal system; *i.e.*, admits dominant, dissonances, and second inversions. The glee is the most distinctive form of English music. The best glees belong to the eighteenth century and the first part of the nineteenth. They have been largely superseded by the part-song.
Gli (It.) (*lee*). The.
Glide. (1) To connect two sounds by sliding. (2) A modern variety of the waltz.
Glissando, Glissato, Glissicato, Glissicando (It.). To play a scale on the pianoforte by drawing the finger along the keys. Only possible in the natural scale. In violin playing, to slide the finger rapidly from one "stop" to the next.
Glissé (Fr.) (*glis-seh*). See *Glissando.*
Glisser (Fr.) (*glis-seh*). To slide.
Glockenspiel (Ger.). Bell play; a small instrument consisting of bells tuned to the diatonic scale, played by small hammers or by means of a keyboard. Steel bars are sometimes used in place of bells.
Gong. A pulsatile instrument consisting of a disc of bronze, struck with drumstick with soft head.

Gernsheim, F. (*gurns-heim*). Pianist, composer, conductor; Germany. B. 1839.
Gerster, Etelka (*gehrs-ter*). Soprano; Hungary. B. 1855.
Gibbons, Orlando. Composer, organist; England. B. 1583; d. 1625.
Gibbons, Christopher, his son. Organist; B. 1615; d. 1676.
Gilchrist, W. W. Composer; U. S. A. B. 1846.
Gilmore, P. F. Conductor; Ireland. B. 1829; d. 1890.
Giordani, Tomaso (*jee-or-dah-nee*). Composer and singing teacher; Italy. B. 1744; d. 18—.
Giuglini, A. (*jeul-ee-nee*). Tenor; Italy. B. 1826; d. 1865.
Gladstone, F. E. Organist, composer; England. B. 1845; d. 1892.
Glareanus, H. (*glah-reh-ah-nus*). Theorist; Germany. B. 1488; d. 1563.

Gleason, F. Grant. Composer; U. S. A. B. 1848; d. 1903.
Glimes, J. B. J. de (*gleem*). Pianist; Brussels. B. 1814; d. 1881.
Glinka, M. I. Composer; Russia. B. 1804; d. 1857.
Glover, C. W. Composer of songs; England. B. 1806; d. 1863.
Glover, Stephen. Composer of songs; England. B. 1812; d. 1870.
Glover, Sarah A. Founder of tonic-sol-fa method; England. B. 1785; d. 1867.
Glover, William H. Composer, journalist; England. B. 1819; d. 1875.
Gluck, Ch. W. von. Opera composer; Austria. B. 1714; d. 1787.
Godard, Ben. L. P. (*go-dahr*). Composer, violinist; France. B. 1849; d. 1895.
Goddard, Arabella. Pianist; England. B. 1836.

GORGHEGGI 43 GREGORIAN CHANT

Gorgheggi (It.) (*gor-ghed'-je*). Florid singing, with runs, trills, etc.
Grace Note. See *Appoggiatura*.
Graces. The ornamental notes first used in harpsichord playing; they are now nearly all obsolete, or if used are written in full by the composer.
Gracieux (Fr.) (*grah-see-oo*), **Gracieuse** (Fr.) (*grah-see-oos*), **Gracile** (It.) (*gra-chee-leh*). Graceful; delicate.
Gradevole (It.) (*grah-deh'-vo-leh*). Grateful.
Graduellement (It.) (*grah-doo-el-mong*). By degrees.
Gran cassa (It.). Great drum; long drum.
Gran gusto (It.), con. With grand expression.
Gran tamburo (It.). The big drum.
Grand barré (Fr.). See *Barré*.
Grand jeu (Fr.) (*zhen*), **Grand choeur** (*koor*). Full organ.
Grand Piano. Properly, the long, wingshaped pianoforte with keyboard at the wide end; commonly applied to all varieties of piano with three strings to each key.
Grande orgue (Fr.) (*org*). Great organ.
Grandezza (It.) (*gran-det'-za*), con. With grandeur.
Grandioso (It.) (*gran-de-o'-so*). Grandly.
Grave [Fr., *grahv*: It., *grah-veh*]. Deep in pitch; slow; solemn.

Gravecembalum (Lat.),**Gravicembalo** (It.) (*gra-vee-chembalo*). The harpsichord.
Gravement (Fr.) (*grahv-mong*), **Gravemente** (It.) (*grah-veh-men-teh*). Slowly; seriously.
Gravita (It.) (*gra-vee-tah*), con. With dignity.
Grazia (It.) (*grat-se-a*), con. With grace; elegance.
Grazioso (It.) (*grat-si-oso*), **Graziosamente** (*grat-si-osa-men-teh*). Gracefully; elegantly.
Great Octave. The sounds from

Great Organ. The division of an organ that contains the most powerful stops, generally operated by the middle keyboard or manual, the upper being the swell organ, the lower the choir organ
Greater. Major; as, greater third, greater sixth. In old usage the major scale is called the scale with the greater third.
Greek Music. The Greek system of music is still a subject of controversy about which very little is known. The best attempts at its elucidation may be found in Chappel's "History of Music" and Munro's "Greek Music." Its interest is purely antiquarian.
Gregorian Chant. See *Plain Song*.

Godefroid, Felix (*gode-froa*). Composer, harpist; France. B. 1818; d. 1897.
Godfrey, D. Dance writer, band-master; England. B. 1831; d. 1903.
Goetz, H. Composer; Germany. B. 1840; d. 1876.
Goldbeck, Robert. Composer, pianist; Germany. B. 1835; d. 1908.
Goldmark, Karl. Composer; Germany. B. 1832.
Goldschmidt, Otto. Conductor and composer, husband of Jenny Lind; Germany. B. 1829; d. 1907.
Gollmick, Adolf. Composer, pianist; Germany. B. 1825; d. 1883.
Goltermann, G. E. Violoncellist; Germany. B. 18 4; d. 1898.
Goovaerts, A. I. M. A. (*goo-vehrts*). Composer; Netherlands. B. 1847.
Goria, A. E. (*go'-ree-ah*). Pianist; France. B. 1823; d. 1860.
Goss, Sir John. Composer, organist; England. B. 1800; d. 1880.
Gossec, F. J. (*gos-sek*). Composer; France. B. 1733; d. 1829.
Gottschalk, L. M. Pianist; U. S. A. B. 1829; d. 1869.

Goudimel, Claude (*goo'-dee-mel*). Composer; France. B. 1510; d. 1572.
Gounod, Ch. F. (*goo - no*). Composer; France. B. 1818; d. 1893.
Gouvy, Theo. (*goo'-vee*). Composer; France. B. 1819; d. 1898.
Gow, Neil. Violinist, dance writer; Scotland. B. 1727; d. 1807.
Grancino, G. (*gran-chee-no*). Violin maker; Italy.
Grancino, P. Violin maker. B. 16—; d. 17—.
Graun, J. G. Composer; Germany. B. 1698; d. 1771.
Graun, Karl H., his brother. Composer. B. 1701; d. 1759.
Greatorex, Th. Organist, composer; England. B. 1758; d. 1831.
Grétry, A. E. (*greh-tree*). Composer; Belgium. B. 1741; d. 1813.
Grieg, Ed. (*greeg*). Composer, pianist; Sweden. B. 1843; d. 1907.
Griepenkerl, F. C. (*gree - pen - kerl*). Theorist; Germany. B. 1782; d. 1849.
Grisi, Mme. (*gree-see*). Soprano; Italy. B. 1812; d. 1869.
Grove, Sir George. Author of dictionary; England. B. 1820; d 1900.

Groppo (It.), **Groppetto** (It.). A turn; a group.

Grosse (Ger.) (*gros-seh*). (1) Major, applies to intervals. (2) Great or grand, as, grosse Sonate. (3) An octave below standard pitch, as, grosse Nazard, an organ stop an octave below the twelfth.

Grosse-caisse, Gros tambour. See *Drum*.

Grosso (It.). Great; large; as, grosso concerto.

Grottesco (It.) (*grot-tes'-ko*). Grotesque; comic.

Ground Bass. A bass of four or eight bars, constantly repeated, each time with varied melody and harmony. The ground bass was generally used as the basis of the chaconne and passacaglio.

Group. (1) A series of rapid notes grouped together. (2) One of the divisions of the orchestra, as string group, brass group, wood group.

Gruppo, Grupetto. See *Groppo, Groppetto*.

G-Schlüssel (Ger.) (*gay-shlues-sel*). G clef.

Guaracha (Sp.) (*gwah-rah'-chah*). A lively Spanish dance in triple time.

Guerriero (It.) (*gwer-reeh'-ro*). Martial; warlike.

Guida (It.) (*gwee-dah*). Guide; the subject of a canon or fugue.

Guidonian Hand. A diagram consisting of a hand, with the syllables written on the tips of the fingers and on the joints, intended to assist in memorizing the hexachord scales.

Guidonian Syllables. The syllables applied by Guido to the notes of the hexachord, *ut, re, mi, fa, sol, la*. When the octave scale was adopted *si* was added for the seventh note; *ut* was changed to *do* as a better syllable for vocalizing.

Guitar. A string instrument with fretted fingerboard, played by plucking the strings with the fingers of the right hand, one of the oldest and most widespread of instruments. It probably originated in Persia, where it is called *tar* or *si-tar*, passed from thence to Greece, and to the rest of Europe and North Africa. The guitar now in general use is called the Spanish guitar. It has six strings tuned thus:—

but their actual sound is an octave below the written notes.

Gusto (It.), **con.** With taste.

Gustoso. Tastefully.

Gut. The material (sheep's entrails) of which violin, guitar, and other strings are made, commonly called catgut.

Gut (Ger.) (*goot*). Good. **Guter Taktteil,** lit., good bar part; the accented part of the bar.

Grützmacher, F. (*greetz-macher*). Violoncellist; Germany. B. 1832; d. 1903.

Guarnerius, A. (*gwar-neh-ree-us*). Violin maker; Italy. B. 1683; d. 1745.

Guglielmi, P. (*gool-yel-mee*). Composer; Italy. B. 1727; d. 1804.

Guido (*gwee-do*). Theorist; Italy. Eleventh century.

Guilmant, F. A. (*geel-mong*). Organist, composer; France. B. 1837.

Guiraud, E. (*gwee-ro*). Composer; France. B. 1837; d. 1892.

Gungl, J. (*goongl*). Dance writer; Bohemia. B. 1810; d. 1889.

Gurlitt, C. Pianist, composer; Germany. B. 1820; d. 1901.

Gutmann, A. Composer; Germany. B. 1818; d. 1882.

Gyrowetz, A. (*gee-ro-vets*). Composer; Bohemia. B. 1763; d. 1850.

H

H. Abbreviation for Hand. Hah (Ger.), the note B♮, B♭ being called B (*bay*). It is this system of nomenclature that makes possible the fugues on the name of Bach, written by Bach, Schumann, and others:—

Hackbrett (Ger.). Literally, chopping-board. The dulcimer.

Halb (Ger.) (*halp*). Half.

Halbe Cadenz (Ger.). Half cadence.

Halbe Note. Half-note.

Halber Ton. Half-tone.

Half-Note.

Half-Rest.

Half-Shift. On the violin, the position of the hand between the open position and the first shift.

Half-Step. Half-tone.

Half-Tone. The smallest interval in modern music.

Hallelujah (Heb.). The Greek form **Alleluia** is often used "Praise ye Jehovah."
Halling. A Norwegian dance in triple time.
Hals (Ger.). Neck, as of violin, guitar, etc.
Hammerklavier (Ger.). A name for the P. F. (used by Beethoven in the great sonata, Op. 106).
Hanacca. A Moravian dance in $\tfrac{3}{4}$ time, somewhat like the polonaise.
Hardiment (Fr.) (*har-dee-mong*). Boldly.
Harmonic Flute. See *Flute*.
Harmonic Scale. The series of natural harmonics; the scale of all brass instruments without valves or pistons.
Harmonic Stops. Organ-stops with pipes of twice the standard length pierced with a small hole at the middle, causing them to sound the first overtone instead of the sound that the whole length would produce.
Harmonica. (1) An instrument invented by Benjamin Franklin, the sounds of which were produced from glass bowls. (2) An instrument consisting of plates of glass struck by hammers. (3) A mixture-stop in the organ.
Harmonici (Gr.) (*har-mon-i-kee*). The followers of Aristoxenus, as opposed to the **Canonici** (*ka-non-i-kee*), the followers of Pythagoras. The former taught that music was governed by its appeal to the ear, the latter that it was a matter for mathematical and arithmetical study only.
Harmonicon. A toy instrument with free reeds, blown by the mouth.
Harmonics, Overtones, Partial Tones.
(1) The sounds produced by the division of a vibrating body into equal parts; it is upon the presence or absence and relative intensity of the overtones that the quality of the sound depends. Open pipes, strings, brass instruments, and instruments with double reed (bassoon and hautboy) give the following series:—

```
           1 2 3 4 5 6 7 8 9
C          C G C E G B♭ C D E, etc.
generator  ½ ⅓ ¼ ⅕ ⅙ ⅐ ⅛ ⅑ 1/10
Closed pipes and beating reeds (clarionet)
```

omit all the even numbers in this series. (2) The sounds produced on the violin by touching the string lightly at one of the points of division; those produced by thus touching the open string are called natural harmonics. Artificial harmonics are produced by stopping the string with the first finger and touching it lightly with the fourth, at the interval of a fourth above; the resulting harmonic is two octaves above the stopped note. In writing music this is indicated by writing thus:—

The lozenge-shaped notes indicate the notes to be lightly touched. Natural harmonics are frequently used on the harp, guitar, and mandolin.
Harmonie-Musik (Ger.). Harmony music; music for wind instruments. A band composed of brass and wood instruments is called a harmony band.
Harmonist. One who is an expert in the art of harmony.
Harmonium. A keyboard instrument with free reeds. It differs from the reed organ in that the air is forced through instead of drawn through the reeds, giving a stronger, rougher quality of tone. In harmonium music, published in Europe, the stops are indicated by figures placed in a circle. Each stop is divided at the middle. The figure in circle, placed below the bass staff, refers to the lower half of the stop; above the treble staff, to the upper half. The cor anglais and flute form one stop, marked ①

below for cor anglais, ① above for flute.

2 means bourdon, below; clarionet, above.
3 " clarion, " piccolo, "
4 " bassoon, " hautboy, "

Habeneck, F. A. Violinist, conductor; France. B. 1781; d. 1849.
Haberbier, Ernst (*hahl'-behr-beer*). Pianist, composer; Germany. B. 1813; d. 1869.
Hale, Adam de la (*hahl*). Troubadour; France. B. 1240; d. 1287.
Halévy, J. F. (*hah-leh-vee*). Composer; France. B 1799; d. 1862.
Halle, Sir Ch. (*hal-leh*). Pianist, conductor; Hagen. B. 1819; d. 1896.
Halm, A. (*hahm*). Pianist, composer. B. 1789; d. 1872.
Hamerik, Asgar. Composer; Denmark. B. 1843.

Händel, G. F. Composer; Germany. B. 1685; d. 1759.
Hanslick, Ed. Critic; Bohemia. B. 1825; d. 1904.
Hardegen, J. von. Composer, pianist; Austria. B. 1834; d. 1867. (Jules Egghard.)
Hartnock, Carl E. Pianist. B. 1775; d. 1834.
Hartog, Edward. Pianist, composer; Holland. B. 1828.
Hartvigson, Anton. Pianist, composer; Sweden. B. 1845.
Hartvigson, Fritz. Pianist, composer; Sweden. B. 1851.

Harmony [from Gr., *harmo*, to join]. The art of combining sounds. The study of harmony in its fullest extent is that which treats of the combination of sounds, consonant and dissonant, and their succession. The so-called laws of harmony have all been arrived at empirically, hence have been subject to change, each new composer of sufficient originality and genius modifying them to suit his purposes. Harmonic combinations may be either consonant or dissonant. The consonant combinations consist of the common (perfect) chord and its derivatives. The dissonant combinations all include some dissonant interval, viz., 7th or 2d, augmented 4th, diminished or augmented 5th, augmented 6th or diminished 3d, or 9th. The movement of consonant combinations is perfectly free; that of dissonant combinations is subject to the rules governing the resolution of the dissonant sounds they contain. Two classes of dissonances are recognized: (1) Those that belong to the overtone series, called essential; (2) those that result from the employment of suspensions, retardations, changing and passing notes.

Harp. A string instrument of very ancient origin, probably first suggested by the bow. The earliest forms of Egyptian harps resemble that weapon, the front bar or support being wanting. The modern harp, by means of contrivances for altering the tension of the strings, controlled by pedals, has the complete chromatic scale. The harp is extensively used in the modern orchestra; its clear, "glassy" tones form a striking and effective contrast to the rest of the orchestra. It is most effective when used to give "arpeggios," or broken chords, particularly in soft passages. Scales are ineffective on the harp, and the chromatic scale is impossible. The compass of the modern harp extends from the second C♭ below the bass staff to the second F2 above the treble staff, six and one-half octaves. The natural harmonics, produced by touching the middle of the string lightly with one hand, are extremely effective in very soft passages.

Harpe (Fr.), **Harfe** (Ger.). The harp.

Harpsichord, Harpsicol, Clavicin (Fr.), **Cembalo** (It.), **Clavicembalo** (It.), **Flügel** (Ger.). A string instrument with keyboard, in shape like the modern grand piano. The sound was produced by pieces of quill, leather, or tortoise-shell, which scratched across the strings when the keys were struck. Harpsichords were often made with two rows of keys and with stops, by means of which the tone might be modified.

Haupt (Ger.) (*howpt*). Head; chief; principal.

Hauptmanuel. Great organ.

Hauptnote. Essential note in a turn, mordent, etc.

Hauptsatz. Principal theme in a sonata or rondo, etc.

Hauptwerk. Great organ.

Hautbois (Fr.) (*hote-boa*). See *Oboe*.

Hautbois d'amour. A small variety of the hautboy.

H dur (Ger.). B major.

H moll (Ger.) (*hah moll*). B minor.

Head. The membrane of a drum; the peg-box of violin, guitar, etc.

Head Voice. See *Voice*.

Heftig (Ger.). Impetuous. Literally, heavily.

Heimlich (Ger.). Mysteriously; secretly.

Heiss (Ger.). Ardent.

Heiter (Ger.). Clear; calm.

Heptachord [Gr., *hepta*, seven; *korde*, string]. A scale or lyre with seven diatonic sounds.

Haslinger, Tobias. Composer, publisher; Austria. B. 1787; d. 1842.

Hasse, Faustina (*has-seh*). Soprano; Italy. B. 1700; d. 1783.

Hasse, J. A., her husband. Composer; Saxony. B. 1699; d. 1783.

Hatton, John L. Composer; England. B. 1809; d. 1886.

Hauck, Minnie (*howk*). Soprano; U. S. A. B. 1852.

Haupt, Carl (*howpt*). Theorist, organist; Germany. B. 1810; d. 1891.

Hauptmann, Moritz (*howpt-man*). Theorist, teacher; Germany. B. 1792; d. 1868.

Haweis, Rev. H. R. Essayist; England. B. 1838; d. 1901.

Haydn, Josef (*highdn*). Composer; Austria. B. 1732; d. 1809.

Haydn, Michael. Composer; Austria. B. 1737; d. 1806.

Hayes, Catherine. Soprano; Ireland. B. 1825; d. 1861.

Hegner, Otto. Pianist. B. 1877.

Heller, Stephen. Pianist, composer; Pesth. B. 1814; d. 1888.

Helmholtz, H. L. F. Acoustician; Germany. B. 1821; d. 1894.

Henkel, H. Pianist, teacher, composer. B. 1822; d. 1899.

Hennes, Aloys. Teacher, pianist; Germany. B. 1827; d. 1889.

Henrion, Paul (*hong-ree-ong*). Composer, pianist; France. B. 1819.

Henschel, Geo. Composer, singer, conductor; Germany. B. 1850.

Herabstrich or **Herstrich** (Ger.). Down bow.

Heraufstrich or **Hinaufstrich** (Ger.). Up bow.

Hidden Fifths or **Octaves.** Called also concealed. These occur when two parts or voices take a 5th or 8th in parallel motion.

The rule forbidding hidden 5ths and 8ths is now very little regarded.

His (Ger.). B sharp.

Hoboe, Hoboy. See *Oboe*.

Hochzeitsmarsch (Ger.) (*hoch-tseits*). Literally, high time. A wedding march.

Hohlflöte (Ger.) (*hole-fla-teh*). Hollow flute; an organ-stop of 8-foot tone, soft, full quality; a stop of the same character a fifth above the diapason is called **Hohlquinte** (*kvinteh*).

Holding Note. A sustained note; a pedal point.

Homo′phony, Homo′phonic, Homo′phonous [Gr., *homo*, one or single; *phonos*, sound]. Music in which one part (melody) is the most important factor, the remaining parts being entirely subsidiary, that is, simply accompaniment.

Horn [It., *Corno;* Fr., *Cor;* Ger., *Horn* or *Waldhorn*]. A generic term for instruments of brass or other metal, wood, or animal horns sounded by means of a cup-shaped mouth-piece. In modern usage applied only to the orchestral horn, called also French horn. A brass instrument with a long, narrow tube bent into a number of circular curves, with a large bell. The modern horn is provided with pistons, which make it a chromatic instrument. The custom is now almost universal of using the horn in F, the part for which is written a fifth higher than the actual sounds. Before the application of pistons to the horn its part was always written in C, and the key was indicated by writing: Corni in B♭ or E♭, etc., as the case might be. Many composers retain this method of writing, but the horn-players generally transpose the part *vista* to suit the F-horn.

Horn Band. In Russia, a band of performers, each one of whom plays but one sound on his horn.

Hornpipe. An old English dance of a lively, rapid character.

Horn-Sordin (Ger.). A contrivance placed in the mouth of the horn to deaden the tone.

Humoresque (Fr.) (*oo-mo-resk*). **Humoreske** (Ger.). A caprice; humorous fantastic composition.

Hunting Horn [Fr., *Cor de Chasse;* It., *Corno di Caccia*]. The horn from which the orchestral horn was developed.

Hymn Tune. A musical setting of a religious lyric poem, generally in four parts.

Henselt, A. Composer, pianist; Germany. B. 1814; d. 1889.

Hering, Carl G. Teacher, pianist; Germany. B. 1765; d. 1853.

Herold, Louis J. F. (*heh-rold*). Composer; France. B. 1791; d. 1833.

Herz, Henry (*herts*). Pianist; Austria. B. 1806; d. 1888.

Hesse, Ad. F. (*hes-seh*). Organist; Germany. B. 1809; d. 1863.

Heuschkel, J. P. (*hoysh-kel*). Pianist, teacher; Germany. B. 1773; d. 1853.

Hiller, Ferd. Composer, conductor, pianist; Frankfort. B. 1811; d. 1885.

Hiller, Johann A. Conductor, composer; Görlitz. B. 1728; d. 1804.

Himmel, F. H. Composer; Germany. B. 1765; d. 1814.

Hofmann, H. Composer, pianist; Germany. B. 1842; d. 1902.

Hofmann, Joseph. Composer, pianist; Germany. B. 1877.

Hol, Richard. Composer, pianist. B. 1825; d. 1885.

Horsley, Wm. Composer; England. B. 1774; d. 1858.

Horsley, Ch. E., his son. Composer; England. B. 1821; d. 1876.

Huber, Hans. Pianist, teacher; Germany. B. 1852.

Hucbald. Theorist; Flanders. Tenth century.

Hullah, John P. Teacher of singing, composer; England. B. 1812; d. 1884.

Hüllmandel, N. (*heel-man-del*). Pianist, composer; Alsace. B. 1751; d. 1823.

Hummel, J. N. Composer, pianist; Pressburg. B. 1778; d. 1837.

Hünten, Franz. Composer, teacher; Germany. B. 1793; d. 1878.

I

Idée fixée (Fr.) (*e-deh fix-eh*). Fixed idea; a name given by Berlioz to a short theme used as the principal motive of an extended composition.

Idyl [Fr., *Idylle;* Gr., *Eidullion*]. A small image or form; a short, tender piece of music generally of a pastoral character.

Il piu (It.) (*eel peu*). The most. Il piu forte possibile, as loud as possible.

Imitando (It.). Imitating; as, Imitando la voce, imitating the voice; a direction to the instrumentalist to imitate the vocalist.

Imitation. A device in counterpoint; a musical phrase being given by one voice is immediately repeated by another voice. There are many varieties of imitation: (1) By augmentation, when the imitating part is in notes of twice or four times the value of those in the theme. (2) By diminution, when the value of the notes is reduced one-half or one-fourth. (3) By inversion, when the intervals are given by the imitating part in inverted order. Imitation is called Canonic when the order of letters and intervals is exactly repeated, thus:—

$$C\ D\ \widehat{E\ F} \qquad G\ A\ \widehat{B\ C}$$

Strict, when the order of letters only is repeated, as:—

$$C\ D\ \widehat{E\ F} \qquad A\ \widehat{B\ C}\ D$$

Free, when the theme is slightly altered, but not enough to destroy the resemblance. The theme is called the antecedent; the imitation, the consequent. There are other varieties of imitation, but they are now generally obsolete, being more curious than musical.

Immer (Ger.). Ever; continuously; always.

Impaziente (It.) (*im-pah-tse-en-teh*). Impatient; restless.

Impazientemente (It.). Vehemently; impatiently.

Imperfect Cadence. Same as *Half Cadence*.

Imperfect Consonance. Major and minor thirds and sixths.

Imperfect Fifth. The diminished fifth.

Imperioso (It.). Imperiously; with dignity.

Impeto (It.) (*im'-peh-to*). con. With impetuosity.

Impetuoso (It.), Impetuosamente (It.). Impetuously.

Implied Intervals. Those not expressed in the figuring.

Incledon, Ch. B. Tenor; England. B. 1763; d. 1826.

Imponente (It.) (*im'-po-nen-teh*). Emphatic; pompous.

Impromptu. (1) An extemporaneous performance. (2) A piece of music having the character of an extemporaneous performance.

Improvisation. Unpremeditated music.

Improvise. To play unpremeditated music.

Improviser (Fr.) (*im-pro-vee-seh*), Improvvisare (It.). To extemporize.

Improvvisatore (It.). An improviser (male).

Improvvisatrice (It.) (*im-prov-vi-sa-tree-cheh*). An improviser (female).

In alt (It.). The notes in the first octave above the treble staff.

In altissimo (It.). All notes above the octave *in alt*.

In nomine (Lat.). In the name; a sort of free fugue.

Incalzando (It.) (*in-cal-tsan-do*). To chase; pursue hotly, with constantly increasing vehemence.

Indeciso (It.) (*in-deh-chee-so*). With indecision; hesitating.

Infinite Canon. See *Canon*.

Inganno (It.). Deceptive. Cadenza inganno, deceptive cadence.

Inner Parts. The parts that are neither at the top nor the bottom, as the alto and tenor in a chorus.

Inner Pedal. A sustained note in an inner part.

Innig (Ger.). Heartfelt; fervent.

Innigkeit (Ger.), mit. With fervor; intense feeling.

Inniglich (Ger.). See *Innig*.

Inno (It.). Hymn.

Innocente (It.) (*in-no-chen'-teh*), Innocentemente. Innocent; natural.

Innocenza (*inno-chent'-sah*), con. With artlessness.

Inquieto (It.) (*in-quee-eh-to*). Unquiet; restless.

Insensibile (It.) (*in-sen-si-bee-leh*), Insensibilmente (It.). By imperceptible degrees; gradually.

Insistendo (It.), Instante (It.), Inständig (Ger.). Urgent; pressing.

Instrument. Any mechanical contrivance for the production of musical sounds. Instruments are classified as follows: String instruments, wind instruments, pulsatile in-

Isouard, Nicolo (*e-soo-ar*). Composer; Malta. B. 1775; d. 1818.

struments. String instruments are divided into bow instruments, violin class; instruments the strings of which are plucked by the fingers—harp, guitar, etc.; plectral, *i. e.*, the strings struck by a rod or thin strip of wood, metal, etc., as mandolin, zither; strings struck by hammers held in the hand—cymbal; strings struck by hammers operated by keyboard—piano-forte. Wind instruments are divided as follows: (1) Vibrating column of air—flutes and flue-stops of organ. (2) Single reed—clarionet, saxophone, basset horn, reed-stops in the organ. (3) Double reed—oboe, bassoon. (4) Free reed—harmonium, vocalion, cabinet organ. (5) Brass instruments in which the lip of the player acts as a reed—trumpet, horn, etc. Pulsatile instruments — drums, triangles, cymbals, bells, xylophone. The small or chamber orchestra includes the following instruments: String — first violins, second violins, violas, violoncellos, contrabassi. Wood-wind — pair of flutes (It., *flauti*), pair of hautboys (It., *oboi*), pair of clarionets (It., *clarionetti*), pair of bassoons (It., *fagotti*). Brass-wind — pair of trumpets (sometimes omitted) (It., *clarini*), pair of horns (It., *corni*), pair of kettle-drums (It., *timpani*). The addition of three trombones changes this to the full or grand orchestra, which is often augmented by the addition of the following instruments: Wood-wind — piccolo or octave flute, English horn (It., *corno Inglese*), alto or bass clarionet, double bassoon (It., *contra fagotto*). In the brass quartet the horns are increased to four, and the alto, tenor, and bass trombones are added and the bass trombone reinforced by the bass tuba. Three or more kettle-drums are frequently employed, also the following pulsatile instruments: large drum, snare drum, triangle, and cymbals. The harp has almost become an essential in the modern orchestra, whether large or small.

Instrumentation. The art of using a number of instruments in combination; the manner of arranging music for the orchestra.

Instrumento or **Stromento** (It.). An instrument.

Instrumento or **Stromento di corda** (It.). String instrument.

Instrumento or **Stromento di fiato** (It.). Wind instrument.

Interlude, Intermède (Fr.) (*in-ter-made*), **Intermedio** (It.) (*in-ter-meh-deo*). A short piece of music between the acts of a drama or the verses of a hymn.

Intermezzo (It.) (*in-ter-medzo*). An interlude; a short movement connecting the larger movements of a symphony or sonata.

Interrupted Cadence. See *Cadence*.

Interval. The difference in pitch between two sounds. The name of an interval is determined by the number of letters it includes (counting the one it begins with and the one it ends with). Seconds may be minor (E, F), major (E, F♯), augmented (E♭, F♯). Thirds may be minor (E, G), major (E, G♯), diminished (E, G♭). Fourths may be perfect (E, A), augmented (E, A♯), diminished (E, A♭). The inversion of an interval produces one of the opposite kind except when it is perfect. Inversion of minor 2d produces major 7th, and since all intervals lie within the octave, and the octave contains twelve half-tones, it follows that an interval and its inversion must together make an octave or twelve half-tones. Intervals are further divided into consonant and dissonant, the consonant into perfect and imperfect. The perfect consonances are the 4th, 5th, and octave. They are called perfect because any alteration of them produces a dissonance. The imperfect consonances are the major and minor 3d and 6th, called imperfect because equally consonant whether major or minor. All other intervals are dissonant, that is, one or both the sounds forming them must move in a certain direction to satisfy the ear. If the dissonant is minor or diminished the sounds must approach each other (except minor 2d); if major or augmented they must separate (except major 7th, which may move either way). Intervals are augmented when greater than major or perfect. Intervals are diminished when less than major or perfect. The prime or unison is often called an interval and if altered, as, C C♯, is called an augmented unison or prime; it is more properly a chromatic semitone. Natural intervals are those found in the major scale. Chromatic intervals are those found in the harmonic minor scale and in chords that include sounds foreign to the scale or key.

Intimo (It.) (*in'-tee-mo*). Heartfelt; with emotion.

Intonation. (1) The correctness or incorrectness of the pitch of sounds produced by the voice or by an instrument. (2) The notes which precede the reciting notes of the Gregorian chant.

Intoning. In the Anglican Church the singing of prayers, etc., in monotone.

Intrada (It.). An introduction or interlude.

Intrepido (It.) (*in-tre-pee-do*), **Intrepidezza, con** (It.) (*in-treh-pee-detza*), **Intrepidamente** (It.) (*in-treh-pee-da men-teh*). Boldly; with daring; dashingly.

Introduction. A preparatory movement to a piece of music, symphony, oratorio, etc., sometimes very short, sometimes a long, elaborate movement in free style.

4

Introduzione (It.) (*in-tro-doo-tse-onch*). Introduction.

Introit. A short anthem sung before the administration of the communion in the Protestant Episcopal Church; in the Roman Catholic Church before the celebration of the mass.

Invention. A name given by Bach to a set of thirty pieces in contrapuntal style.

Inversion. (1) Of intervals. See *Interval*. (2) Of chords, when any member of the chord but the root is used as a bass. (3) Of themes. See *Imitation*.

Ira (It.) (*e-rah*), con. With anger.

Irato (It.) (*e-rah'-to*). Angrily.

Irlandais (Fr.) (*ir-lan-day*). In the Irish style.

Ironico (It.) (*e-ron'-e-co*). Ironicamente (It.). Ironically; sardonically.

Irresoluto (It.) (*ir-reh-so-lu'-to*). Undecided; irresolute.

Islancio (It.) (*is-lan'-chee-o*). Same as *Slancio*.

Istesso (It.). Same. **L'istesso tempo**, the same time, *i. e.*, rate of movement.

Italian Sixth. See *Augmented Sixth*.

Italienne (Fr.) (*e-ta-lee-en*), **Italiano** (It.) (*e-tal-yah-no*). In Italian style.

J

Jack. The short, upright piece of wood at the end of the key of the harpsichord or spinet, to which the quill was attached which struck the strings.

Jagdhorn (Ger.) (*yagd-horn*). Hunting horn.

Jägerchor (Ger.) (*yay-ger-kore*). Hunting chorus.

Jaleo (Sp.) (*hah-leh-o*). A Spanish dance in triple time.

Janko Keyboard (*yanko*). The invention of Paul Janko, arranged like a series of steps, six in number. Each key may be struck in three places, some on the 1st, 3d, and 5th steps, the rest on the 2d, 4th, and 6th, thus enabling the performer to select the most convenient for the passage to be executed. The chief advantages claimed for this keyboard are: that all scales may be fingered alike; that the thumb may be placed on any key, black or white; that the extended chords are brought within easy reach.

Janissary Music. Instruments of percussion, as small bells, triangles, drums, cymbals.

Jeu (Fr.) (*zhoo*). Literally, play. A stop on the organ.

Jeu d'anche (*d'ongsh*). Reed stop.

Jeu de flute. Flue stop.

Jeu demi (*deh-mee*). Half power; mezzo forte.

Jeu doux (*doo*). Soft stops.

Jeu forts (*fort*). Loud stops.

Jeu grand. Full organ.

Jeu plein (*plane*). Full power.

Jig [It., *Giga;* Fr. and Ger., *Gigue;* comes either from Geige, an obsolete variety of fiddle, or from Chica, a rapid Spanish national dance]. Now a rapid rustic dance of no fixed rhythm or figures. In the classic suite the jig is the last movement, written in $\frac{6}{8}$ time and often very elaborately treated in fugal form.

Jodeln (Ger.) (*yo-deln*). A manner of singing cultivated by the Swiss and Tyrolese; it consists of sudden changes from the natural to the falsetto voice.

Jota (Sp.) (*ho-ta*). A Spanish national dance in triple time.

Jour (Fr.) (*zhoor*). Day. An open string is called corde à jour.

Jubal (Ger.) (*yoo-bal*). An organ-stop of 2- or 4-foot pitch.

Jungfernregal (Ger.) (*yung-fern-reh-gal*). See *Vox angelica*.

Just Intonation. Singing or playing in tune.

Jackson, Wm. Organist, composer; England. B. 1730; d. 1803.

Jacobsohn, S. E. (*yah-cob-sone*). Violinist; Germany. B. 1839.

Jadassohn, S. (*yah-das-sone*). Composer, theorist; Germany. B. 1831; d. 1902.

Jaell, Alfred (*yale*). Pianist; Austria. B. 1832; d. 1882.

Jahn, Otto (*yahn*). Essayist; Germany. B. 1813; d. 1869.

Janiewicz, Felix (*yah-nee-vich*). Violinist; Poland. B. 1762; d. 1848.

Janssens, J. F. (*yahn-sens*). Composer; Belgium. B. 1810; d. 1890.

Jarvis, Ch. H. Pianist; U. S. A. B. 1836; d. 1895.

Jensen, Adolf (*yen-sen*). Composer; Germany. B. 1837; d. 1879.

Joachim, J. (*yo-a-kim*). Violinist; Hungary. B. 1831; d. 1907.

Jomelli, N. (*yo-mel-lee*). Composer; Italy. B. 1714; d. 1774.

Joncières, Victorin de (*zhon-see-ehr*). Real name, T. L. Rossignol. Composer; France. B. 1839; d. 1903.

Joseffy, Raphael (*yo-sef-fee*). Pianist; Hungary. B. 1852.

Josquin, Després (*zhos-kang, deh-preh*). Composer; France. B. 1450; d. 1521.

Jullien, L. A. (*zhool-leang*). Composer and conductor; France. B. 1812; d. 1860.

Jungmann, A. (*yoong-man*). Composer, pianist; Germany. B. 1814; d. 1892.

K

Kalamaika (*ka-la-my-ka*). A Hungarian dance; rapid 2/4 time.
Kammer (Ger.). Chamber.
Kammerconcert. Chamber concert.
Kammermusik. Chamber music.
Kammerstil. Chamber-music style.
Kammerton. Concert pitch.
Kanon, Kanonik (Ger.). See *Canon*.
Kanoon. A Turkish dulcimer, played like the psalterion by means of plectra attached to thimbles.
Kantate (Ger.). Cantata.
Kanzone (Ger.), **Kapodaster** (Ger.), **Capotasto, Kassation** (Ger.), **Kavatino** (Ger.). See same words under *C*.
Kapellmeister (Ger.). The leader of a band or chorus attached to a royal or noble household.
Kapellmeister-Musik (Ger.). A contemptuous term for music that is dull and unoriginal but correct and pedantic.
Keckheit (Ger.). Boldness. **Mit Keckheit,** with boldness.
Kehrab or **Kehraus** (Ger.). Lit., turn out. The last dance at a ball.
Kent Bugle. A wind instrument generally made of copper, with cup-shaped mouthpiece, furnished with keys.
Keraulophon [from Gr., *keras*, horn ; *aulos,* flute; and *phone*, sound]. A soft flue-stop of 8-foot pitch.
Keren. A Hebrew trumpet.
Kettle-drum. A half-sphere of copper, the head made of vellum, which may be tightened or loosened by means of screws or braces. The kettle-drum is the only drum from which sounds of definite pitch may be obtained. They are generally used in pairs in the orchestra, and are tuned to the tonic and dominant of the key, but modern writers adopt various other methods of tuning; it is also quite usual now to use three drums. The larger drum may be tuned to any note from

The smaller

In old scores the drum part was always written in C and the sounds wished were indicated by writing Timpani in F, B♭, etc. The modern custom is to write the actual sounds.
Key. (1) A series of sounds forming a major or minor scale. See *Scale*. (2) A piece of mechanism by means of which the ventages of certain wind instruments, as flute and clarionet, are closed or opened. (3) A lever by which the valves of the organ are opened or the hammers of the piano-forte put in motion. (*A Table of Signatures and Names of all the Major and Minor Keys on the following page.*)
Keyboard, Klavier (Ger.) (*kla-feer*). The rows of keys of the organ or piano; those for the hands are called manuals, for the feet, pedals.
Keynote. The sound or letter with which any given scale begins; tonic. See *Scale.*
Kinderscenen (Ger.) (*kin-der - stsa - nen*). Child-pictures; a name given by Schumann to a collection of little pieces for the piano.
Kinderstück (Ger.). Child's piece.
Kirchenmusik (Ger.). Church music.
Kirchenstil. Church style.
Kirchenton. Ecclesiastical mode.

Kafka, J. C. Violinist; Austria. B. 1747; d. 1800.
Kafka, J. N. Composer and pianist; Bohemia. B. 1819; d. 1886.
Kalkbrenner, F. W. M. (*kalk-brenner*). Pianist, composer; Germany. B. 1784; d. 1849.
Kalliwoda, J. W. (*kal-lee-vo'-dah*). Composer, violinist; Bohemia. B. 1800; d. 1867.
Kastner, J. G. (*kast-ner*). Composer; Alsatia. B. 1810; d. 1867.
Kéler Béla, A. von (*keh-ler beh-la*). Composer, band-master; Germany. B. 1820; d. 1882.
Kellogg, Clara Louisa. Singer; U. S. A. B. 1842.
Kerl, J. C. (*kerl*). Composer, organist; Bavaria. B. 1628; d. 1690.
Kiel, Fredk. (*keel*). Composer; Germany. B. 1821; d. 1885.
Kiesewetter, R. G. von. Essayist; Germany. B. 1773; d. 1850.
King, Julie Rive. Pianist; U. S. A. B. 1856.
Kircher, A. Historian; Germany. B. 1602; d. 1680.
Kirnberger, J. P. (*keern-behr-ger*). Theorist; Germany. B. 1721; d. 1783.

TABLE OF SIGNATURES AND NAMES OF ALL THE MAJOR AND MINOR KEYS.

Key-signature.	English.	German.	French.	Italian.	
	C-major A-minor	C dur A moll	Ut majeur La mineur	Do maggiore La minore	Natural key.
	G-major E-minor	G dur E moll	Sol majeur Mi mineur	Sol maggiore Mi minore	
	D-major B-minor	D dur H moll	Ré majeur Si mineur	Re maggiore Si minore	
	A-major F-sharp minor	A dur Fis moll	La majeur Fa dièse mineur	La maggiore Fa diesis minore	Keys with sharps.
	E-major C-sharp minor	E dur Cis moll	Mi majeur Ut dièse mineur	Mi maggiore Do diesis minore	
	B-major G-sharp minor	H dur Gis moll	Si majeur Sol dièse mineur	Si maggiore Sol diesis minore	
	F-sharp major D-sharp minor	Fis dur Dis moll	Fa dièse majeur Ré dièse mineur	Fa diesis maggiore Re diesis minore	
	G-flat major E-flat minor	Ges dur Es moll	Sol bémol majeur Mi bémol mineur	Sol bemolle maggiore Mi bemolle minore	
	D-flat major B-flat minor	Des dur B moll	Ré bémol majeur Si bémol mineur	Re bemolle maggiore Si bemolle minore	
	A-flat major F-minor	As dur F moll	La bémol majeur Fa mineur	La bemolle maggiore Fa minore	Keys with flats.
	E-flat major C-minor	Es dur C moll	Mi bémol majeur Ut mineur	Mi bemolle maggiore Do minore	
	B-flat major G-minor	B dur G moll	Si bémol majeur Sol mineur	Si bemolle maggiore Sol minore	
	F-major D-minor	F dur D moll	Fa majeur Ré mineur	Fa maggiore Re minore	

Kit, Pochette (Fr.), **Taschengeige** (Ger.). A small pocket-fiddle used by dancing-masters.
Klangfarbe (Ger.). Lit., sound-color. Quality of tone; timbre (Fr., *tambr*).
Klavier or **Klaviatur** (Ger.) (*kla-feer'*, *klah-fee-a-toor'*). Keyboard.
Klavierauszug. Piano-forte arrangement.
Klaviermässig. Suited to the piano.

Kittl, J. F. Organist; Bohemia. B. 1806; d. 1868.
Kjerulf, Halfdan (*kcrroolf, hofdan*). Composer; Norway. B. 1815; d. 1868.
Klein, Michel R. (*kline, meechel*). Pianist; Silesia. B. 1846.

Klaviersatz. In piano-forte style.
Klavierspieler. Pianist.
Klein (Ger.). Small; minor.
Klein gedeckt. Small stopped diapason.
Knee-stop. A lever controlled by the knees of the performer, used in the harmonium or cabinet organ either to operate the swell or to put on or off the full power of the instrument.

Klengel, A. A. Composer, pianist. B. 1784; d. 1852.
Klindworth, C. (*klint-worth*). Pianist; Germany. B. 1830.
Köhler, L. Pianist, composer; Germany. B. 1820; d. 1886.

Koppel (Ger.). A coupler. Koppel ab, coupler off. Koppel an, coupler on.
Kosakisch (Ger.). Cossack dance in $\frac{3}{4}$ time.
Kraft (Ger.). Force; power.
Kräftig (Ger.). Vigorous; powerfully.
Krakowiak (*kra-ko-viak*). Cracovienne.
Kreuz (Ger.) (*kroyts*). A sharp.
Kriegerisch (Ger.). Martial.
Kriegerlied (Ger.). War-song.

Kontski, A. de (*kont-skee*). Composer, pianist; Poland. B. 1817.
Kontski, Appolinaire. Violinist; Poland. B. 1825; d. 1879.
Kotzeluch, J. A. (*kots-eh-loock*). Composer; Bohemia. B. 1738; d. 1814.
Kotzeluch, L. K. Composer; Bohemia. B. 1748; d. 1814.
Kotzwara, F. (*kots-vah-rah*). Violinist; Bohemia. B. 1750; d. 1791.
Krebs, J. L. Composer, organist; Germany. B. 1713; d. 1780.
Krebs, R. A. Composer; Germany. B. 1804; d. 1880.
Krebs, Marie, daughter of last. Pianist. B. 1851.
Kreutzer, A. Auguste (*kroit-zer*). Violinist; France. B. 1781; d. 1832.
Kreutzer, Conrad. Composer; Germany. B. 1780; d. 1849.
Kreutzer, Rudolph, brother of A. Violinist; France. B. 1766; d. 1831.
Kreutzer, Leon, son of R. Violinist; France. B. 1817; d. 1868.

Krummhorn (Ger.). Crooked horn; the cremona stop.
Kunst (Ger.). Art.
Kunstlied (Ger.). An artistic song; the reverse of a popular song or Volkslied.
Kurz (Ger.) (*koorts*). Short; staccato.
Kurz und bestimmt. Short and emphatic.
Kyrie [Gr., *Lord*]. The first word of the mass; used as a name for the first division.

Krüger, Wm. (*kree-ger*). Pianist; Germany. B. 1820; d. 1883.
Krumpholz, J. B. (*kroomp-holts*). Harpist; Bohemia. B. 1745; d. 1790.
Krumpholz, W., brother of J. B. Harpist; Bohemia. B. 1750; d. 1817.
Kücken, F. W. (*kee-ken*). Song writer; Germany. B. 1810; d. 1882.
Kufferath, H. F. (*koof-e-raht*). Germany. Pianist; composer. B. 1808; d. 1882.
Küffner, J. (*kef-ner*). Pianist; Germany. B. 1776; d. 1856.
Kuhe, W. (*koo-eh*). Pianist; Bohemia. B. 1823.
Kuhlau, F. D. R. (*koo'-low*, Ger. *au* like *ow* in *town*). Composer, flutist; Denmark. B. 1786; d. 1832.
Kuhnau, J. (*koo'-now*). Composer, organist; Germany. B. 1667; d. 1722.
Kullak, Adolf (*kool-lak*). Composer, essayist; Germany. B. 1823; d. 1862.
Kullak, Theo., brother of above. Pianist. B. 1818; d. 1882.
Kummer, F. A. (*koom-mer*). 'Cellist; Germany. B. 1797; d. 1879.

L

L. H. Abbreviation for left hand; in German, *linke Hand*.
La. The sixth Aretinian syllable; the name in French and Italian of the sound A.
Labial [Lat., *labium*, lip]. A flue-stop.
Labialstimme (Ger.). A flue-stop.

Labitsky, Josef (*lah-bit'-skee*). Composer; Schönfeld. B. 1802; d. 1881.
Lablache, Luigi (*lah-blash'*). Basso; Naples. B. 1794; d. 1858.
Lachner, Franz (*lach'-nehr*). Conductor, composer; Bavaria. B. 1804; d. 1890.
Lachner, Theodor (*lach'-nehr*), brother of above. Organist; Bavaria. B. 1798; d. 1877.
Lachner, Ignaz (*lach'-nehr*), brother of above. Composer, conductor; Bavaria. B. 1807; d. 1895.

Lacrimoso or Lagrimoso (It.) [from *lagrima*, tear]. Tearfully; mournfully.
Lamentabile, Lamentabilmente, Lamentando, Lamentevolmente, Lamentevole, Lamentato [It., from *lamentare*, to lament]. Mournfully; complainingly.

Lachner, Vincenz (*lach'-nehr*), brother of preceding. Organist, conductor; Bavaria. B. 1811; d. 1893.
La Grange, Anna (*lah-gronzh*). Soprano; Paris. B. 1825.
Lalo, Edward (*lah-lo*). Composer, violinist; France. B. 1823; d. 1892.
Lambillote, Louis (*lam-bee-yote*). Composer; France. B. 1797; d. 1855.
Lamoureux, Ch. (*lah-mo-roo*). Violinist, conductor; France. B. 1834; d. 1899.
Lamperti, F. (*lam-pehr'-tee*). Singer; Italy. B. 1813; d. 1892.

Lancers. The name of a variety of the contra dance.

Ländler (Ger.) (*laynd-ler*). A slow waltz of South German origin.

Langsam (Ger.). Slow. **Etwas langsam,** rather slow (poco adagio). **Ziemlich** (*tseem-lich*) **langsam,** moderately slow (andante). **Sehr langsam,** very slow (adagio).

Language. The diaphragm of a flue-pipe.

Languendo (It.) (*lan-gwen'-do*), **Languente** (It.) (*lan-gwen'-teh*) [from *languire*, to languish], **Languemente** (It.) (*lan-gweh men'-teh*). In a languishing style.

Largamente (It.). Broadly; slowly; with dignity.

Largando (It.). Gradually slower and broader.

Largement (Fr.) (*larzh-mong*). Largamente.

Larghetto (It.) (*lar-get-to*). Rather slow.

Larghissimo (It.) (*lar-gis-sim-mo*). Slowest possible time.

Largo (It.). Lit., large; broad. Very slow, stately movement is indicated by this term.

Largo assai. Slow enough.

Largo di molto. Very slow.

Largo ma non troppo. Slow, but not too much so.

Larigot (Fr.) (*larigo*). An organ-stop of 1⅓-foot pitch, that is, a twelfth-stop.

Lauftanz (Ger.). Running dance; the coranto.

Launig (Ger.) (*low-nig*). Gay; light; facile.

Lavolta (It.). An old Italian dance resembling the waltz.

Lay [Ger., *Lied;* Fr., *lai*]. A song.

Leader. Conductor; principal violinist in an orchestra; principal clarionet in a wind band; principal cornet in a brass band.

Leading Motive. In German, *Leitmotiv*, *q. v.*

Leading Note. The 7th note of a scale; in the major scale the 7th is naturally a half-tone below the keynote, in the minor scale it is naturally a whole tone below, and must be raised by an accidental (see *Minor Scale*); called also sub-tonic.

Leaning Note. See *Appoggiatura*.

Leap. To move from one tone to another more than one degree distant; the reverse of diatonic or chromatic.

Lebendig (Ger.) (*leh-ben'-dig*), **Lebhaft** (Ger.) (*lehb'-hahft*). Lively; with animation.

Ledger Line. See *Leger Line*.

Legato (It.) (*leh-gah'-to*), **Legando** (It.) (*leh-gan'-do*) [from *legare*, to tie or bind]. Passages thus marked are to be played with smoothness, without any break between the tones. **Legatissimo,** as smooth as possible, the tones slightly overlapping. Legato is indicated by this sign ⌒ called a slur. The proper observance of Legato is of the utmost importance in phrasing.

Legatura (It.) (*leh;gah-too'-ra*). A tie.

Legatura di voce (*de-vo-chch*). A group of notes sung with one breath; a vocal phrase.

Legend, Légende (Fr.) (*leh-zhend*), **Legende** (Ger.) (*leh-ghen'-deh*). A name given to an extended lyric composition, somewhat in the manner of "program music." [*Cf.* Chopin's Légendes.]

Leger, Legere (Fr.) (*leh'-zhehr*). Light.

Leger Line. Short lines used for notes which are above or below the staff.

Legerment (*leh-zhehr-mong*). Lightly.

Leggeramente (*led-jehr-a-men'-teh*). Lightly.

Leggerezza (It.) (*led-jeh-ret'-za*). Lightness.

Leggero (*led-jeh-ro*), **Leggiero** (*led-jee-ro*). Light; rapid.

Leggiadramente (It.) (*led-jah-drah-men'-teh*), **Leggiaramente** (*led-jah-rah-men'-teh*), **Leggiermente** (*led-jeer-men'-teh*). All these terms (derived from the same root—*leggiere*, light, quick, nimble,) indicate a light, rapid style of performance without marked accent.

Lang, Ben. J. Composer, pianist, conductor; U. S. A. B. 1840; d. 1909.

Lange, Gustav (*lang'-eh*). Composer, pianist; Germany. B. 1830; d. 1889.

Lanner, Jos. F. K. (*lan'-ner*). Composer; Austria. B. 1801; d. 1843.

Laport, Ch. P. (*lah-port*). Composer; Paris. B. 1781; d. 1839.

Lassen, Eduard. Composer; Denmark. B. 1830; d. 1904.

Lavalee, Calixa (*lah-vah-leh*). Composer, pianist; Canada. B. 1842; d. 1888.

Le Carpentier, Adolphe C. (*le car-pong-tee-eh*). Composer, pianist; Paris. B. 1809; d. 1869.

Léclair, Jean M. (*leh-clare*). Composer, violinist; France. B. 1687; d. 1764.

Lecocq, Alex. Ch. (*le-kok*). Composer; Paris. B. 1832.

Lecouppey, Félix (*le-coop-pay*). Composer, pianist; Paris. B. 1814; d. 1887.

Le Duc, Alphonse. Composer, pianist; France. B. 1804; d. 1868.

Lefébure-Wély, Louis J. A. (*le-feh-boor-veh-lee*). Composer, organist; Paris. B. 1817; d. 1869.

Lemmens, Nicholas J. Organist; Holland. B. 1823; d. 1881.

Lemoine, Henri. Composer, pianist; Paris. B. 1786; d. 1854.

Legno (It.) (*lehn-yo*). Wood. **Col legno**, with the wood. A direction in violin playing to strike the strings with the wooden part of the bow.
Leicht (Ger.). Light; easy.
Leichtbewegt (Ger.) (*beh-vehgt*). Light; with motion.
Leidenschaft (Ger.). Passion; fervency.
Leidenschaftlich (Ger.). Passionately.
Leierkasten. Barrel-organ.
Leiermann. Organ-grinder.
Leise (Ger.) (*lei'-seh*). Soft; piano.
Leiter (Ger.). Ladder. **Tonleiter**, toneladder; scale.
Leitmotiv (Ger.). Leading motive; a name given by Wagner to certain striking phrases used to indicate certain emotions, characters, or situations.
Leitton (Ger.). Leading note.
[NOTE. *-ei* in German is sounded like *eye* in English.]
Lenezza (It.) (*leh-net'-za*). Gentleness.
Leno (It.) (*leh'-no*). Faint; feeble.
Lentamente (*len-tah-men-teh*). Slowly.
Lentando. Growing slower; retarding.
Lentezza (*len-tet-za*). Slowness.
Lento (It.). Slow, between adagio and grave.
Lesser. Minor is sometimes so called, as key of C with lesser third; C minor.
Lesson. A name used in England for the suite, or the various members of it.
Lesto (It.) (*leh'-sto*). Lively; brisk.
Letter Name. The letter used to designate a degree of the scale, key of piano or organ, line or space of the staff.
Levé (Fr.) (*leh-veh*). Raised; up-beat.
Leyer or **Leier** (Ger.). Lyre.
Liaison (Fr.) (*lee-eh-song*). A tie.
Libellion. A variety of music-box.
Liberamente (It.) (*lee-beh-ra-men'-teh*), **Librement** (Fr.) (*leebr-mong*). Freely.

Libretto (It.) (*lee-bret to*). Little book; the book of an opera or oratorio, etc.
License, Freiheit (Ger.), **Licence** (Fr.), **Licenza** (It.) (*lee-chentza*). An intentional disregard of a rule of harmony or counterpoint.
Liceo (It.) (*lee-cheh'-o*). Lyceum; academy of music.
Lie (Fr.) (*lee-eh*). Tied; bound; legato.
Lieblich (Ger.). Sweet; lovely.
Lieblich gedacht. Stopped diapason.
Lied (Ger.) (*leed*). Song. **Durchkomponiertes Lied** (all through composed), a song with different melody, etc., to every stanza. **Strophenlied**, the same melody repeated with every stanza. **Kunstlied**, art song; high class of song. **Volkslied**, people's song; national song.
Lieder-Cyclus. Song-circle (as Schubert's Müllerin).
Liederkranz. A singing-society.
Liederkreis. Song circle; collection of songs.
Liederspiel. Song-play; operetta; vaudeville.
Liedertafel (song-table). A social singing-society.
Ligato. See *Legato*.
Ligature. A tie. See *Legatura*.
Ligne (Fr.) (*leen*), **Linea** (It.) (*lee' neh-ah*), **Linie** (Ger.) (*lee-nee-eh*). Line.
Lingua (It.) (*ling-wah'*). Tongue; reed of organ-pipe.
Linke Hand (Ger.). Left hand.
Lip. The upper and lower edges of the mouth of an organ pipe. To lip, the act of blowing a wind instrument.
Lippenpfeife or **Labialpfeife** (Ger.). A flue pipe-organ.
Lira (It.) (*lee'-ra*). Lyre.
Lirico (It.) (*lee'-ree-co*). Lyric.
Liscio (It.) (*lee'-sho*). Smooth.
L'istesso (It.) (*lis-tes'-so*). See *Istesso*.

Lemoine, Jean B. (*le-mo-ane*). Composer; France. B. 1751; d. 1796.
Leschetitsky, Theodor (*leh-shay-tit'-skee*). Composer, pianist; Austria. B. 1831.
Leslie, Henry D. Composer, conductor; London. B. 1822; d. 1896.
Leybach, Ignace (*li'-bach*). Composer, pianist; Alsace. B. 1817; d. 1891.
Lickl, J. G. Composer, organist; Germany. B. 1769; d. 1841.
Liebling, Emil (*leeb-ling*). Pianist; Silesia. B. 1851.
Lille, Gaston de (*leel*). Composer; France. B. 1825.

Lind, Jenny. Vocalist; Sweden. B. 1820; d. 1887.
Lindley, Rob. Violoncellist; England. B. 1776; d. 1855.
Lindley, Wm., son of R. Violoncellist; England. B. 1802; d. 1869.
Lindpaintner, Peter J. von. Composer; Coblenz. B. 1791; d. 1856.
Linley, George. Composer; England. B. 1798; d. 1865.
Linley, Thomas. Composer; England. B. 1732; d. 1795.
Linley, William. Composer; England. B. 1767; d. 1835.

Litany [from Gr., *litaino*, to pray]. A form of prayer consisting of alternate petitions and responses by priest and people, frequently sung or chanted.

Livre (Fr.) (*leevr*). Book. **A libre ouvert,** "at open book;" to sing or play at sight.

Lobgesang (Ger.). Song of praise.

Loco (It.). Place; play as written. Used after *8va*.

Lontano (It.), **Da lontano.** As if from a distance.

Lösung or **Auflösung** (Ger.) (*lay-soonk*) [from Ger., *lösen*, to free]. Resolution.

Loud Pedal. A name for the damper-pedal.

Loure (Fr.) (*loor*). (1) A slow dance in $\frac{6}{4}$ or $\frac{3}{4}$ time. (2) An old name for a variety of bag-pipe.

Louré (Fr.) (*looreh*). Legato; slurred.

Low. (1) Soft. (2) Deep in pitch.

Lugubre [Fr., *loo-groobr;* It., *loo-goo-breh*]. Mournful.

Lullaby. Cradle song; berceuse.

Lunga (It.). Long. **Lunga pausa,** long pause.

Luogo (It.). See *Loco*.

Lusingando (It.) (*loos-in-gan'-do*), **Lusingante** (It.) (*loo-sin-gan'-teh*), **Lusinghevolmente** (It.) (*loo-sing-eh-vol-men'-teh*), **Lusinghiere** (It.) (*loo-sin-gee-eh-reh*). Coaxing; caressing; seductive. [From It., *lusingare*, to coax or flatter.]

Lustig (Ger.) (*loos-tig*). Merry; gay; lively.

Lipinski, Karl J. (*lip-in'-skee*). Violinist; Poland. B. 1790; d. 1861.
Lisle, Rouget de (*leel*). Composer; France. B. 1760; d. 1836.
Listemann, B. F. (*lis'-teh-man*). Violinist; Germany. B. 1841.
Liszt, Franz (*list*). Composer, pianist; Hungary. B. 1811; d. 1886.
Litolff, Henri C. (*lee'-tolf*). Pianist; England. B. 1818; d. 1891.
Logier, J. B. (*lo-jeer*). Composer; Germany. B. 1780; d. 1846.
Lortzing, Gustav A. (*lort-zing*). Composer; Germany. B. 1803; d. 1851.

Lute, Luth (Ger.) (*loot*). A string instrument of the guitar family of very ancient origin. It was brought into Europe by the Moors. In shape it resembled the mandolin, and was strung with from six to twelve or more strings of gut. The bass strings were wire-covered and did not pass over the fingerboard. For several centuries the lutes held the foremost place as fashionable instruments. They were made of several sizes. The larger varieties were called Theorbo, Arch Lute, or Chittarone. Music for the lute was written in a system of notation called tablature, *q. v*.

Luth (Ger.) (*loot*). Lute.

Luthier (Ger.) (*loot-eer*). A lute-maker; also given to makers of all string instruments of the guitar or violin families.

Luttosamente. Mournfully. [From It., *luttare*, to mourn; struggle.]

Luttoso (It.) (*loot-to-so*). Mournful.

Lyre. A Greek string instrument of the harp family.

Lyric. Song-like. In poetry, a short poem of a simple, emotional character. The term has been borrowed by music to designate musical works of like character.

Lyric Form. A composition the themes of which are not treated in the manner of the rondo or sonata, *q. v*.

Lyric Stage. The operatic stage. This term will hardly apply to the modern "music drama."

Löschhorn, Albert (*lesh'-horn*). Pianist, composer; Germany. B. 1819; d. 1905.
Louis (Prince Ludwig F. C., of Prussia). Composer. B. 1772; d. 1806.
Löwe, Johann C. G. (*leh'-veh*). Composer; Cöthen. B. 1796; d. 1869.
Lucca, Pauline. Vocalist; Austria. B. 1841; d. 1908.
Lully, Jean Bap. de (*lul-lee*). Composer; Italy. B. 1633; d. 1687.
Lumbye, Hans C. (*loom'-bee*). Composer; Denmark. B. 1808; d. 1874.
Lysberg, Ch. S. (*lis-berg*). Composer, pianist; Switzerland. B. 1821; d. 1873.

M

M. Abbreviation for Mano or Main, the hand.
M. D. Abbreviation for Main Droite or Mano Destra, the right hand.
M. F. Abbreviation for Mezzo Forte, half loud.
M. G. Abbreviation for Main Gauche, left hand.

M. M. Abbreviation for Maelzel's Metronome.
M. V. Abbreviation for Mezzo Voce.
Ma (It.). But.
Machine Head. The screw and wheel contrivance used instead of pegs in the guitar, etc.

Madre (It.) (*mah'-dreh*). Mother; the Virgin Mary.

Madrigal. A word of uncertain origin. A name given to contrapuntal compositions in any number of parts. They differ from the motet only in being written to secular words, generally amatory. This style of composition was cultivated with great success in England in Elizabeth's reign.

Maesta (It.) (*mah'-es-ta*), con, **Maestade** (*mah'-es-tah-deh*), con, **Maestevole** (*mah'-es-ta-vo-leh*), **Maestevolmente** (*vol-ment-e*), **Maestosamente** (*mah'-es-to sah-ment'-teh*). All mean the same thing:— Dignified; with dignity.

Maestoso (It.) (*mah-es-to'-so*). Majestic; with dignity.

Maestrale (It.) (*mah-es-trah-leh*). "Masterful;" the stretto of a fugue when written in canon.

Maestro (It.) (*mah-es-tro*). Master.

Maestro al cembalo. Old term for conductor of orchestra, so called because he conducted seated at the cembalo, or harpsichord.

Maestro del coro. Master of the chorus or choir.

Maestro del putti (*del poot'-tee*). Master of the boys (choir boys).

Maestro di capella. Master of the church; choir-master; also conductor of the music in the household of a great personage.

Magadis (Gr.). A string instrument tuned in octaves.

Magas (Gr.). A bridge.

Maggiolata (It.) (*madjo-lah'-tah*). A spring song (from Maggio-May).

Maggiore (It.) (*mad-jo'-reh*), **Majeur** (Fr.) (*mah-zhoor*), **Dur** (Ger.) (*duhr*). Major.

Maggot. Old English name for a short, slight composition of fanciful character.

Magnificat (Lat.). Doth magnify; opening word of the hymn of the Virgin Mary.

Main (Fr.) (*mang*). Hand. **M. D. or droite,** right hand; **M. G. or gauche,** left hand.

Maitre (Fr.) (*mehtr*). Master.

Maitrise (Fr.) (*meh-trees*). A cathedral music school.

Maas, Louis. Composer, pianist; Germany. B. 1852; d. 1889.

MacDowell, Ed. A. Composer, pianist; U. S. A. B. 1861; d. 1908.

Macfarren, Sir G. A. Composer, theorist; London. B. 1813; d. 1887.

Macfarren, Walter C. Composer, pianist; London. B. 1826; d. 1905.

McKenzie, A. C. Composer, violinist; Scotland. B. 1847.

Majestätisch (Ger.) (*mah-yes-tay'-tish*). Majestically.

Major (Lat.). Greater.

Major Chord or Triad. One in which the third over the root is major, *i.e.*, two whole tones above the root.

Major Scale. One in which the third of the scale is a major third above the keynote.

Major Key, or Mode, or Tonality, has the same meaning.

Malinconia (It.) (*mah-lin-co-nee'-a*), **Malinconico, Malinconoso, Malinconioso, Malinconicamente.** Melancholy; in a sad, melancholy manner.

Mancando (It.) [from *mancare*, to want; fail]. Decreasing; dying away in loudness and speed.

Manche (Fr.) (*mansh*), **Manico** (It.) (*mah'-nee-ko*). Handle; neck of violin, etc.

Mandola (It.), **Mandora.** A large mandolin.

Mandolin, Mandolino (It.) (*man-do-lee-no*). A string instrument of the lute family, strung with eight wire strings tuned in pairs; the tuning same as the violin; played by means of a small plectrum; fingerboard fretted like the guitar.

Mandolinata (It.). Resembling the mandolin in effect.

Manichord [from Lat., *manus*, hand, *chorda*, string]. Supposed to be the earliest form of a string instrument, with keyboard, possibly the same as the clavichord.

Manier (Ger.) (*mah-neer'*). A harpsichord grace.

Maniera (It.) (*man-yeh'-ra*). Manner; style.

Männerchor (Ger.) (*man'-ner-kor*). A men's chorus.

Männergesangverein. Lit., men's song-union.

Mano (It.). Hand. **D.** or **destra,** right hand; **S.** or **sinistra,** left hand.

Manual [from Lat., *manus*, hand]. An organ keyboard.

Marcando, Marcato. Decided; marked, with emphasis.

Marcatissimo. As decided as possible.

Maelzel, J. N. (*male-tsel*). Inventor of the metronome; France. B. 1772; d. 1838.

Maggini, G. P. (*mad-jee'-nee*). Violin-maker; Italy. B. 1581; d. 1632.

Malibran, Maria F. (*mah'-lee-bran*). Soprano; Paris. B. 1808; d. 1836.

Marchesi, Mathilde de C. (*mar-keh'-see*). Soprano; Germany. B. 1826.

Maretzek, Max. Composer, conductor; Brunn. B. 1821; d. 1897.

March, Marche (Fr.) (*marsh*), **Marcia** (It.) (*mar-chee-a*), **Marsch** (Ger.) (*marsh*). A composition with strongly marked rhythm, designed to accompany the walking of a body of men. Marches vary in tempo from the slow, funeral march to the "charge." The following are the principal varieties: Parade March (Ger., *Paraden-Marsch*; Fr., *pas-ordinaire*); Quick-march or Quick-step (Ger., *Geschwind-Marsch*; Fr., *pas redoublé*); Charge (Ger., *Sturm-Marsch*; Fr., *pas-de-charge*). The funeral march and parade march are generally in $\frac{4}{4}$ time; the quick marches often in $\frac{6}{8}$ time.

Mark. A sign, *q. v.*

Markiert (Ger.) (*mar'-keert*), **Marqué** (Fr.) (*mar-kay*). See *Marcato*.

Marseillaise (Fr.) (*mar-sel-yase*). The French national song, composed by Rouget di Lisle.

Martelé (Fr.) (*mar-tel-leh'*), **Martellato** (It.) (*mar-tel-lah'-to*). Hammered. In piano music indicates a heavy blow with stiff wrist; in violin music, a sharp, firm stroke.

Marziale (It.) (*mart-se-a'-leh*). Martial.

Maschera (It.) (*mas-kay'-ra*). A mask.

Mascherata (It.) (*mas-kay'-ra-ta*). A mask.

Masque. Mask. A species of musical and dramatic entertainment founded on mythical or allegorical themes.

Mass, Missa (Lat.), **Messa** (It.), **Messe** (Fr. and Ger.). The communion service in the Roman Catholic Church. In music, that portion of the service consisting of the Kyrie, Gloria, Sanctus, and Agnus Dei, which are sung. The word mass is generally explained as being derived from the words "*Ite missa est*," used to dismiss non-communicants before the service. High Mass is used on feasts and festivals. Low Mass on ordinary occasions, sometimes without music.

Mario, G. (*mah'-ree-o*). Tenor; Italy. B. 1812 (?); d. 1883.

Marmontel, A. F. Pianist, composer; France. B. 1816; d. 1898.

Marpurg, F. W. Composer; Germany. B. 1718; d. 1795.

Marschner, H. (*marsh'-nehr*). Composer, conductor; Germany. B. 1795; d. 1861.

Martini, G. B. (*mar-tee'-nee*). Composer, theorist; Italy. B. 1706; d. 1784.

Marx, Ad. B. Theorist; Germany. B. 1799; d. 1865.

Mason, Lowell. Composer, writer; U. S. A. B. 1792; d. 1872.

Mason, William (son of L.). Composer, pianist; U. S. A. B. 1829; d. 1908.

Massenet, Jules F. E. (*mas-seh-neh*). Composer; France. B. 1842.

Mässig (Ger.) (*may'-sig*). Moderate; moderato.

Massima (It.). Whole note.

Master Chord. The dominant chord.

Master Fugue. One without episodes.

Master Note. The leading note.

Masure (*mah-soo-re*), **Masurek, Masurka, Mazurka.** A Polish dance in $\frac{3}{4}$ time.

Matelotte (Fr.). A sailors' hornpipe dance in $\frac{2}{4}$ time.

Matinée (Fr.) (*ma-tee-neh'*). A morning concert.

Mean. Old name for an inner part in music for voices; also for inner strings of viol, lute, etc. The C clef was also called the mean clef.

Measure. (1) Old name for any slow dance. (2) The portion of music enclosed between two bars. (3) Rhythm. (4) Tempo.

Mechanism, Mecanisme (Fr.), **Mechanik** (Ger.). (1) A mechanical appliance. (2) Technical skill.

Medesimo (It.) (*mee-deh'-see-mo*). The same as. **Medesimo tempo,** the same time.

Mediant. The third degree of the scale.

Mediation. That part of a chant (Anglican) between the reciting note and the close.

Meisterfuge (Ger.). See *Master-fugue*.

Meistersänger (Ger.). Master-singers; the successors of the minnesingers or Troubadours; the most renowned was Hans Sachs, of Nuremberg, the hero of Wagner's opera, "Der Meistersänger." The meistersänger first appeared in the 14th century. They were for the most part workingmen, differing in this respect from their predecessors, the minnesingers, who numbered royal and noble singers in their ranks. The meistersänger only became extinct in 1839, when their last society in Ulm was dissolved.

Materna, Amalie. Soprano; Germany. B. 1847.

Mathews, W. S. B. Writer, pianist; U. S. A. B. 1837.

Mattei, Tito (*mat-teh'-ee, tee'-to*). Composer, pianist; Italy. B. 1841.

Maurel, Victor (*mo-rel*). Baritone; France. B. 1847.

Mayer, Karl. Composer, pianist; Germany. B. 1799; d. 1862.

Mayseder, J. (*my'-seh-der*). Violinist; Austria. B. 1789; d. 1863.

Mazas, J. F. (*mah'-zah*). Violinist; France. B. 1782; d. 1849.

Mazzinghi, J. (*mat-zin-gee*). Composer; London. B. 1765; d. 1844.

Mehlig, Anna. Pianist; Germany. B. 1846.

Melancolia (It.), **Mélancholic** (Fr.). See *Malinconia*.

Mélange (Fr.) (*meh-lonzh*). A medley.

Melisma (Gr.). (1) A song; melody. (2) A run; roulade.

Melismatic. Florid vocalization. A melismatic song is one in which a number of notes are sung to one syllable, as in the florid passages in Händel's solos.

Melodeon. The precursor of the cabinet organ; an instrument with free reeds, operated by suction.

Melodia (It.). (1) Melody. (2) An organ-stop of 8- or 4-foot pitch; soft, flute-like quality.

Melodic. Pertaining to melody, as opposed to harmonic.

Melodico, Melodicoso (It.). Melodiously.

Mélodie (Fr.). Melody; air.

Melodrama. A play abounding in romantic and dramatic situations, with or without musical accompaniment. Melodramatic music is music used to accompany and "intensify" the action of a drama. The term is also applied to instrumental music abounding in startling changes of key or sudden changes of loud and soft.

Melody. An agreeable succession of single sounds, in conformity with the laws of rhythm and tonality. In music for voices the melody is generally in the soprano, or, if for male voices, in the first tenor, but there are many exceptions to this. In orchestral music it is even less necessary that the melody should be in the highest part, as the varying "tone color" of the instruments used is enough to give it the necessary prominence.

Melograph. A mechanical device for recording improvisation on the piano-forte. Many attempts have been made to produce such a machine, but with only partial success.

Melopiano. A piano-forte in which a continuous tone was produced by a series of small hammers which struck rapidly repeated blows on the strings. Invented by Caldara in 1870. It was re-invented in 1893 by Hlaváč of St. Petersburg, and exhibited at the Columbian Exposition, where it attracted great attention.

Melos (Gr.). Melody. Used by Wagner as a name for the recitative in his later works.

Même (Fr.) (*mame*). The same.

Men. (It.). Abbreviation for **Meno**, less; as, **Meno mosso**, slower, less motion.

Menestral (Fr.). Minstrel; Troubadour.

Ménétrier (Fr.) (*meh-neh'-tree-eh*). A fiddler.

Mehul, E. N. (*may-ool*). Composer; France. B. 1763; d. 1817.

Mendelssohn, J. L., Felix B. Composer, pianist; Germany. B. 1809; d. 1847.

Mente (It.) (*men-teh*). Mind. **Alla mente**, improvised.

Menuet (Fr.) (*me-noo-eh*), **Menuett** (Ger.), **Minuetto** (It.). Minuet; a slow, stately dance in $\frac{3}{4}$ time, retained as one of the members of the sonata, quartet, symphony, etc., until Beethoven changed it into the scherzo.

Mescolanza (It.) (*mes-co-lant'-sa*). A medley.

Messa di voce (It.) (*messa-dee-vo-cheh*). Swelling and diminishing on a sustained sound; literally, "massing of the voice."

Mestizia (It.) (*mes-tit'-sia*), con. With sadness.

Mesto (It.) (*mehs-to*). Gloomy; mournful.

Mestoso, Mestamente. Mournfully; sadly.

Mesure (Fr.) (*meh-soor*). Measure. **A la mesure**, in time.

Metal Pipes. Organ-pipes made of tin, zinc, etc.

Metallo (It.). Metal; a metallic quality of tone. **Bel metallo di voce**, fine, "ringing" quality of voice.

Method, Méthode (Fr.) (*meh-tode*), **Metodo** (It.). (1) System of teaching. (2) Manner of using the voice, or of performing on an instrument.

Metre or **Meter** [Gr., *metron*, a measure]. Properly belongs to poetry, from whence it is transferred to music. In poetry it has two meanings: (1) As applied to a group of syllables; (2) as applied to the number of these groups in a line. English prosody recognizes four groups of syllables, called feet: (1) The Iambus, consisting of a short or unaccented syllable followed by a long or accented syllable, as, be-fore͞; (2) the Trochee, which is just the reverse, as, mu͞-sic; (3) the Anapest, two short followed by a long, as, re-pro-duce͞; (4) the Dactyl, which is just the reverse, as, fear͞-ful-ly. As applied to lines (verses), **Long Meter** signifies four iambic feet in every line; **Common Meter** (also called Ballad Meter) an alternation of four and three iambic feet; **Short Meter**, two lines of three feet, one of four, and one of three in every stanza. Trochaic, Anapestic, and Dactyllic Meters are indicated by figures giving the number of syllables in each line, as 8, 6, 8, 6, etc. It is important to the musician to become thoroughly familiar with prosody, lest he fall into the too common error of setting short syllables to the accented beats of the measure, or the reverse.

Menter, Sophie. Pianist; Bavaria. B. 1848.

Mercadante, S. (*mehr-ka-dan'-teh*). Composer; Italy. B. 1795; d. 1870.

Metronome [Gr., *metron*, measure; *nomos*, rule]. A mechanical device for determining the time-value of the beat. The one in ordinary use is attributed to Maelzel, whose name it bears. It consists of a pendulum with two bobs, one of which is movable, driven by clockwork; back of the movable bob is a graduated scale. It is used as follows: If the metronomic indication at the beginning of a piece of music in ¾ time is ♩ = 100 (¼-note equal to 100), the movable bob is slid along the rod until it is opposite the figures 100, the pendulum is set in motion, and one swing — indicated by a sharp click — is allowed to every beat.

Mettez (Fr.) (*met-teh*). Put; in organ music used in the sense of "draw" or "add" any stop or stops.

Mezzo or **Mezza** (It.) (*med-zo*). Half.

Mezzo Aria. A style of singing in which the distinctness of recitative is aimed at; also called **Aria parlante**, "speaking aria."

Mezzo Forte. Half loud.

Mezzo Piano. Half soft.

Mezzo Soprano. The female voice between the alto and soprano.

Mezzo Tenore. A tenor with range of baritone.

Mezzo Voce. Half voice.

Mi (It.) (*mee*). The name of E in French, Italian, and Spanish. **Mi contra fa** (mi against fa), the interval from F to B♮; the tritone; three whole tones.

Middle C. The C half way between the fifth line of the bass staff and first line of the treble staff; the C always indicated by the C clef:

Militairemente (Fr.) (*mee-lee-tehr-mong*), **Militarmente** (It.) (*mee-lee-tar-men-teh*). Military style.

Military Band. Consists of (1) brass instruments only; (2) saxophones; (3) brass instruments and clarionets; (4) brass, wood, and saxophones.

Minaccivole (It.) (*min-nat-chee'-vo-leh*), **Minnacivolmente** (*min-nat-chee-vol-men'-teh*), **Minnacciando** (*min-nat-chee-an'-do*), **Minnacciosamente** (*min-nat-chee-o-sa-men'-teh*), **Minnaccioso** (*min-nat-chee-o'-so*). Menacing; threatening.

Mineur (Fr.) (*mee-noor*). Minor.

Minim. A half note.

Merkel, Gustav. Organist, composer; Germany. B. 1827; d. 1885.

Merz, Carl (*merts*). Composer, writer; Germany. B. 1834; d. 1893.

Meyer, Leopold von. Pianist; Austria. B. 1814; d. 1883.

Minnesänger (Ger.). German name for Troubadour; literally, love-singer.

Minor (Lat.). Lesser.

Minor Chord. The third above the root minor.

Minor Interval. One half-tone less than major.

Minor Scale. The third degree, a minor third above the key-note.

Minstrel. See *Troubadour*. Minstrel has been adopted as the name of the imitation Ethiopians who sing songs supposed to be illustrative of the manners and customs of the plantation negroes in the days of slavery.

Minuet. See *Menuet*.

Mise de voix (Fr.) (*meese de vo-a*). See *Messa di voce*.

Mise en scene (Fr.) (*meese ong scayne*). The "getting up;" putting on the stage of a play, opera, etc.

Misteriosamente. Mysteriously.

Misterioso (It.). Mysterious.

Misurato (It.) (*mee-soo-rah'-to*). Measured; in strict time.

Mit (Ger.). With.

Mit Begleitung (*be-gley'-toonk*). With accompaniment.

Mixed Cadence. A close, consisting of subdominant, dominant, and tonic chords, so called because it includes the characteristic chords of both the plagal and authentic cadences, viz.: subdominant and dominant.

Mixed Chorus, } Male and female voices
Mixed Voices. } together.

Mixolydian. See *Mode*.

Mixture. An organ-stop with from three to six small pipes to each note, tuned to certain of the overtones of the fundamental (diapason) used in full organ only.

Mobile (It.) (*mo'-bee-leh*). With motion; mobile.

Mode [Lat., *modus*, manner, way]. (1) A scale in Greek and ecclesiastical music. (2) In modern music used only in conjunction with the terms major and minor, as Major Mode, Minor Mode. **Greek Modes**; the scale system of the Greeks is not yet quite satisfactorily made out. According to Chappel, who is considered the best authority, the succession of whole and half tones was the same in all the modes, their only difference being in pitch. He gives

---

Meyerbeer, G. Composer; Germany. B. 1791; d. 1864.

Mills, S. B. Composer, pianist; England. B. 1839; d. 1898.

Mohr, Hermann. Composer, conductor; Germany. B. 1830; d. 1896.

the following as the initial notes of the principal modes: Dorian (the standard mode) D, Phrygian E, Lydian F♯, Mixolydian G. Those modes the initial notes of which are below the Dorian were distinguished by the prefix *hypo*, beneath, as Hypolydian C♯, Hypophrygian B, Hypodorian A. The succession of sounds was like that of the natural scale of A minor. Church (or ecclesiastical), or Gregorian, or Ambrosian modes were derived from the Greek modes, but discarded the chromatic sounds. Thus the Dorian and Phrygian were the same, that is, had the same initial sounds, but the Lydian began on F instead of F♯. There are other differences between the Greek and the Church modes, viz.: The first four are called authentic; those the initial notes of which are below the Dorian are called plagal; each plagal mode is considered as the relative of the authentic mode, beginning a 4th above it. The final of a plagal is always made on the initial note of its related authentic mode. If the interpretation of the Greek modes is to be trusted, the church modes seem to have arisen from a misunderstanding of the Greek modes.

Moderatamente (*mod-e-rah-tah-men'-teh*). Moderately.

Moderatissimo (*mod-e-rah-tis'-see-mo*). Very moderate.

Moderato (It.) (*mod-e-rah'-to*). Moderate.

Moderazione (It.) (*mo-deh-rat-se-o'-neh*), con. With moderation.

Modificazione (It.) (*mo-dee-fee-cat-se-o'-neh*). Modification; light and shade.

Modinha (Port.) (*mo-deen'-ya*). Portuguese love-song.

Modo (It.). Mode; style.

Modulation. (1) Gradation of sound in intensity. (2) Change of key or tonality. Diatonic modulation moves from one key to another by means of chords from related keys; chromatic modulation, by means of chords from non-related keys; enharmonic modulation, by substituting ♯ for ♭, or the reverse. A passing or transient modulation is one followed by a quick return to the original key; the signature is not changed in a modulation of this kind. A final modulation is one in which the new key is retained for some time, or permanently; it is generally indicated by a change of signature following a double bar.

Modus (Lat.). Mode; scale.

Moll (Ger.) [Lat., *mollis*, soft]. Minor.

Molique, B. (*mo-leek*). Composer, violinist; Bavaria. B. 1803; d. 1869.

Molloy, J. L. Composer; Ireland. B. 1837; d. 1909.

Monteverde, C. (*mon-teh-ver'-deh*). Composer; Italy. B. 1568; d. 1643.

Moll-Akkord. Minor chord.
Moll-Tonart. Minor key or mode.
Moll-Tonleiter. Minor scale; literally, tone-ladder.

Molle (Lat.). Soft; mediæval name for B♭, B♮ being called B durum (hard). The German words for minor and major (*moll, dur*) are derived from these terms, also the French and Italian names for the flat sign, viz., French, *bémol;* Italian, *bemolle*.

Mollemente (It.) (*mol-leh-men-teh*). Softly; sweetly.

Molto (It.). Very much. **Di molto,** exceedingly; as Allegro di molto, exceedingly rapid.

Monferina (It.) (*mon-feh-ree'-nah*). Italian peasant dance in 6/8 time.

Monochord [Gr., *monos*, one; *chorda*, string]. An instrument consisting of a single string stretched over a sound board, on which is a graduated scale giving the proportionate divisions of the string required for the production of perfect intervals. A movable bridge is placed at the points indicated on the scale. The Monochord was formerly used as a means for training the ear. It is now used only for acoustic experiments.

Monody. (1) A song for a single voice unaccompanied. (2) In modern usage it denotes a composition in which the melody is all-important, the remaining parts simply accompaniment; called also Homophony and Monophony,—the antithesis of Polyphony.

Monotone. Recitative on a single sound.

Montre (Fr.) (*mongtr*). Lit., displayed. The open diapason, so called because the pipes are generally placed in the front of the case and ornamented.

Morceau (Fr.) (*mor-so*). A "morsel;" a short piece; an extract.

Mordent, Mordente (It.), Beisser (Ger.). A sign 𝄾 indicating a single rapid stroke of the auxiliary note below the principal followed by a return to the principal. Thus—

Played.

When the sign is used without the dash through it, thus 𝄾 it is called an Inverted Mordent, or Pralltriller, and con-

Morgan, G. W. Organist; England. B. 1823; d. 1895.

Moscheles, Ignaz (*mosh'-e-lehs*). Composer, pianist; Bohemia, Germany. B. 1794; d. 1870.

 Played.

The Mordent proper is not used in modern music, and the word Mordent is now by common usage applied to the inverted Mordent, or Pralltriller.

Morendo (It.) [from *morire*, to die]. Dying away; gradually growing softer and slower.

Morisca (It.). Morris dance.

Mormorando, Mormorevole, Mormorosa (It.). Murmuring.

Morris Dance. A rustic dance of Moorish origin.

Mosso (It.). Moved. **Piu mosso,** faster. **Meno mosso,** slower.

Mostra (It.). A direct ⁀, generally used in manuscript music to indicate an unfinished measure at the end of a brace.

Moteggiando (It.) (*mo-ted-jan'-do*). Bantering; jocose.

Motett, Motetto (It.). A vocal composition to sacred words, written in strict contrapuntal style. The madrigal differs only in being set to secular words. Many modern compositions to sacred words (not metric) are called motetts, but would more properly be called anthems.

Motif (Fr.), **Motivo** (It.), **Motiv** (Ger.). Motive. (1) A short, marked musical phrase. (2) A theme for development. See *Leitmotiv*.

Motion, Moto (It.). **Conjunct Motion,** movement by degrees. **Disjunct Motion,** movement by skips. **Direct, Similar, or Parallel Motion,** when two parts ascend or descend together. **Contrary Motion,** when two parts move in opposite directions. **Oblique Motion,** when one part is stationary while the other moves.

Mouth. The opening in the front of an organ flue-pipe.

Mouth-organ. The harmonica; Pandean pipes.

Mouth-piece. In brass instruments the cup-shaped part applied to the lips; in oboe, clarionet, etc., the part held between the lips. [Fr., *embouchure*; It., *imboccatura*; Ger., *Mundstück*.]

Movement, Mouvement (Fr.) (*move-mong*). (1) Tempo. (2) One of the members of a sonata, symphony, etc. (3) The motion of a part or parts.

Movimento (It.). Movement; tempo. **Doppio movimento,** double movement; when a change of time signature from ⁴⁄₄ to 𝄴 occurs, and it is desired to preserve the same rate of movement, or tempo, *i. e.*, the quarter-note beat becomes the half-note beat.

Munter (Ger.). Lively; brisk; allegro.

Murky. An old name for a piece of harpsichord music with a bass of broken octaves.

Musars. Troubadour ballad singers.

Musette (Fr.). (1) A bagpipe. (2) An old dance. (3) In the suite the second part or "trio" of the gavotte, etc., is frequently so called, and is written in imitation of bagpipe music. (4) A soft reed-stop in the organ.

Music, Musica (Lat. and It.), **Musique** (Fr.), **Musik** (Ger.) [from Gr., *mousike*, from *mousa*, muse]. Originally any art over which the Muses presided, afterward restricted to the art that uses sound as its material.

Music Box. An instrument in which steel tongues are vibrated by means of pins set in a revolving cylinder.

Musical Glasses. An instrument consisting of a number of goblets, tuned to the notes of the scale, vibrated by passing a wetted finger around the edge.

Musician. (1) One who makes a livelihood by playing, singing, or teaching music. (2) A member of a regimental or naval band. (3) A composer of music. "Musician" is a very elastic term; it includes every grade from the drummer and fifer to Mozart.

Musikant (Ger.). A vagabond musician.

Musiker, Musikus (Ger.). A musician. (Generally used in a derogatory sense.)

Mutation Stop. Any organ-stop not tuned to the diapason or any of its octaves, as the tierce, quint, twelfth, larigot, etc. Stops of this kind (also mixtures, cornets, sesquialteras) are used for the purpose of "filling up" the volume of tone and giving it greater brilliancy.

Mute [It., *sordino*; Fr., *sourdine*; Ger., *Dämpfer*]. A small contrivance of wood or metal placed on the bridge of the violin, etc., to deaden the sound; a cone or cylinder of pasteboard, leather, or wood placed in the bell of a brass instrument for the same purpose.

Mutig (Ger.) (*moo-tig*). Bold; spirited; vivace.

Moszkowski, M. (*mosh-kow'-skee*). Composer, pianist; Poland. B. 1854.

Mozart, Leopold (*mo'-tsart*). Violinist; Austria. B. 1719; d. 1787.

Mozart, Wolfgang A. (son of L.). Composer, pianist; Austria. B. 1756; d. 1791.

Mozart, W. A. (son of preceding). Composer, pianist. B. 1791; d. 1844.

Murska, Ilma de. Soprano; Croatia. B. 1835; d. 1889.

Mysleweczek, J. (*mis'-leh-vch-chek*). Composer; Bohemia. B. 1737; d. 1781.

N

Nacaire (Fr.) (*nah-kehr'*). A large drum.
Nacchera (It.) (*nak-keh'-rah*). Military drum.
Nach (Ger.). After; according to; resembling.
Nach Belieben. At pleasure; ad libitum.
Nach und nach. By degrees; poco a poco.
Nachahmung. Imitation.
Nachdruck. Emphasis.
Nachlassend. Retarding.
Nachsatz. Closing theme; coda.
Nachspiel. Postlude.
Nachthorn (Ger.). Night-horn. An organ-stop; large-scale closed pipes, generally 8-foot tone.
Naïf (Fr.), masc. (*nah-if*), fem. **Naïve** (*nah-eve*). Simple; natural; unaffected.
Naiv (Ger.) (*nah-if*). See *Naïf*.
Naïvement (Fr.) (*na-eve-mong*). Artless.
Naïveté (Fr.) (*na-eve-teh*). Simplicity.
Naker. A drum. (Obsolete.)
Narrante (It.) (*nar-ran-teh*). Narrating. A style of singing in which especial attention is given to distinctness of enunciation, rather than to musical effect.
Nasard, Nazard, or **Nassat.** An organ-stop tuned a twelfth above the diapason.
Nason Flute. A soft, closed stop, 4-foot pitch.
Natural. A sign ♮ which restores a letter to its place in the natural scale. In the ancient system of music the only changeable note in the scale was B. The sign for that sound was ♭, the old form of the letter; it signified the sound we call B flat and was called B rotundum, *i. e.*, round B. When it was to be raised a half tone a line was drawn downward at the right side, thus ♮, and it was called B quadratum, *i. e.*, square B. In our modern music these have been retained as the signs for flat and natural.
Natural Horn or **Trumpet.** Those without valves or slides. The sounds produced are called natural harmonics, and are the same as may be produced by touching lightly a vibrating string at any point that will cause it to divide into equal parts, as 2, 3, 4, etc.

Natural Major Scale. The scale of C major.
Natural Minor Scale. A minor; also any minor scale with unchanged 6th and 7th.
Natural Pitch. The sounds produced by flute, clarionet, etc., without overblowing. The flute, oboe, and bassoon overblow at the octave above their fundamental. The clarionet at the 12th.
Naturale (It.) (*nah-too-rah'-leh*), **Naturel** (Fr.) (*nah too-rel'*). Natural; unaffected.
Neapolitan Sixth. A name given to a chord consisting of the subdominant with minor 3d and minor 6th, as F, A♭, D♭; used in both major and minor keys.
Neben (Ger.) (*neh'-ben*). Subordinate; accessory.
Neben-Dominant (Ger.). The dominant of the dominant.
Neben - Gedanken (Ger.). Accessory themes.
Nebensatz (Ger.). An auxiliary theme in sonata, etc.
Nebenwerk. The second manual of the organ.
Neck [Ger., *Hals*; Fr., *manche* (mongsh)]. The "handle" of violin, guitar, etc.; on its top is the fingerboard; at its end, the peg-box.
Negli (It.) (*nehl-yee'*), **Nei, Nel, Nell, Nella, Nelle, Nello.** In the manner of.
Negligente (It.) (*neg-lee-gen'-teh*). Careless.
Negligentimente (It.) (*neg-lee-gen-te-men-teh*). Carelessly.
Negligenza (*neg-lee-gent-sa*), con. With carelessness.
Nel battere (It.) (*bat-teh-reh*). At the beat.
Nel stilo antico. In the antique style.
Nenia or **Nænia** (Lat.). A funeral dirge.
Nettamente (It.) (*nett-a-men-teh*). Neatly; clearly.
Netto (It.). Neat; exact.
Neuma, Neumes. Signs used in mediæval notation.
Nineteenth. An organ-stop; two octaves and a fifth above the diapason.

Nägeli, J. G. (*nay'-ge-lee*). Composer, writer; Switzerland. B. 1768; d. 1836.
Naumann, Emil (*now-mann*). Composer, writer; Germany. B. 1827; d. 1888.
Neefe, Ch. G. (*neh'-feh*), Organist, composer; Saxony. B. 1748; d. 1798.
Néruda, J. B. G. (*neh-roo'-da*). Composer, violinist; Bohemia. B. 1707; d. 1780.
Néruda, Wilhelmina (Norman). Violinist; Austria; B. 1840.
Neukomm, S. Chev. (*noy'-kom*). Composer, pianist; Austria. B. 1778; d. 1858.
Nicode, J. L. (*nee-ko-day*). Composer; Polish Silesia. B. 1853.
Nicolai, Otto (*nee-ko-lie*). Composer, organist; Germany. B. 1810; d. 1849.

Ninth. An interval one degree beyond the octave, being the second removed an octave; it may, like the second, be minor, major, or augmented. The minor and major ninths are essential dissonances, that is, sounds derived from the fundamental; with the augmented ninth the lower sound is really the ninth, thus, G, B, D, F, A or A♭, are overtones of G, but C, D♯ arise from B, D♯. F♯, A, C, chord of ninth. A chord consisting of root major 3, per. 5, minor 7, and major or minor ninth may have either major or minor ninth in major keys, but only the minor ninth in minor keys.

Nobile (It.) (*no-bee-leh*). Noble; grand.

Nobilita (It.) (*no-bee'-lee-ta*), con. With nobility.

Nobilmente (It.) (*no-bil-men-teh*). Nobly.

Noch (Ger.). Still; yet; as, **noch schneller**, still faster.

Nocturne (Fr.) (*noc-toorn*), **Notturno** (It.), **Nachtstück** or **Nokturne** (Ger.) (*noktoor'-neh*). Literally, night-piece; a quiet, sentimental composition, usually in Lyric form, but under the title Notturno important compositions for several instruments or full orchestra have been written containing several movements.

Nocturns. Night services in the R. C. Church, at which the psalms are chanted in portions, also called nocturns.

Node. A line or point of rest in a vibrating body. A node may be produced in a vibrating string by touching it lightly. (*Cf.* under Natural Horn.) The sounds thus produced, called harmonics, are often used on instruments of the violin family and on the harp.

Noël (Fr.) (*no-el*), **Nowell** (Eng.). "Good news;" "Gospel." Christmas eve songs or carols.

Noire (Fr.) (*no-ar*). Black; quarter note.

Nonet [It., *nonetto;* Ger., *Nonett*]. A composition for nine voices or instruments.

Nonuplet. A group of nine notes to be played in the time of six or eight of the same value.

Normal Pitch. The pitch of a sound, generally A or C, adopted as a standard. This standard for the sound A, second space, has varied from 404 vibrations per second in 1699 to 455 in 1859. By almost universal consent the modern French pitch is now adopted, viz., A = 435 vibrations per second.

Nicolini, E. (*nik-o-lee'-nee*). Tenor; France. B. 1834; d. 1898.

Niedermayer, L. Composer; France. B. 1802; d. 1861.

Nilsson, Christine. Soprano; Sweden. B. 1831.

Notation. The various signs used to represent music to the eye, as staff, clefs, notes, rests, etc. The earliest attempts at the representation of musical sounds of which we have any knowledge were made by the Greeks, who used the letters of their alphabet, modified in various ways to represent the series of sounds they employed. Their series of sounds is supposed to have begun on the note A, first space in the bass clef. From this system music has retained the name of A for this sound. The next development was the adoption of a series of signs called neumæ. These signs, although curiously complicated, were yet very defective in precision, being inferior to the letters as indications of pitch. The great want, both of the letter system and the neumæ, was that neither gave any indication of the duration of the sounds. The next step was the adoption of the staff. At first use was made only of the spaces between the lines, and, as notes had not yet been invented, the syllables were written in the spaces; this gave exactness to the relative pitch of the sounds but no indication of their duration. The next step was to use the lines only, indicating the sounds by small square notes called points. The letter names of the lines, of which eight was the number, were indicated by Greek letters placed at the beginning. This, though an improvement on the plan of dislocating the syllables, was still wanting in that no duration was indicated. This desideratum was secured by the invention of the notes, attributed to Franco of Cologne. Invention was now on the right track. The expression of pitch and relative duration were now determined with exactness. The system of notation now in use is substantially the same, modified and improved to meet the requirements of modern musical complexity.

Note. A sign which, by its form, indicates the relative duration of a sound, and by its position on the staff the pitch of a sound.

Notenfresser (Ger.). "Note devourer." A humorous title for a ready sight reader; generally implies one whose playing is more notes than music.

Nourri (Fr.) (*nour-ree*). Nourished; *un son nourri*, a well-sustained sound. Generally applied to vocal sounds.

Novelette. A name invented by Schumann and given by him to a set of pieces without formal construction, with numerous con-

---

Nohl, Carl F. L. Author; Germany. B. 1831; d. 1885.

Nottebohm, M. G. (*not'-teh-bome*). Composer, writer; Germany. B. 1817; d. 1882.

Nourrit, Louis (*noor-ree*). Tenor; France. B. 1780; d. 1831.

stantly changing themes, giving expression to a very wide range of emotions.

Novemole (Ger.) (*no-veh-mo'-leh*). Nonuplet.

Nuance (Fr.) (*noo-ongs*). Shading; the variations in force, quality, and tempo, by means of which artistic expression is given to music.

Number. (1) A movement of a symphony or sonata. (2) A solo, chorus, or other separate part of an opera or oratorio, etc. (3) A given piece on a concert programme. (4) The "opus" or place in the list of an author's works as to order of composition.

Nunsfiddle [Ger., *Nonnen-Geige*]. Called also Tromba Marina. An instrument with a distant resemblance to a double bass, furnished with one string and a peculiarly constructed bridge. The harmonic sounds only are used. It gets its name from the fact that it was formerly used in Germany and France in the convents to accompany the singing of the nuns.

Nuovo (It.) (*no'-vo*), **Di nuovo.** Over again; repeat.

Nut [Ger., *Sattel*, saddle; Fr., *sillet*, button; It., *capo tasto*, head-stop]. (1) The ridge at the end of the fingerboard next the peg-box; its purpose is to raise the strings slightly above the fingerboard of instruments of violin and guitar families. (2) [Ger., *Frosch*, frog; Fr., *talon*, heel]. The piece at the lower end of violin bow, etc., in which the hair is inserted and tightened or slackened by means of a screw.

Nourrit, Adolphe (son of L.) (*noor-ree*). Tenor; France. B. 1802; d. 1839.

Novello, Vincent. Composer, organist; England. B. 1781; d. 1861.

Novello, Clara A. (daughter of V.). Soprano; England. B. 1818.

Novello, Mary S. (daughter of V.). Soprano; England. B. 18—.

Novello, Jos. A. (son of V.). Bass; England. B. 1810.

Nunn, John H. Composer, organist; England. B. 1827; d. 1905.

O

O (It.). Or; also written od.

Ob. Abbreviation of oboe and obbligato.

Obbligato (It.) (*ob-blee-gah'-to*). An essential instrumental part accompanying a vocal solo.

Ober (Ger.) (*o'-behr*). Over; upper.

Oberwerk. The uppermost manual of an organ.

Obligé (Fr.) (*o-blee-zheh*). Obbligato.

Oblique Motion. When one part is stationary while the other ascends or descends.

Oboe (It.) (*o-bo-eh*), plural, oboi (*o-bo-ee*); (Fr.) **Hautbois** (*ho-boa*); (Eng.) Hautboy or Hoboy [from the French word which means, literally, "high-wood"]. A wind instrument with double reed, formerly the leading instrument in the orchestra, filling the place now taken by the violins. A pair are generally employed in the modern orchestra. The oboe is one of the most ancient and widely disseminated of musical instruments. It is the general opinion of students of antiquity that many of the instruments called by the general name "flute" by the Greeks were oboi.

Oboe. A reed-stop in the organ, of 8-ft. pitch, voiced to resemble the oboe.

Oboe d'amore (It.) (*dah-mo'-reh*). Oboe "of love;" a small soft-toned oboe.

Oakeley, Sir H. S. Composer, organist; England. B. 1830; d. 1903.

Oboe di caccia (It.) (*cat'-cheea*). Oboe of the chase; a large oboe, used formerly as a hunting signal.

Oboist, Oboista (It.). An oboe player.

Ocarine, Ocarina (It.). A small wind instrument of terra cotta, with flute-like quality of tone,—more of a toy than a musical instrument.

Octave, Ottava (It.). **Oktave** (Ger.). (1) The interval between a given letter and its repetition in an ascending or descending series. The diapason of the Greeks. (2) An organstop of 4-ft. pitch.

Octave Flute. The piccolo.

Ottava bassa. An octave lower than written; the sign: 8va Ba............

Ottava alta (It.). At the octave above; indicates that the passage is to be played an octave higher than written, indicated by the sign: 8va ....

A return to the natural position of the notes is signified by the word *loco* (place), or frequently by the cessation of the dotted line thus: 8va..................

Octet, Octuor, Ottetto (It.), **Oktett** (Ger.), **Octette** (Fr.). A composition for eight solo voices or instruments.

Oberthür, Ch. (*o'-behr-teer*). Harpist, composer; Bavaria. B. 1819; d. 1895.

Octo basse (Fr.). A large double bass going a third lower than the ordinary instrument, furnished with a mechanism of levers and pedals for stopping the strings,—an important addition to the orchestra.

Octuplet. A group of eight notes played in the time of six of the same value.

Ode Symphonie (Fr.). Choral symphony.

Odeon (Gr.), **Odeum** (Lat.). A building in which public contests in music and poetry were held. In modern use as a name for a concert-hall or theatre.

Oder (Ger.). Or.

Œuvre (Fr.) (*öuvr*). Work; opus.

Offen (Ger.). Open.

Offertory, Offertorio (It.), **Offertoire** (Fr.) (*of-fer-twar*), **Offertorium** (Ger. and Lat.). (1) The collection of the alms of the congregation during the communion service. (2) The anthem or motet sung by the choir at this time. (3) A piece of organ music performed during this time.

Ohne (Ger.) (*o'-neh*). Without, as ohne Ped., without pedal.

Olio [Sp., *olio*, from Lat., *olla*, pot. A mixture of meat, vegetables, etc., stewed together]. Hence, a medley of various airs; a potpourri.

Olivettes (Fr.) (*o-lee-vet*). Dance after the olive harvest.

Omnes or **Omnia** (Lat.). All. Same as *Tutti.*

Omnitonic, Omnitonique (Fr.). All sounding, *i.e.*, chromatic; applied to brass instruments.

Ondeggiamento (It.) (*on-ded-ja-men'-to*), **Ondeggiante** (It.) (*on-ded-jan'-teh*), **Ondulation** (Fr.) (*on-doo-lah-siong*), **Ondulé** (Fr.) (*on-doo-leh*), **Ondulieren** (Ger.)'(*on-doo-leet'-ren*). Waving, wavy; undulating; tremolo.

Ongarese (It.) (*on-gah-reh'-seh*). Hungarian.

Open Diapason. See *Diapason.*

Open Harmony. An equidistant arrangement of the notes of the chords.

Open Notes. (1) The sounds produced by the strings of a violin, etc., when not pressed by the finger. (2) The natural sounds of horn, trumpet, etc., *i.e.*, without valves.

Open Pipe. An organ-pipe without stopper.

Open Score. One in which each voice or instrument has a separate staff assigned to it.

Open Strings. See *Open Notes* (1).

Oesten, Theodor. Composer, pianist; Germany. B. 1813; d. 1870.

Offenbach, Jacques. Composer, conductor, violoncellist; Germany. B. 1819; d. 1880.

Opera (It.) [from Lat., *opus*, work]. A combination of music and drama in which the music is not merely an incidental, but the predominant element. The opera originated in an attempt to revive what was supposed to be the manner in which the classic Greek drama was performed. The efforts of the group of musical enthusiasts who made this attempt culminated in the production of "Euridice," in 1600, the first Italian opera ever performed in public. The ground being broken, new cultivators soon appeared, and the new plant grew rapidly. Peri, the composer of "Euridice," was succeeded first by Gagliano, then by Monteverde,—one of the great names in music. In his hands the opera developed with extraordinary rapidity. Before the close of the 17th century a host of opera-writers appeared, led by Scarlatti. The next important development in the form of opera was made by Lulli, the court-musician of Louis XIV. No very striking advance was now made until Händel appeared. He did little in the way of developing the form, but infused so much genius into the received form that it gave it a new life. In this respect Händel resembled Mozart, who, at a later stage of the development of the opera, was quite satisfied to take the then received form, which his genius sufficed to make immortal. The first decided departure from the traditional form was made by Gluck, whose theory of dramatic music is strongly akin to the modern theory of Wagner. The opera since Mozart has grown with so much luxuriance, in such a diversity of forms, that even a slight sketch of it would be impossible in our limits. Appended will be found the names of the principal varieties.

Opera Buffa. Comic opera. (Fr., *Opera Bouffe.*)

Opera Comique (Fr.). Comedy (not comic) opera.

Opera drammatica (It.). Romantic opera. In modern German usage the term "Musikdrama" has been adopted to distinguish the modern from the old form of opera.

Opera Seria. Grand opera; serious opera; tragic opera.

Operetta (It.). An opera with spoken dialogue.

Ophicleide, Oficleide (It.) [from Gr., *ophis*, snake, and *kleis*, key. Lit., "keyed snake," in allusion to its contorted shape]. A large brass instrument of the bugle family, *i. e.*, with keys, now little used. The

Onslow, G. Composer; France. B. 1784; d. 1852.

Osborne, G. A. Composer, pianist; Ireland. B. 1806; d. 1893.

best example of its use by a great composer will be found in Mendelssohn's "Midsummer Night's Dream" music.

Oppure (It.) (*op-poo'-reh*). See *Ossia*.

Opus (Lat.). Work; used by composers to indicate the order in which their works were written.

Oratorio (It.) [from Lat., *oratorius*, pertaining or belonging to prayer; a place for prayer]. A composition consisting of solos and concerted pieces for voices, the theme of which is taken from the Bible or from sacred history. The name arose from the fact that St. Philip Neri gave discourses intermingled with music in his oratory about the middle of the 16th century. The term Oratorio is also used for secular works written on the same plan, such as Haydn's "Seasons," and Bruch's "Odysseus," but is manifestly inappropriate. The oratorio is descended from those middle-age dramatic performances founded on biblical or moral themes, known as mysteries, moralities, or miracle plays. It took its rise about the same time as the opera, from which it differs chiefly in that it affords an opportunity for the highest developments of the contrapuntal art, whereas the opera is essentially monodic. The oratorio has not gone through the manifold changes and diversities that have marked the development of the opera, nor has it attracted anything like the number of composers that have devoted themselves to the opera. The first writer of any prominence in this field was Carissimi. He was followed by A. Scarlatti; then Händel appeared and stamped for all time the form of the oratorio. His great contemporary, Bach, equaled, if he did not surpass him, but in a different style. Händel has had but two successors worthy to be named with him,— Haydn and Mendelssohn, each of whom has stamped a new character on the oratorio without descending from the high plane on which this class of composition should stand. The taste for the oratorio seems to be on the wane, as no composer of any mark has of late years devoted his attention to it.

Orchestra, Orchestre (Fr.), **Orchester** (Ger.) [from Gr., *orchester*, a dancer]. Originally the place where the dancing took place in the Greek theatre. (1) The place where the instrumentalists are placed. (2) The company of instrumentalists. (3) The collection of instruments used at any performance. See *Instrument*.

Orchestrate. To write music for the orchestra.

Orchestration. The art of writing for the orchestra.

Orchestrion. A mechanical organ designed to imitate, by means of various stops, the instruments of the orchestra.

Ordinario (It.) (*or-dee-nah'-ree-o*). Usual; ordinary; as tempo ordinario, the usual time, used in the sense of moderate.

Organ, Organo (It.), **Orgue** (Fr.), **Orgel** (Ger.) [from Gr., *organon*, tool, implement, instrument]. An instrument consisting of a large number of pipes grouped according to their pitch and quality of tone into "stops." A large bellows supplies the compressed air or "wind" to the various air-tight boxes called sound-boards, on which the pipes are placed. By means of a key mechanism the "wind" is allowed to enter the pipes corresponding to any given pitch at will. The set or sets of pipes it is desired to sound are controlled by means of "registers" which, when drawn, allow the "wind" to enter the pipes of the "stop," the name of which is marked on the knob of the register. Organs are built with from one to four, and even more, "manuals," or keyboards, placed one above the other. Three manuals is the usual number. The lowest is called the "choir organ," the middle the "great organ," the upper the "swell organ." When a fourth manual is added it is called the "solo manual," a fifth the "echo organ;" there is also a keyboard for the feet called the "pedal organ."

Organ Point, Point d'orgue (Fr.), **Orgelpunkt** (Ger.). A succession of harmonies belonging to the key, written over a prolonged holding of the dominant or tonic, or both; an organ point is generally at the bass.

Organetto (It.). Small organ; bird-organ.

Organum (Lat.), **Organon** (Gr.). An early attempt at part-writing in which the parts moved in fourths or fifths with each other.

Orguinette. A small mechanical reed-organ.

Orpharion. A lute with wire strings.

Osservanza (It.) (*os-ser-van'-tsa*), con. With care; with exactness.

Ossia (It.) (*os'-see-a*). Or else; otherwise; as ossia piu facile, or else more easily.

Ostinato (It.) (*os-tee-na'-to*). Obstinate. Basso ostinato is a name given to a frequently repeated bass with a constantly varied counterpoint, called also ground bass; frequently used by the old composers as the foundation for the passacaglia.

Osgood, Emma A. Soprano; U. S. A. B. 1849.

Otto, Ernst J. Composer; Germany. B. 1804; d. 1877.

Otto, Otto (brother of E.). Composer; basso; Germany. B. 1806; d. 1842.

Oublicheff, Alex. von (*oo'-blee-chef*). Writer; Germany. B. 1795; d. 1856.

Otez (Fr.) (*o-teh*). Take off; a direction in organ music to push in a given register.

Ottavino (It.) (*ot-ta-vee-no*). The piccolo.

Ottavo (It.). See *Octave*.

Ottetto (It.). See *Octet*.

Ou (Fr.) (*oo*). See *Ossia*.

Ouvert (Fr.) (*oo-vehr*). Open. See *Open Notes*. A livre ouvert, literally, "at open book;" at sight.

Overblow. To blow a wind instrument in such a manner as to make it sound any of its harmonics. In the organ a pipe is overblown when the air-pressure is too great, causing it to sound its octave or twelfth.

Overspun. Said of strings covered with a wrapping of thin wire.

Ouseley, Rev. F. A. G. Organist, writer; England. B. 1825.

Overstring. Arranging the stringing of a piano in such a way that one set crosses the rest diagonally.

Overtone. The sounds produced by the division of a vibrating body into equal parts.

Overture, Overtura (It.), **Ouverture** (Fr.), **Ouverture** (Ger.). A musical prelude to an opera or oratorio. Independent compositions are also written under the name of concert overtures, generally with some descriptive title. In its highest form the overture is developed in the sonata form without repeating the first part. Many overtures are nothing but a medley of airs in various tempos.

Ovvero. See *Ossia*.

P

P. Abbreviation for piano. Soft (positive degree).

PP. Abbreviation for piu piano. Softer (comparative degree).

PPP. Abbreviation for pianissimo. Softest (superlative degree).

P. F. Abbreviation for pianoforte (when capital letters are used). p. f. Abbreviation for poco forte, a little loud; or piu forte, louder. In French organ music **P.** signifies posatif, *i. e*, choir-organ.

Padouana (It.) (*pah-doo-ah'-nah*), **Paduana, Padovana, Padovane** (Fr.) (*pah-o-van*). See *Pavan*.

Pæan (Gr.). A song of triumph, originally in praise of Apollo.

Paired Notes. A succession of thirds, sixths or eighths on the piano.

Palco (It.). The stage of a theatre.

Pallet. The valve that controls the admission of "wind" to the pipes of the organ, harmonium, etc.

Pallettes (Fr.). The white keys of the piano, etc. The black keys are called *feintes* (faints).

Pandean Pipes or Pan's Pipes. The syrinx; a series of small pipes made from reeds, sounded by blowing across the open top. An instrument of unknown antiquity and universal use. The ancient Peruvians carved them out of stone. The Fijians and the South American Indians make them with a double set of pipes—one set open, the other closed at one end, thus producing octave successions.

Pantalon (Fr.). One of the numbers in a set of quadrilles. The old set of quadrilles consisted of five or six numbers called: (1) pantalon; (2) été; (3) poule; (4) pastourelle; (5) finale. If there were six, the other was called trénis.

Parallel Keys. The major and minor scales beginning on the same keynote.

Parallel Motion. When two parts or voices ascend or descend together.

Pachmann, Vladimir de. Pianist; Russia. B. 1848.

Pacini, G. (*pah-chee'-nee*). Composer; Italy. B. 1796; d. 1867.

Paderewski (*pah-droof'-skee* or *pah-dref'-skee*). Pianist; Poland. B. Nov. 6, 1859.

Paganini, N. (*pah-gah-nee'-nee*). Violinist; Italy. B. 1784; d. 1840.

Paine, J. K. Composer, organist; U. S. A. B. 1839; d. 1906.

Paisiello, G. (*pah-e-se-el'-lo*). Composer; Italy. B. 1741; d. 1816.

Paladilhe, Emile (*pah-lah-deel*). Composer; France. B. 1844.

Palestrina, G. P. da (*pah-les-tree'-nah*). Composer; Italy. B. 1515; d. 1594.

Palmer, H. R. Composer; U. S. A. B. 1834; d. 1907.

Panofka, H. Composer, violinist; Breslau. B. 1807; d. 1887.

Panseron, A. (*pan-seh-rong*). Composer, vocalist; France. B. 1796; d. 1859.

Pape, Wm. B. (*pah'-peh*). Composer, pianist; U. S. A. B. 1850.

Paraphrase. An elaborate arrangement of a piece of music for the piano, originally written for the voice, or for some other instrument. An orchestral paraphrase is a like arrangement of a vocal or pianoforte composition.

Parlando, Parlante (It.) (*par-lan'-do, par-lan'-teh*). Declaiming; singing in recitative style; playing in imitation of vocal recitative.

Part. (1) The series of sounds allotted to a single voice or instrument, or a group of voices or instruments of identical kind in a musical composition. (2) One of the counterpoints of a polyphonic composition for piano or organ, as a three- or four-part fugue. (3) One of the divisions of an extended form as indicated by double bars.

Part-Song. A composition for equal or mixed voices, unaccompanied, consisting of a melody to which the other parts are subordinated, in this respect differing from the glee and madrigal, which are contrapuntal, *i.e.*, all the parts are of equal importance.

Part-Writing. Counterpoint.

Partial Tones. See *Overtone*.

Partita (It.) (*par-tee'-tah*). See *Suite*.

Partition (Fr.) (*par-tee'-syong*), **Partitur** (Ger.) (*par-tee-toor'*), **Partitura** (It.) (*par-tee-too'-rah*), **Partizione** (It.) (*par-teetz-eo'-neh*). [From It., *partire*, to divide.] In allusion to the division by bars of the page; in English "scoring;" an orchestral or vocal score.

Paspy [from Fr., *passepied*], **Passamezzo** (It.) (*passa-med'-so*). A dance resembling the minuet, but more rapid in its movement.

Passacaglio (It.) (*pas-sa-cal'-yo*), **Passacaglia**, (*pas-sa-cal'-ya*), **Passecaille** (Fr.) (*pass-ea-ee*), **Passe-rue** (Fr.) (*pass-roo*), **Passa-calle** (Sp.) (*pas-sa-cal'-leh*), **Gassenhauer** (Ger.) (*gas-sen-how-er*). Literally, "running the street." An old dance in triple time, generally written on a ground bass.

Passage. (1) A musical phrase. (2) The figure of a melodic sequence. (3) A brilliant run or arpeggio.

Passaggio (It.) (*pas-sad'-jeo*). Passage.

Passing Note. An ornamental melodic note foreign to the harmony; when these notes fall on the beat or the accent they are called changing notes.

Passione (It.). Passion-music; a musical setting of the closing scenes in the life of the Saviour in the form of an oratorio, originally with dramatic action. The Oberammergau passion-play is a survival of this custom.

Passione (It.) (*pas-se-o'-neh*), **Passionato** (It.) (*nah-to*), **Passionatamente** (It.), **Passione** (Fr.) (*pas-si-o'-neh*), con. With passion; intensity; impassioned; with intense passion.

Pasticcio (It.) (*pas-tit'-che-o*), **Pastiche** (Fr.) (*pas-tish*). A "composition" made up of airs, etc., borrowed from different sources.

Pastoral, Pastorale (It) (*pas-to-rah'-leh*). (1) A rustic melody in ⁶⁄₈ time. (2) Used to designate an extended composition intended to portray the scenes and emotions of rustic life, as pastoral symphony, pastoral sonata.

Pastorella (It.) (*pas-to-rel'-lah*), **Pastorelle** (Fr.) (*pas-to-rel*). A little pastoral.

Pastourelle. A figure in the quadrille. See *Pantalon*.

Pateticamente (It.) (*pa-tch-tee-cah-men'-teh*), **Patetico** (It.) (*pa-teh'-tee-co*), **Pathétiquement** (Fr.) (*pa-tch-teek-mong*), **Pathétique** (Fr.) (*pa-teh-teek*). Pathetic; pathetically.

Patimento (It.) (*pah-tee-men-to*). Suffering. Con espressione di patimento, with an expression of suffering.

Patouille (Fr.) (*pah-too-ee*). Claquebois; xylophone.

Pauke (Ger.) (*pow-keh*), pl., **Pauken**. Kettle-drum.

Pausa (It.) (*paw-sa*), **Pause** (Fr.) (*paws*). A rest or pause; a bar's rest.

Pavan. A stately dance in ¼ time. The name is derived either from *pavo*, a peacock, in allusion to its stately character, or from *pavana*, the abbreviated form of *Padovana*, the Latin name of Padua, where the dance is said to have originated.

Pavana (It.), **Pavane** (Fr.). Pavan.

Paradies, Maria T. von. Pianist; Austria. B. 1759; d. 1824.

Parepa, Rosa. Soprano; Scotland. B. 1836; d. 1874.

Parker, J. C. D. Organist, composer; U. S. A. B. 1828.

Parry, C. Hubert H. Composer; England. B. 1848.

Parsons, A. R. Composer, pianist; U. S. A. B. 1847.

Pasdeloup, J. E. (*pah-de-loo*). Conductor; France. B. 1819; d. 1887.

Pasta, G. Soprano; Italy. B. 1798; d. 1865.

Patti, Adelina. Soprano; Spain. B. 1843.

Patti, Carlotta (sister of A.). Soprano; Italy. B. 1840; d. 1889.

Pauer, Ernst (*power*). Composer, pianist, writer; Austria. B. 1826; d. 1905.

Paventato (It.) (*pa-ven-tah' to*), **Paventoso** (*pa-ven-to-so*) [from Lat., *pavidus*, fearing]. Timid; with fear; timidly.

Pavillon (Fr.) (*pa-vee-yong*). The bell of a horn, clarionet, etc.

Pavillon chinois (*shee-no-a*). A staff of small bells. Flute à pavillon, an organ-stop with "bell-mouthed" pipes.

Pedal, abbreviated Ped. [from Lat., *pes*, a foot]. (1) Any mechanism controlled by the foot; in the piano, the contrivance for raising the dampers; also that for shifting the action (una corda). In square and upright pianos, the soft pedal, when depressed, interposes small strips of soft leather between the hammers and strings. The sostenuto pedal is a contrivance by means of which one or more sounds in the lower register of the piano may be prolonged at will. In the organ, the keyboard for the feet, the levers for opening and closing the swell (swell pedal) and for operating various groups of stops (combination pedals).

Pedal Check. A mechanism in the organ, controlled by a hand-knob, which prevents the movement of the pedals. **Crescendo Pedal,** a mechanism in the organ by means of which the full power may be put on or off. **Balancing Swell Pedal** is one that remains in whatever position it may be when the foot leaves it.

Pedal Harp. The mechanical contrivances by means of which certain strings are tightened or slackened to change the key, as F♯ ped., B♭2-ped., etc.

Pedal Pipes. The organ-pipes sounded by the pedal keyboard.

Pedal Point or **Organ Point.** See *Organ Point.*

Pédale (Fr.). Pedal.

Pedale doppio (It.) (*peh-dah'-leh dop'-yo*). Pedal in octaves; organ music.

Pedalflügel (Ger.). A grand piano with pedal keyboard.

Peg. The wooden or metal pins around which one end of the strings of the violin, etc., are wound, by turning which the pitch of the strings is raised or lowered; in the pianoforte they are generally called pins.

Pensieroso (It.) (*pen-see-eh-ro'-so*). Pensive; thoughtful.

Pease, Alfred H. Composer, pianist; U. S. A. B. 1842; d. 1882.

Pepusch, J. C. Composer; Germany. B. 1667; d. 1752.

Perabo, Ernst. Pianist, composer; Germany. B. 1845.

Pergolesi, G. B. (*pehr-go-leh'-see*). Italy. B. 1710; d. 1736.

Pentatone. An interval of five whole tones; augmented 6th.

Pentatonic Scale. See *Scale.*

Per (It.) (*pehr*). For, or by; as, **Per il violino,** for the violin.

Percussion Stop. A hammer which, striking the reed of a harmonium or organ-pipe, causes it to vibrate promptly when the key is depressed.

Percussive Instruments. Drums, cymbals, triangles, etc.

Perdendo (It.) (*pehr-den'-do*), **Perdendosi** (*pehr-den-do'-see*) [from *perdere*, to lose]. Gradually dying away, both in speed and power. (Abbr., Perd. or Perden.)

Perfect Cadence. See *Cadence.*

Perfect Concord. Root, minor or major 3d, and perfect 5th.

Perfect Consonances. See *Interval.*

Périgourdine (Fr.) (*peh-ree-goor-deen*), **Périjourdine** (*peh-ree-zhoor-deen*). An old French dancing-song in ¾ time.

Period, Periode (Fr.) (*peh-ree-ode*), **Periodo** (It.) (*peh-ree-o-do*). A complete musical sentence, generally eight measures.

Perlé (Fr.) (*per-leh*), **Perlend** (Ger.). "Pearled," like a string of pearls. A metaphorical expression for a clear, delicate execution; also a direction that the passage is to be played in a "pearly" manner.

Pesante (It.) (*peh-san'-teh*). Heavy; weighty.

Petite (Fr.) (*peh-teet*). Small; little.

Petite Flute. The piccolo.

Petite mesure à deux temps. ¾ time.

Petite Pedale. Soft-pedal in organ music.

Petites Notes. Grace notes.

Petto (It.). Chest.

Peu à peu (Fr.). (This sound cannot be reproduced in English; it resembles *oo*, but is not so broad.) Little by little; by degrees.

Pezzi (It.) (*pet-see*). Pieces.

Pezzi concertanti. (1) Concerted pieces. (2) A "number" of an opera, concert, etc.

Pezzi di bravura (*bra-voo-ra*). Showy, brilliant pieces.

Perkins, Chas. C. Author, etc.; first president of Boston Händel and Haydn Society; U. S. A. B. 1823; d. 1886.

Perkins, J. E. B. Vocalist; U. S. A. B. 1845; d. 1875.

Peschka-Leutner, Minna (*pesh'-ka-loit'-ner*). Soprano; Austria. B. 1839; d. 1890.

Petersilea, Carlyle. Pianist; U. S. A. B. 1848; d. 1903.

Pezzo (It.) (*pet'-so*). A piece; phrase. Beethoven uses the following sentence as a direction in one of his pianoforte sonatas: "Questo pezzo si deve trattare con più gran delicatezza,"—Every phrase must be treated with the greatest delicacy.

Pfeife (Ger.) (*pfei-feh*). Pipe; fife.

Phantasie (Ger.). See *Fantasia*.

Phantasieren (Ger.) (*fan-ta-see'-ren*). To improvise.

Phantasiestück. A piece devoid of form.

Phrase. Technically, an incomplete musical sentence.

Phrasing. The art of dividing a melody into groups of connected sounds so as to bring out its greatest musical effect, including also the placing of accent — cres. and decres., rall. and accel., rubato, etc.,—and in pianoforte music, the varieties of touch. In vocal music, it refers chiefly to the breathing places; in violin music, to the bowing.

Phrygian Mode. One of the Greek scales, generally supposed to be E—E. In the ecclesiastical scales, the octave scale from

Phrygian Cadence.

Physharmonica. (1) The predecessor of the melodeon. (2) A free reed-stop in the organ.

Piacemento (It.) (*pe-aht-chee-men'-tō*). See *Piacere*.

Piacere, à (It.) (*pe-aht-chee'-reh*). At pleasure, *i. e.*, the tempo at the will of the performer.

Piacevole (It.) (*pe-aht-cheh'-vo-leh*). Smoothly; quietly.

Piacevolezza (It.) (*pe-aht-cheh-vo-let'-za*), con. With smoothness.

Piacevolmente (It.) (*pe-aht-cheh-vol-men'-teh*). Smoothly.

Pianette (Fr.), **Pianino** (It.) (*pee-ah-nee-no*). A small piano; upright piano.

Piangendo (It.) (*pee-an-jen'-do*), **Piangevole** (*pee-an-jeh'-vo-leh*), **Piangevolmente** (*pee-an-jeh-vol-men'-teh*). "Weeping;" plaintively wailing.

Piatti, A. (*pee'-at-tee*). Composer, 'cellist; Italy. B. 1822; d. 1 01

Piano (It.) (*pee-an'-no*). Soft. (Abbreviation, P.; pianissimo, PP.)

Pianoforte (It.) (*for'-teh*). In common usage, piano, without the forte. An instrument strung with steel wire (formerly brass wire was largely used), provided with a keyboard; the depression of the keys causes the hammers to strike the strings. The name pianoforte was given to it because the volume of sound was under the control of the performer. Three forms of pianoforte are made: The grand piano [in Fr., *piano à queue*, lit.. "piano with a tail;" Ger., *flügel*, in allusion to its wing shape]; the square, and the upright. The pianoforte is descended from the dulcimer in the same sense that the harpsichord is descended from the psalterion. In form the dulcimer and psalterion were identical, differing only in that the former was played by means of hammers, the latter by means of "plectra." The adaptation of mechanism to control the hammers developed the piano out of the dulcimer, and the adaptation of mechanism to control the "plectra" developed the harpsichord out of the psalterion. The hammer action was first made practically effective by Cristofori of Padua, in 1711. About the same time an English monk, "Father Wood," made one in Rome. This instrument came into the possession of the celebrated Fulke Greville, and became well known as Mr. Greville's pianoforte. In 1717, a German youth of eighteen, named Schröter, invented the pianoforte independently; his invention was copied by Silberman of Strasburg, who submitted two of his instruments to Bach, who liked the mechanism but not the tone, preferring that of the clavichord. The growth of the pianoforte has been rapid since the beginning of the present century, and has now reached a point beyond which it hardly seems possible to advance.

Piatti (It.) (*pe-at'-tee*). Cymbals.

Pibroch. A sort of fantasia for the bag-pipe of the Scotch Highlanders; supposed to represent the incidents of a fight.

Piccolo. A small flute an octave higher than the ordinary flute; a 2-foot organ-stop.

Piccolo-piano. A small upright pianoforte.

Picco-pipe. A small instrument resembling a flageolet; gets its name from an Italian peasant, Picco, who produced astonishing results from it.

Piece. A composition; a single instrument, as, "a band of twenty pieces."

Pièce (Fr.) (*pee-ace*). A member of a suite, *q. v.*

Pieno-piena (It.) (*pe-eh'-no*). Full.

Piccini, N. (*pit-chee'-nee*). Composer; Italy. B. 1728; d. 1800.

Pietoso (It.) (*pe-eh-to'-so*), **Pietosamente** (*pe-ch-to-sa-men'-teh*). Tender; pitiful; tenderly.

Pifferaro (It.) (*pif-feh-rah-ro*). A player on the piffero.

Piffero or **Piffaro** (It.). Old form of the hautboy, still used in Italy. The same form of instrument exists all through Asia,— probably the "*aulos*" of the Greeks.

Pincé (Fr.) (*pang-seh'*). (1) Pinched. See *Pizzicato*. (2) A mordent.

Pipe. The tubes of wood or metal in the organ. They are classified as follows:— Open pipes, open at the top; closed or stopped pipes, with a movable plug; flue pipes, those constructed on the principle of the whistle or flageolet; reed pipes, those in which a beating reed is combined with the pipe. Pipes are also classified by length, the open diapason being the standard. An open pipe must be eight feet long to sound

A closed pipe four feet long gives the same sound; both are said to have an 8-foot tone. If a pipe has a 4-foot tone, its sound is an octave higher than the diapason; if a 2-foot tone, it is two octaves above the diapason.

Piqué (Fr.) (*pee-keh'*). A manner of bowing the violin, indicated by combined slur and dots:

Piquieren (Ger.)(*pik-eet'-ren*). To play piqué.

Piston (Fr.), **Ventil** (Ger.). Valve; a device used in brass instruments to lengthen the tube, thus depressing the pitch.

Pitch. Relative pitch is the interval between a given sound and some other sound. Absolute pitch is the number of vibrations per second necessary to produce a given sound. Standard 'pitch is the number of vibrations per second adopted as the pitch of a given sound. The standard (now almost universal) is 𝄞 = 435. which is known as the French "diapason normal." Between 1699 and 1859 the standard rose from 404 to 455.

Pitch Pipe. A wooden pipe used to give the keynote. A small tube containing a free reed is now generally used.

Piccini, L. (*pit-chee'-nee*) (son of N.). Composer; Italy. B. 1766; d. 1827.

Pinsuti, Ciro (*pin-soo'-tee, chee-ro*). Composer; Italy. B. 1829; d. 1888.

Plaidy, Louis (*play'-dee*). Pianist, writer; Germany. B. 1810; d. 1874.

Piu (It.). More; as, **Piu forte**, louder.

Piva (It.) (*pee-vah*). A bagpipe; also a piece of music in imitation of the bagpipe.

Pizzicato (It.) (*pits-e-cah'-to*), **Pincé** (Fr.), **Gekneipt** (Ger.). Lit., "pinched." A direction in music for bow instruments to pluck the strings with the finger, as in the guitar. (Abbr., **Pizz.**)

Placidamente (It.) (*plah-chee-dah-men'-teh*). Placidly; quietly.

Placido (It.) (*plah-chee'-do*). Placid; quiet.

Plagal Cadence. From subdominant to tonic:

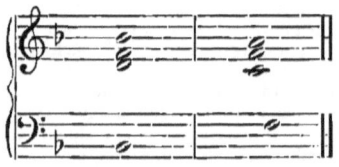

Plagal Scales or Modes. In the ecclesiastical system, those scales beginning a fourth below the authentic scales, but ending on the keynotes of their related authentic scales. They are distinguished by the prefix *hypo* [Gr., ὑπο, below], as Dorian (authentic) D-D, ending on D; hypo-Dorian (plagal) A-A, ending on D.

Plain Chant. Plain song. **Cantus planus,** or **Cantus choralis** (Lat.), the early music of the church, written in the ecclesiastical modes (also called Ambrosian) and Gregorian scales. In the 12th century the unrhythmic melodies of the early forms of plain song were largely superseded by the rhythmic cantus mensurabilis, or measured song, which came into existence upon the invention of notes by Franco of Cologne. Before this invention the musical rhythm depended entirely on the rhythm of the words to which it was sung.

Plainté (Fr.). Elegy; lament.

Plaisanterie (Fr.) (*play-zong-te-ree*). A lively fantasia in which various dance-tunes are introduced.

Planxties. Laments; music of Irish harpers to celebrate the departed.

Plectrum [Gr., *plectron*]. A small rod of metal, bone, ivory, etc., or a flat strip of wood or tortoise shell, or a ring with a projecting piece, used to strike the strings of the lyre, Japanese guitar, mandolin, zither, etc.

Pleyel, Ignaz J. Composer; Germany. B. 1757; d. 1831.

Pleyel, Marie F. D. M. (wife of above). Pianist; France. B. 1811; d. 1875.

Pole, Will. Author, theorist; England. B. 1814; d. 1900.

Plein jeu (Fr.) (*plane zhoo*). Full power; full organ.

Pneuma (Gr.). Breath. See *Neuma*.

Pneumatic Action. A contrivance in large pipe-organs by means of which a small bellows, called pneumatic bellows, is made to do the work of opening the palettes in place of the fingers.

Pochettino (It.) (*po-ket-tee-no*). Very little.

Pochetto (It.) (*po-ket'-to*). A little; (not so much as *Poco*).

Pochissimo (It.) (*po-kis-see-mo*). The "least little bit;" as **Cres. pochissimo**, the least degree louder.

Poco (It.). A little; rather; as, **Poco lento**, rather slow.

Poco a poco. By degrees; as, *Rall. poco a poco*.

Poggiato (It.) (*pod-je-ah'-to*). Dwelt upon; lit., leaned upon.

Poi (It.) (*po-ee*). Then; afterward. **P. poi f.**, soft, then loud.

Point (Fr.) (*po-ang*). A dot (Eng.). A phrase for imitation.

Point d'orgue (Fr.). Pedal point.

Pointé (Fr.) (*po-ang-teh*). Dotted.

Poitrine (Fr.) (*po-a-treen*). Chest. **Voix de poitrine**, chest voice.

Polacca. A Polish dance in $\frac{3}{4}$ time; polonaise.

Polka. A dance in $\frac{2}{4}$ time, originated among the peasants of Bohemia.

Polka Mazurka. A mazurka danced with the polka-step.

Polonaise. See *Polacca*.

Polska. Swedish dance in triple time.

Polyphonic [from Gr., *polus*, many; and *phone*, a voice]. Music written contrapuntally, as opposed to music written harmonically with a single melody.

Polyphony. "Many voices." Counterpoint in several parts.

Pommer. A large instrument of the hautboy family; bombard.

Pomposamente (It.) (*pom-po-sah-men'-teh*). Dignified; majestic.

Pomposo (It.). Pompous.

Ponderoso (It.). Ponderous; strongly marked.

Ponticello (It.) (*pon-tee-chel-lo*). The bridge of the violin, etc.

Polko, Elise. Soprano; Germany. B. 1831; d. 1899.

Ponchielli, A. (*pon-kee-el-lee*). Composer; Italy. B. 1834; d. 1886.

Poniatowski, Prince J. M. F. X. J. (*pone-ya-tow'-skee*). Composer, tenor; Italy. B. 1816; d. 1873.

Port de voix (Fr.). (1) Portando la voce. (2) An obsolete grace in harpsichord music.

Portamento (It.) (*por-tah-men'-to*). Sliding or "carrying" the voice from one sound to another; also on bow instruments, sliding the finger along the string from one place to another.

Portando la voce. Same as *Portamento*.

Portunal Flute. Organ-stop with wooden pipes which "flare," *i. e.*, get wider from the mouth to the top.

Portunen (Ger.) (*por-too'-nen*). The bourdon stop.

Posatif (Fr.) (*po-sa-teef*). The choir organ.

Posato (It.) (*po-sah'-to*), **Posément** (Fr.) (*po-seh-mong*). Quiet; sedate; grave.

Posaune (Ger.) (*po-zown-eh*). The trombone; a powerful reed-stop in the organ, of 8-, 16-, or 32-foot pitch.

Position. (1) Of chords. The common chord may be written in three positions, called the octave, tierce, and quint.

Octave. Tierce. Quint.

As given in this example it is called the close position of the chord; the following example is called the open position:—

(2) On instruments of the violin and guitar family, "Position" refers to the part of the fingerboard on which the left hand is placed.

Possibile (It.) (*pos-see'-bee-leh*). Possible; as, **Il piu forte possibile**, as loud as possible.

Postlude, Postludium (Lat.), **Nachspiel** (Ger.), **Clôture** (Fr.). The concluding voluntary on the organ; lit., after-play.

Potpourri (Fr.) (*po-poor-ee*). A number of tunes strung together.

Popper, David. Composer, 'cellist; Bohemia. B. 1846.

Porpora, Niccolo. Composer; Italy. B. 1686; d. 1767.

Potter, Cipriani. Pianist, composer; England. B. 1792; d. 1871.

Poule, la. See *Quadrille*.

Poussé (Fr.) (*poos-seh*) "Push." Upbow.

Prächtig (Ger.) (*praych-tig*). Grand; majestic.

Pralltriller (Ger.),

now commonly called the Mordent. The sign for the mordent proper is ∧∧. It always means that the auxiliary note is to be below the principal. When the line that crosses the sign was omitted it was called the Inverted Mordent or Pralltriller. The original form of the mordent is never used by modern writers.

Precentor. In the English church, the clerical head of the choir; his side of the chancel is called the cantoris side. In the Scotch Presbyterian church, the singer who stands in front of the pulpit and "gives out" the psalm tunes.

Precipitoso (It.), **Precipitato** (It.), **Precipitazione, con** (It.), **Precipitamente** (It.), **Precipité** (Fr.). A rapid, precipitate, hurried style of execution.

Prelude, Preludium (Lat.), **Vorspiel** (Ger.). An introduction; an opening voluntary; a composition which may or may not be in some regular form.

Premier (Fr.) (*preh-mee-eh*). First. **Première fois,** first time.

Preparation. The prolongation, in the same voice, of a sound from one chord in which it is a member into a chord in which it is not a member.

Prepared Trill. One preceded by a gracenote or turn.

Pressante (It.) (*pres-san'-teh*), **Pressieren** (Ger.) (*pres-seer'-ren*), **Pressez** (Fr.) (*pres-seh*). Pressing on; hurrying.

Prestant (Ger. and Fr.). 4-foot metal open stop. Same as *Principal*.

Prestezza (It.) (*pres-tet'-za*), con. With rapidity.

Prestissimo (It.) (*pres-tis'-see-mo*), **Prestissimamente** (It.) (*pres-tis-se-ma-men'-teh*). As fast as possible.

Presto (It.). Fast.

Prelleur, Peter (*prel-loor*). Composer, organist; England. B. 17—; d. 1758.

Proch, Heinrich. Composer, violinist; Germany. B. 1809; d. 1878.

Proksch, J. (*proksh*). Teacher; Bohemia. B. 1794; d. 1864.

Prick-song. Old name for written music. The first notes used were small, square marks without stems, called pricks, or points.

Primary Accent. The first member of the measure. When there are two or more accents in the measure, the first is the primary, the rest are called secondary.

Prima donna. First lady; the leading soprano.

Prima vista. At first sight.

Prima volta. First time; lit., first turn.

Prime. The first note of a scale; keynote; the generator of an overtone series; unison.

Primo (masc.), **Prima** (fem.) (It.) (*pree-mo, pree-ma*). First.

Primo tenore. First tenor.

Principal (Eng.). 4-foot open metal stop.

Principale (It.) (*prin-chee-pah-leh*), **Principal** (Fr.), **Prinzipal** (Ger.). The open diapason.

Probe (Ger.) (*pro-beh*). Rehearsal.

Program or Programme. A list of compositions to be performed at a musical entertainment.

Program-music. Music designed to "tell a story," or illustrate some action or event.

Progression. (1) Melodic—from note to note. (2) Harmonic—from chord to chord.

Progressive Stop. An organ-stop in which the number of pipes to each key increases as the pitch rises; a variety of mixture-stop.

Prontamente (It.) (*pron-tah-men'-teh*), **Promptement** (Fr.) (*prompt-mong*). Promptly; exactly; strictly.

Pronto (It.). Prompt; strict.

Pronunziato (It.) (*pro-nuntz-ee-ah'-to*), **Prononcé** (Fr.) (*pro-nong-seh*). Pronounced; emphatic. **Ben pronunziato** (It.), **Bien prononcé** (Fr.), well marked; strongly accented.

Prova (It.). Rehearsal.

Psaltery, Psalterium (Lat.), **Salterio** (It.), **Psalterion** (Fr.), **Psalter** (Ger.) [from Gr., *psaltein*, to harp]. Ancient instrument, consisting of a square, oblong, or triangular flat box, with wire strings stretched across it, played by the fingers, each of which is armed with a ring with a short projecting plectrum. The same instrument is called a dulcimer when played by two small hammers, held one in each hand.

Prout, E. Theorist, composer; England. B. 1835; d. 1910.

Prudent, F. B. (*proo-dong*). Composer, pianist; France. B. 1817; d. 1863.

Prume, F. H. (*proom*). Violinist, composer; France. B. 1816; d. 1849.

Pulsatile. Instruments played by drumsticks or by clashing them together; as drums, cymbals, etc. [From Lat., *pulsare*, to beat.]
Pulse. A beat.
Punkt (Ger.) (*poonkt*). Dot; point.
Punta (It.) (*poon'-tah*). The point. **Colla punta del-'arco**, with the point of the bow.
Puntato (It.) (*poon-tah'-to*). Pointed; staccato.
Purfling. The thin strips of wood (a white strip between two black) around the border of the back and belly of the violin, etc.
Pyramidon. An organ-stop with pipes shaped like an inverted pyramid, closed at top. From its peculiar shape a pipe not three feet long will produce 16-foot C.
Pyrophone [from Gr., *pur*, fire, *phone*, sound]. An instrument the sounds of which are produced by gas jets burning just inside of the lower end of glass tubes open at both ends. Invented by Kastner.

Puget, Loisa (*poo-zheh*). Composer; Paris. B. 1810; d. 1890.
Purcell, Henry. Composer; England. B. 1658; d. 1695.
Pyne, J. Kendrick. Tenor; England. B. 1785; d. 1857.
Pyne, J. Kendrick, 2d (son of 1st). Composer, organist; England. B. 1810; d. 1893.
Pyne, J. Kendrick, 3d (son of 2d). Composer, organist; England. B. 1852.
Pyne, Louisa F. Soprano; England. B. 1832.

Q

Quadrate, B quadratum, *i. e.*, B squared. Old name for B♮ — retained as the sign for a ♮.
Quadratum (Lat.). A breve ▢.
Quadrible or Quatrible. An ancient species of counterpoint, consisting of a succession of 4ths over a cantus.
Quadrille. A "square dance." See *Pantalon*.
Quadruple Counterpoint. A four-part counterpoint so constructed that the parts may change places without involving any false progressions.
Quadruple croche (Fr.) (*crosh*). A 64th-note.
Quadruplet. A group of four notes played in the same time of three or six of the same value.
Quality of Tone [Ger., *Klangfarbe* or *Tonfarbe;* Fr., *Timbre;* It., *Timbro*]. That which enables us to distinguish between different instruments. The character of a tone quality depends largely upon the presence or absence and relative intensity of its overtones; thus, the tone of a clarionet differs entirely from that of a violin, although all violins and all clarionets do not sound alike. The differences in tone quality that are found among violins, for example, depend on other factors, as the construction, material, weight of strings, individuality of the performer, and many more. The tone qualities of the voice are dependent largely on the accurate contact of the vocal cords, the size and shape of the cavity of the mouth and nostrils, and the management of the breath.
Quart. Interval of 4th. [It. and Lat., *Quarta*.]
Quart (Fr.) (*kart*). Quarter.
Quart de soupir (*soo-pee*). A 16th-rest.
Quart de mesure (Fr.) (*meh-zoor*). A 4th-rest.
Quartfagott (Ger.). A bassoon a 4th lower than the ordinary instrument.
Quartflöte (Ger.). A flute a 4th higher than the ordinary instrument.
Quarte du ton (Fr.) (*kart doo tong*). A 4th of the scale; subdominant.
Quarter Note ♩.
Quartet. A composition for four solo performers. **String Quartet** is composed of first and second violins, viola, and violoncello. **Piano Quartet** is composed of violin, viola, violoncello, and piano. **Vocal Quartet** may be either for male or female or mixed voices.
Quartett (Ger.) (*kvar-tet'*), **Quatuor** (Fr.) (*qua-too-or*), **Quartetto** (It.) (*quar-tet'-to*). Quartet in English, sometimes spelled quartette.
Quartole (Ger.) (*kvar-to'-le*). Quadruplet.
Quasi (It.) (*quah'-see*). As if; in the manner of; like; as, *Quasi allegro*, like allegro; *Quasi sonata*, resembling a sonata.
Quatre mains (Fr.) (*katr mang*). For four hands.
Quatrible. See *Quadrible*.

Quantz, J. J. Composer, flutist; Germany. B. 1697; d. 1773.
Quidant, Joseph (*kee-dong*). Pianist, composer; France. B. 1815; d. 1893.

Quattro mani (It.) (*quat-tro man-nee*). Four hands.

Quatuor. See *Quartet*.

Quaver. An eighth-note.

Querflöte (Ger.) (*kvehr-fla'-teh*), **Flauto traverso** (It.). " Cross-flute." The flute played by blowing across it, as distinguished from the old flute, blown at the end.

Queue (Fr.) (*koo*). Tail-piece of violin; stem of a note.

Quickstep. A rapid march, generally in ⁶⁄₈ time.

Quinable. An old species of counterpoint, consisting of a succession of fifths above the cantus.

Quint. (1) A 5th. (2) An organ-stop a 5th above the diapason.

Quint Viola. An organ-stop of the Gamba species a 5th or 12th above the diapason.

Quintaton. An organ-stop so voiced that it gives two sounds—the fundamental and the 12th. The pipes are of metal, slender and closed.

Quinte (Ger.) (*kvin-teh*). (1) The interval of a 5th. (2) The E-string of the violin.

Quintet. A composition for five solo performers. The string quintet generally consists of first and second violins, first and second violas, and violoncello ; occasionally two violoncellos are used, in which case it is called a Violoncello Quintet to distinguish it from the former. The Piano Quintet consists of a string quartet and the piano.

Quintole (Ger.) (*kvin-to'-leh*). A group of five notes to be played in the time of four of the same value.

Quintuor (Fr.) (*kang-too-or*), **Quintetto** (It.), **Quintett** (Ger.) (*kvin-tet*). Quintet, or quintette.

Quintuplet. Quintole.

Quire and Quirester. Old English for choir and chorister.

Quodlibet (Lat.) (*quod-lee'-bet*). " What you will." A performance in which every participant sings or plays a different tune ; an impromptu fantasia ; a musical jest.

R

R. Abbreviation for Right. In French organ music, for Recit. (swell manual).

Rabbia (It.) (*rab'-be-a*), con. With fury.

Rackett or Rankett. An obsolete instrument resembling the double bassoon ; a 16- or 18-foot stop in old organs.

Raddolcendo (It.) (*rad-dol-chen'-do*), **Raddolcente** (*rad-dol-chen'-teh*), **Raddolcito** (*rad-dol-chee'-to*). Growing gradually softer and sweeter.

Radiating Pedals. A fan-shaped arrangement of the pedal keys of the organ; the narrow end of the fan farthest from the organ. Radiating pedals are generally "concave" at the same time, that is, the pedals at the sides are higher than those in the middle.

Radical Bass. The root of a chord.

Rallentamento (It.) (*ral-len-ta-men'-to*). Slower. Same as *Piu lento*, or *Meno mosso*.

Rallentando (It.) (*ral-len-tan'-do*), **Rallentato** (*ral-len-tah'-to*), **Rallentare** (*ral-len-tah'-reh*). Gradually slower. Abbreviation for the above, Rall.

NOTE.—Rallentando and Ritenuto, although both mean to "get slower," differ somewhat in the manner of using them : Rallentando being used at the end of a piece (movement): Ritenuto in the course of a piece, followed by "A Tempo," when the original pace is to be resumed. Ritardando is used in the same way as Ritenuto. Abbreviation for both is *Rit*.

Raff, J. J. Composer; Germany. B. 1822; d. 1882.

Rank. A row of organ-pipes belonging to one stop. Mixture-stops are of 2, 3, 4, 5, or 6 ranks, according to the number of pipes that "speak" for each key.

Rant. An old dance. In Scotland many dance-tunes are called rants.

Ranz des vaches (Fr.) (*rongs deh vash*). Lit., "row of cows." Tunes played or sung by the Swiss as cattle calls. (In Ger., *Kuhreihen*.) As the Alpine horn is a simple tube, the melodies played on it are formed from the natural harmonic notes. When the *ranz des vaches* are sung, the melodies are varied by adding the characteristic Jodel. Many of these melodies are of great antiquity and exceeding beauty.

Rapidamente (It.) (*rah-pid-a-men'-teh*). Rapidly.

Rapidita (It.) (*rah-pid'-ee-tah*), con. With rapidity.

Rapido (It.) (*rah'-pee-do*). Rapid.

Rasgado (Sp.). In guitar-playing, a direction to sweep the strings with the thumb.

Rattenuto (It.) (*rat-teh-noo'-to*), **Rattenendo** (It.) (*rat-teh-nen-do*). Holding back the movement.

Rauschquinte (Ger.) (*rowsh'-kvin-teh*). A two-rank mixture-stop.

Rameau, J. P. (*rah-mo*). Composer, theorist ; France. B. 1683; d. 1764.

Rauscher (Ger.) (*row-sher*) [from *rauschen*, to rustle]. A repeated note on the piano.

Ravvivando il tempo (It.) (*rav-vee-van'-do*). Lit., " reviving the time." Resuming the original tempo after a rall. or rit.

Re. The second Aretinian syllable; the note D in French, Italian, and Spanish. In tonic sol-fa spelled **Ray**.

Real Fugue. One in which the subject and answer are identical, as opposed to *Tonal Fugue, q. v.*

Rebab, Rebec, Rebeck, Rebibe, Rebible. One of the precursors of the violin in the middle ages.

Recheat. A hunting signal sounded on the horn to recall the hounds.

Recht (Ger.). Right.

Recitando (It.) (*reh-chee-tan'-do*), **Recitante** (*reh-chee-tan'-teh*). In the style of a recitative.

Reci'tative (Eng.), **Recitatif** (Fr.) (*re-cee-ta-teef'*), **Recitativo** (It.) (*rch-chee-ta-tee'-vo*), **Recitativ** (Ger.) (*reh-see-ta-tiv'*). Declamatory singing, resembling chanting somewhat, tand supposed, when invented in 1600, to be a revival of Greek art. Abbreviation **Recit**.

Recitative Accompaniment. The string band is generally used to accompany Recitative. If the accompaniment is at all elaborate the freedom of the singer is greatly curtailed. Modern writers frequently use the whole resources of the orchestra to accompany Recitative.

Recitativo secco. Dry Recitative was accompanied very sparingly with chords. It was customary at one time, during the pauses of the voice, for the violoncello to execute impromptu flourishes.

Reciting Note. In Gregorian chant, the dominant, being the note on which the greater part of the reciting is done.

Recorder. An obsolete instrument of the flageolet family; also an old name for the flute.

Redita (It.) (*reh-dee'-ta*). A repeat.

Redowa, Redowak, Redowazka. A Bohemian dance in ¾ time.

Redundant. Same as *Augmented*.

Ran'degger, A. Composer; Austria. B. 1832.

Rappoldi, E. (*rap-pol'-dee*). Composer, violinist; Austria. B. 1839; d. 1903.

Rappoldi, Laura K. (his wife). Pianiste; Austria. B. 1853.

Ravenscroft, Thos. Composer; England. B. 1582; d. 1635.

Reeves, J. Sims. Tenor; England. B. 1818.

Reed, Zunge (Ger.) (*tsoon'-geh*), **Anche** (Fr.) (*onsh*), **Ancia** (It.) (*an'-che-a*). The technical name for the small thin strip of metal, cane, or wood, the vibration of which causes the sound of a variety of instruments. There are three kinds of reeds: (1) The single beating reed of instruments of the clarionet family; also of the reed-stops of the organ. (2) The double reed of the hautboy and bassoon family, also of the bagpipe; these two varieties are never used except in conjunction with a tube or pipe. (3) The free reed of the cabinet-organ, vocalion, etc. This reed may be used with or without a tube. The effect of the tube when combined with the free reed is analogous to that of a resonator, *i. e.*, the vibration of the contained air is sympathetic, whereas in the other cases the vibration of the reed is controlled by the column of air.

Reed Instruments. Those in which the sound is produced by the vibration of a reed in the mouthpiece.

Reel. A lively dance, nationalized in Ireland and Scotland; supposed to be of Danish origin, as the same kind of dance is found there under the name of Hreol.

Refrain. Burthen. (1) The chorus at the end of every stanza of some ballads. (2) The drone of a bagpipe. (3) The tune sung as an accompaniment to dancing.

Régales de bois (Fr.) (*reh-gal de bo-a*). See *Xylophone*.

Regals, Rigals, Rigoles. Small, portable organs with one or two sets of pipes, carried by a strap round the neck of the player, who worked the bellows with his left hand and manipulated the keyboard with the right.

Register. (1) Same as stop, or rank of pipes. (2) The projecting knobs on which the names of the stops are marked. (3) The compass of a voice. (4) One of the divisions of the voice; as, chest register, head register.

Registration. The combinations and successions of stops used by an organist in the performance of a piece.

Règle de l'octave (Fr.) (*regl de loc-tav*). See *Rule of the Octave*.

Rei'cha, A. J. Composer, theorist; Bohemia. B. 1770; d. 1836.

Reichardt, Alex. Composer, tenor; Germany. B. 1825; d. 1885.

Reichardt, Johann F. Composer, writer; Germany. B. 1752; d. 1814.

Reichardt, Louise (daughter of J.). Composer; Germany. B. 1778; d. 1826.

Reinecke, Carl (*rei'-nek-kuh*). Composer, pianist; Altona. B. 1824; d. 1910.

Relative Chord. A chord whose members are found in the scale.

Relative Key. One whose tonic chord is one of the common chords found in the scale.

Religioso (It.) (*reh-lee-jo'-so*), **Religiosamente** (*reh-lee-jo-sa-men'-teh*). In a devotional manner.

Relish. An obsolete harpsichord grace.

Remote Key. A non-related key.

Remplissage (Fr.) (*rom-plis-sazh*). Filling up. (1) The inner parts. (2) Sometimes used in the same sense as "development" (*durchführung*) in the sonata or rondo. (3) Non-essential (ripieno) parts. (4) Used in a contemptuous sense of a clumsy, overloaded composition.

Rendering. A modern term which is supposed to mean more than saying one "played" or "sang."

Repeat. A double bar with dots, thus signifies that the part before the double bar is to be repeated. If the dots are on both sides it signifies that the parts before and after the double bar are to be repeated.

Repercussion. The re-entry of subject and answer in a fugue, after an episode.

Repetition. (1) The reiteration of a note or chord. (2) A pianoforte action invented by Erard, which admits of the re-striking of a note before the key has risen to its normal position. (3) The re-entry of one of the principal themes of a sonata or rondo.

Répétition (Fr.) (*reh-peh-tis-yong*). A rehearsal.

Repetizione (It.) (*reh-peh-tit-ze-oh'-neh*). Repetition.

Replicate. The recurrence of the same letter in an ascending or descending series; the octave repetitions of a given letter.

Reply, Répons (Fr.) (*reh-pong*), **Réponse** (Fr.) (*reh-pongs*), **Report.** The "answer" to a fugue subject or theme for imitation.

Reprise (Fr.) (*reh-prees*). (1) A repeat. (2) The re-entry of the principal theme in the second part of a sonata; also called **Rentree** (*rong-treh*).

Reinhold, Hugo. Composer; Austria. B. 1854.

Reinthaler, C. M. (*rein'-tah-ler*). Composer, organist; Saxony. B. 1822; d. 1896.

Reissiger, C. G. (*rice'-see-ger*). Composer; Germany. B. 1798; d. 1859.

Requiem (Lat.). "Rest." The first word in the mass for the dead, hence called requiem mass.

Resin or Rosin. The clarified gum of the pitch pine.

Resolution. The movement of a dissonant to a consonant sound.

Rests. Signs indicating silence of the same duration as the notes for which they stand. In all varieties of time the whole rest is used to indicate a silence of one measure.

Whole Half Quarter Eighth Six- Thirty- Sixty-
Rest. Rest. Rests. Rest. teenth second fourth
 Rest. Rest. Rest.

Three forms of quarter-rest are found. No. 1 is generally found in music printed from type, Nos. 2 and 3 in engraved music. No. 2 is the most convenient form in MS. In orchestral parts a rest of two measures is indicated thus:

three   four

Any number of measure rests may be expressed by combining these three signs, but when the number exceeds six it is generally expressed thus: a heavy diagonal line with numeral above it.

Retardation. The prolonging of a sound which is a member of one chord into a chord in which it is not a member, thus producing a dissonance. See *Resolution*.

Reverie. A sentimental name used by some modern writers for composition of like character, generally in lyric form.

Rhapsodie or Rhapsody [from Gr., *rhabdos*, a staff]. The Rhapsodists were wandering reciters who carried a long staff. The term is now applied to an irregular, formless composition which "wanders" from one theme, or key, or tempo to another at the will of the composer.

Rhythm. (1) The recurrence of accents at equal intervals of time. (2) The repetition of a group of sounds (not necessarily

---

Rellstab, H. F. L. Composer, writer; Germany. B. 1799; d. 1860.

Rellstab, J. C. F. (father of H.). Composer, writer; Germany. B. 1759; d. 1813.

Remenyi, Ed. (*reh'-men-yee*). Violinist; Hungary. B. 1830; d. 1898.

melodic) at equal intervals of time. This is an illustration of the first meaning:

This, of the second:

The first may be called the essential rhythm; it is never destroyed, no matter how much it may be divided by the second or ideal rhythm; thus the essential rhythm of the following passage is 1' 2 3; the ideal rhythm varies with each measure:

Rhythm is the first essential of melody; without it we have only an aimless rising and falling of sounds. The essential rhythm is a fixed quantity which will bear very little tampering with. Witness the generally unsatisfactory effect of those compositions in which alternate measures of two and three units are used. Its pace may be changed by acceleration or retardation provided the rhythmical unit is maintained. The ideal rhythm, or rhythm of the melody, is, on the other hand, completely under the composer's control, provided that its melodic motives, phrases, etc, may be "measured" by the rhythmical units adopted as the "time signature."

Ricercata (It.) (*ree-cher-cah'-ta*). A species of fugue very highly elaborated.

Rigadoon. A rapid dance of French origin, generally in ¼ time.

Rigore (It.) (*ree-go'-reh*), con, **Rigoroso** (*ree-go-ro'-so*). With rigor; exactly; in strict time.

Rilasciando (It.) (*ree - lah - she - an' - do*), **Rilasciante** (*ree-lah-she-an'-te*). Relaxing the time; retarding.

Rimettendo (It) (*ree-met-ten'-do*). Holding back; retarding.

Rinforzando (It.) (*rin-for-tzan'-do*), **Rinforzare** (*rin - for - tzah'-reh*), **Rinforzato**

(*rin - for - tzah' - to*). Lit., re-enforcing. Placing a strong accent on a note or passage.

Ripieno (It.) (*ree-pee-eh'-no*). "Filling up." A part that is not essential to the score, added to increase the volume of a tutti.

Ripigliare (It.) (*ree-peel-yah'-reh*), **Riprendere** (*ree-pren'-deh-reh*). To resume.

Ripresa (It.) (*ree-preh'-sah*), **Riprese** (Fr.). A repeat; the sign 𝄋.

Risentito (It.) (*ree-sen-tee'-to*). With energetic expression.

Risolutamente (It.) (*ree-so-lu-ta-men'-te*). Resolutely.

Risoluto (It.) (*ree-so-lu'to*). Resolute.

Risoluzione (It.) (*ree-so-loot-ze-o-neh*), con. With resolution.

Risvegliato (It.) (*ris-vehl-ya-to*). Animated; lively.

Ritardando (It.) (*ree-tar-dan'-do*), **Ritardato** (*ree-tar-dah'-to*), **Ritenuto** (*ree-ten-oo'-to*), **Ritenente** (*ree-ten-en'-teh*). Holding back; retarding. Abbreviation **Rit.**

Ritmo (It.). See *Rhythm*.

Ritmo a due battate. Of two measures.

Ritmo a tre battate. Of three measures. The following passage, which, being written in ¾ (scherzo) time, looks like a six-bar phrase, is in reality a two-bar phrase, founded on the triple unit:

Ritmo a tre battate.

written in ⁹⁄₈ time; or it may be written in ¾ time with triplets.

This example is analogous to the oft-quoted one in the scherzo of Beethoven's ninth symphony.

Rheinberger, J. (*rine'-ber-ger*). Composer, organist; Germany. B. 1839; d. 1901.

Ricci, F. (*rit'-chee*). Composer; Italy. B. 1809; d. 1877.

Ricci, Luigi (brother of F.). Composer; Italy. B. 1805; d. 1859.

Richards, Brinley. Composer, pianist; England. B. 1817; d. 1885.

Richter, E. F. E. Composer, writer; Germany. B. 1808; d. 1879.

Richter, Hans. Composer, conductor; Germany. B. 1843.

Riemann, Hugo (*ree' - man*). Theorist; Germany. B. 1849.

Ries, F. (*rees*). Composer; Germany. B. 1784; d. 1838.

Righini, V. (*ree-gee'-nee*). Composer; Italy. B. 1756; d. 1812.

Rimbault, Ed. F. Composer, organist, writer; England. B. 1816; d. 1876

Rimbault, Stephen F. Composer, organist; England. B. 1773; d. 1837.

Rink, J. C. H. composer, organist; Germany. B. 1770; d. 1846.

Ritornella (It.) (*ree-tor-nel'-la*). Interlude; chorus; burden; tutti in the old concertos.
Robusto (It.) (*ro-bus'-to*). Robust; bold.
Roger de Coverly. Old English country dance in ¾ time.
Röhrflöte (Ger.) (*rare'-flo-teh*). Reed-flute; a flute-stop in the organ.
Rôle (Fr.) (*roll*). The part in an opera or play assigned to any performer.
Roll, Wirbel (Ger.), **Rollo** (It.), **Roulement** (Fr.). The tremolo produced on the drum by the rapid alternation of blows with the drumsticks. On the kettle-drum the roll is produced by single alternating blows; on the side drum, by double alternating blows.
Romance. (1) A ballad. (2) An instrumental piece in lyric form, of romantic character; often used as the slow movement of a sonata, etc.
Romanesca (It.) (*ro-ma-nes'-ca*), **Romanesque** (Fr.) (*ro-man-esk*). Same as *Galliard*.
Romantic. A vague term for that form of art in which the emotional content is considered as of more importance than the form. The term "romantic" is often used as opposed to classic; but the application of "classic" is as vague as is that of "romantic." The element of time seems to be an essential of classicism, the work of a living author never being considered classic. The term romantic may be defined as roughly dividing the music written on harmonic principles from that written before the principles of harmonic combination and succession were discovered; but already the romantic school has been sub-divided into what may be called the classic-romantic and the new-romantic; but since every "new" thing must in time become "o d," this last school must, when its day is past, give place to a newer romanticism.
Rondo, Rondeau (Fr.). One of the forms of composition characterized by the return of the first theme after the presentation of each new theme. The modern rondo partakes of the character of the sonata form, in that its second theme is repeated in the tonic key, having been first given in the dominant key. The following schemes exhibit at a glance the usual forms of the rondo:—

MAJOR KEY.—	I Th. Tonic.	II Th. Dom.	I Th. Tonic	‖ III Th. Subdom. Rel. min. Par. min.	I Th. Tonic.	II Th. Tonic.	I Th. Tonic.
MINOR KEY.—	I Th. Tonic.	II Th. Rel. major.	I Th. Tonic.	‖ III Th. Subdom. of rel. major.	I Th. Tonic.	II Th. Tonic. major.	I Th. Tonic.

Example of Rondo in Major Key,—last movement of Op. 2, No. 2 (Beethoven).
Example of Rondo in Minor Key,—last movement of Sonata Pathetique.

Root. The fundamental or generating note of a chord.
Rosalia (It.) (*ros-al-ya*). The repetition of a melodic phrase several times, each time one degree higher or lower than the last. It gets its name from an Italian folk-song, "Rosalia Mia Cara," the melody of which is constructed in this way. Although not considered good writing, many examples may be found in the works of the greatest composers. Three such repetitions are generally considered allowable. In Germany the Rosalia has the ludicrous name of *Schusterfleck* (cobbler's patch), also *Vetter Michel* (Cousin Michel), from its occurrence in a well-known Volkslied, "Gestern Abend war Vetter Michel da."
Rose. The sound-hole in the belly of the guitar, mandolin, etc.
Rosin. See *Resin*.

Ritter, A. G. Composer, organist; Germany. B. 1811; d. 1885.
Ritter, Fred. L. Composer, writer; Alsace. B. 1831; d. 1892.
Ritter, Fanny Raymond (wife of Fred.). Writer; U. S. A. B. 1840.
Ritter, Theodore. Composer, pianist; France. B. 1841; d. 1886.
Rochlitz, F. J. Composer, critic; Germany. B. 1769; d. 1842.
Rockstro, Will. S. Composer, writer; England. B. 1830; d. 1895.
Rode, J. P. J. Composer, violinist; France. B. 1774. d. 1830.
Roeckel, J. A. Tenor; Germany. B. 1783; d. 1870.
Roeckel, Ed. (son of J. A.). Composer, pianist; France. B. 1816; d. 1876.
Roeckel, J. L. (son of J. A.). Composer, pianist; England. B. 1838. [J. L. Roeckel writes under the pseudonym of Edward Dorn.]
Romberg, Andreas. Composer, violinist; Germany. B. 1767. d. 1821.
Romberg, Bernhard. Composer, 'cellist; Germany. B. 1767; d. 1841.
Ronconi, Sebastian (*ron-ko'-nee*). Baritone; Italy. B. 1814.
Röntgen, Julius. Composer, pianist; Germany. B. 1855.
Root, Geo. F. Composer, writer; U. S. A. B. 1820; d. 1895.

Rota (Lat.). A round.
Rote. Hurdy-gurdy; vielle.
Roulade (Fr.) (*roo-lad*). A brilliant run; an ornamental flourish.
Round. A variety of canon, the imitation being always at the 8*va* or unison.
Roundel, Round, Roundelay. A dance in which a ring with joined hands was formed. Roundelay also means a poem with a constantly reiterated refrain or burden.
Rubato (It.) (*roo-bah'-to*). Robbed; stolen. The direction Rubato, or Tempo Rubato, indicates a style of performance in which the rhythmic flow is interrupted by dwelling slightly on certain melodic notes and slightly hurrying others. This style of performance is used with great effect in the modern intensely emotional school of music.

Rosa, Carl A. N. Violinist, conductor; Germany. B. 1842; d. 1889.
Rosellen, Henri (*ro-sell-len*). Pianist; France. B. 1811; d. 1876.
Rosenhain, Jacob (*ro'-sen-highn*). Composer, pianist; Germany. B. 1813; d. 1894.
Rosenthal, Moritz (*ro'-sen-tal*). Pianist; Germany. B. 1862.
Rossi, Luigi (*ros'-see*). Composer; Italy. B. 15—; d. 16—.
Rossini, G. A. (*ros-see'-nee*). Composer, Italy. B. 1792; d. 1868.
Rousseau, J. J. (*roos-so*). Composer, writer; Geneva. B. 1712; d. 1778.

Ruhig (Ger.) (*roo'-ig*). Calm; quiet; tranquilly.
Rule of the Octave. An old formula for putting chords to the diatonic scale, major or minor.
Run. A passage founded on the scale, generally used in vocal music. The run is generally sung to one syllable.
Rusticano (It.) (*rus-tee-cah'-no*). Rustically.
Rustico (It.) (*rus'-tee-co*). Rustic; pastoral.
Rutscher (Ger.) (*root'-sher*). "Slider." Old name for the galopade.
Ruvido (It.) (*roo'-vee-do*). Rough; harsh.
Rythme (Fr.) (*reethm*), **Bien rythmé** (Fr.), **Ben ritmato** (It.). Well marked; exact.

Roze, Marie P. Soprano; Paris. B. 1846.
Rubini, G. B. (*roo-bee'-nee*). Tenor; Italy. B. 1795; d. 1854.
Rubinstein, Anton G. Composer, pianist; Russia. B. 1830; d. 1894.
Rubinstein, N. (brother of Anton). Composer, pianist; Russia. B. 1835; d. 1881.
Rudersdorff, H. Soprano; Russia. B 1822; d. 1882.
Rudorff, Ernst F. Composer, pianist; Germany. B. 1840; d. 190-(?).
Ruggieri, F. (*rood-jee-eh'-ree*). Violin maker; Italy. B. 16—; d. 17—.
Rummel, Franz. Pianist; England. B. 1853, d. 1901.

S

S. Abbreviation of **Segno** (sign); **Senza** (without); **Sinistra** (left); **Solo**; **Subito** (quickly).
𝄋 A sign used to point out the place from which a repeat is to be made. **Al 𝄋**, to the sign; **Dal 𝄋**, from the sign.
Sabot (Fr.). A "shoe." Part of the mechanism of the double-action harp, consisting of a revolving disk of brass with two projecting studs; when the pedal is depressed the string is caught between the studs and drawn tighter, thus raising its pitch.
Saccade (Fr.) (*sac-cad*). A strong pressure of the violin bow on the strings, causing two or three to sound together.

Sacchini, A. M. L. (*sak-kee'-nee*). Composer; Italy. B. 1734; d. 1786.
Saint-Saëns, Camille (*sangt-sah-ong*). Composer, organist, pianist; Paris. B. 1835.
Sainton-Dolby, Ch. Helen. Composer, contralto, soprano; England. B. 1821; d. 1885.

Sackbut. An old name for a species of the trombone. Sometimes written Sagbut.
Sackpfeife (Ger.). Bagpipe.
Saite (Ger.) (*sy-teh*). A string.
Salicional, Salicet, Salcional [from Lat., *salix*, willow]. A soft, open metal organ-stop.
Salonflügel (Ger.). Parlor grand pianoforte.
Salonstück (Ger.). Parlor piece; salon music.
Saltarello (It.) (*sal-tah-rel'-lo*) [from *saltare*, to leap]. An Italian dance in triple time.
Saltato (It.). "Springing bow" in violin playing.

Sainton, P. P. C. (*sang-tong*) (husband of S.-Dolby). Composer, violinist; France. B. 1813; d. 1890.
Salaman, Ch. K. Composer, pianist; England. B. 1814; d. 1901.
Salieri, A. (*sal-yeh'-ree*). Composer; Italy. B. 1750; d. 1825.

Salto (It.). A skip. A counterpoint that moved by skips was called C. P. di salto; in Lat., *C. P. per saltem*.

Sambuca. Generally supposed to be an ancient variety of the harp. The Sabeca, mentioned in the Bible (Daniel iii: 5, 7, 10, 15), translated "sackbut" in the English version, is supposed to be the same instrument. The derivation of the word is not known.

Sampogna or **Zampogna** (It.) (*sam-pone'-ya*). Bagpipe.

Sanft (Ger.). Soft.

Sans (Fr.). Without.

Saraband, Sarabanda (It.), **Zarabanda** (Sp.), **Sarabande** (Fr.). A slow, stately dance in ¾ time, used as the "slow movement" in the suite. The Saraband is founded on the following rhythm:—

One of the finest examples is the song in "Rinaldo," by Händel, "*Lascia ch' io pianga*," which is said to have been written first as a Saraband, and afterward adapted to the words.

Sarrusophone. A brass wind instrument with a double reed like hautboy.

Satz (Ger.). (1) A theme. **Hauptsatz**, principal theme; **Seitensatz**, secondary theme; **Nebensatz**, auxiliary theme; **Schluss-Satz**, closing theme, or coda. (2) A piece; composition.

Saxhorn. A brass instrument with from three to five cylinders or pistons; invented by A. Sax. Saxhorns are made in seven different keys. A saxhorn band consists of "high horn" (or cornet), soprano, alto, tenor, baritone, bass (or tuba), double bass (or bombardon). The "high horn," alto, and bass are in E♭, the others in B♭.

Saxophone. Brass instrument with clarionet mouthpiece, invented by A. Sax. Made in seven sizes, corresponding to the saxhorns, except that there are two of each kind, differing by a whole tone in pitch;

thus: Sopranino (high saxophone) in F and E♭, soprano in C and B♭, alto in F and E♭, tenor in C and B♭, baritone in F and F♭, bass in C and B♭. The saxophone is extensively used in France in military bands, but has not as yet found its way into the orchestra, as its tone quality is not of a character to mix well with the rest of the orchestra.

Saxtromba. Brass instrument resembling the saxhorn, but differing in tone quality from having a narrower tube.

Saxtuba. The bass saxhorn.

Sbalzato (It.) (*sbalt-zah'-to*). Impetuously; dashing.

Scale. (1) A succession of ascending or descending sounds. **Major Scale**, a series of sounds with a half-tone between 3-4 and 7-8, reckoning upward. **Minor Scale**, a series of sounds with a half-tone between 2-3 and 5-6 in the natural minor, in the Melodic Minor, 7-8, ascending. The Melodic Minor descends, like the Natural Minor; in the Harmonic Minor there are half-tones between 2-3, 5-6, and 7-8, and a tone and a half between 6 and 7. The Minor Scale sometimes descends with raised 6 and 7. Many examples may be found in Bach's music. **Chromatic Scale**, one formed wholly of half-tones. **Pentatonic Scale** [Gr., *penta*, five, *tonos*, sound], one that omits the 4 and 7. The Pentatonic Scale may be major or minor, thus:—

Hungarian Gypsy Scale consists of the following curious succession:—

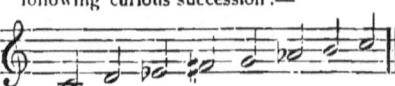

(2) The series of overtones of a simple tube, such as the horn without valves. (3) In organ-pipes, the proportion between the length and the diameter. (4) In the piano,

Salo, Gasparo da. Violin maker; Italy. B. 1542; d. 1609.

Sankey, Ira D. Vocalist; U. S. A. B. 1840; d. 1908.

Santley, Ch. Baritone; England. B. 1834.

Sarasate, P. M. M. Y. N. (*sah-rah-sah'-teh*). Violinist, composer; Spain. B. **1844**; d. 1908.

Sarti, G. (*sar'-tee*). Composer, organist; Italy. B. 1729; d. 1802.

Satter, Gustav. Composer, pianist; Austria. B. 1832.

Sauret, Emile (*saw-ray*). Violinist; France. B. 1852.

Sax, Antoine J. With his father, inventor of saxhorns, saxophones, etc.; France. B. 1814; d. 1894.

Sax, Ch. J. (father of A. J.). With his son, inventor of saxhorns, saxophones, etc.; France. B. 1791; d. 1865.

Scalchi, Sofia (*skal'-kee*). Alto; Italy. B. 1850.

Scarlat'ti, A. Composer; Italy. B. 1659; d. 1725.

Scarlat'ti, Dominico (son of A.). Composer, pianist; Italy. B. 1683; d. 1757.

Scarlat'ti, G. (son of D.). Composer; Italy. B. 1712; d. 1777.

the proportion between the length, weight, and tension of the string, and the pitch of the sound it is meant to give. Piano builders include many other points in the term "scale;" those given are the most important.

Scemando (It.) (*shay-man'-do*). See *Diminuendo*.

Scena (It.) (*shay-nah*). (1) A scene. (2) A solo for voice in which various dramatic emotions are expressed.

Scenario (It.) (*shay-nahr'-yo*). (1) The plot of a drama. (2) The book of stage directions.

Scene. (1) See *Scena*. (2) A division of a dramatic performance. (3) A stage-setting.

Schablonenmusik (Ger.). "Pattern" or "stencil" music, *i. e.*, correct, but uninspired.

Schäferlied (Ger.) (*shay'-fer-leet*). Shepherd song; pastoral.

Schäferspiel (Ger.) (*shay'-fer-speel*). Pastoral play.

Schallbecken (Ger.). "Sound bowls;" cymbals. Frequently called **Becken**.

Schalmy. See *Chalameau*.

Scharf (Ger.). Sharp. A mixture-stop.

Schaurig (Ger.). Weird; dread-inspiring.

Scherz (Ger.) (*sherts*). Droll; playful.

Scherzando (It.) (*sker-tzan'-do*), **Scherzante** (*sker-tzan'-teh*), **Scherzevole** (*sker-tzeh'-vo-leh*), **Scherzoso** (*sker-tzo'-so*). All derived from *scherzo*, and signifying a light, playful style of performance or composition.

Scherzhaft (Ger.). Funny; amusing.

Scherzo (It.) (*skert'-zo*). A "jest." (1) A piece of music of a sportive, playful character. (2) A symphony or sonata movement of this character, taking the place of the minuet. Haydn first changed the character of the minuet, while still retaining its name, by giving it a light, playful character and more rapid tempo. Beethoven discarded the name and adopted that of *Scherzo*, and still further increased the rapidity of the movement; all that he retained of the minuet was the ¾ time. Many composers since Beethoven have made still further departures, Scherzi being now written in ⁶⁄₈ and ²⁄₄ time.

Schiettamente (It.) (*ske-et-ta-men'-teh*). Without ornament.

Schietto (It.) (*ske-et'-to*). Simple; neat.

Schleppend (Ger.). Dragging; retarding.

Schluss (Ger.). End; close.

Schlüssel (Ger.). Key; clef.

Schlussfall (Ger.). Cadence.

Schlussnote (Ger.). Last note.

Schluss-Satz (Ger.). Last movement; last theme; coda.

Schmeichelnd (Ger.). Coaxing; *lusingando*.

Schmelzend (Ger.) (*schmel'-tzend*). Lit., melting; *morendo*.

Schmerz (Ger.) (*schmerts*). Pain; sorrow.

Schmerzlich (Ger.). Painful; sorrowful.

Schnell (Ger.). Quick.

Schneller (Ger.). An inverted mordent (called mordent in modern usage):

with accent on the first note.

Schottische. A dance in ²⁄₄ time resembling the polka.

Schad, Jos. Composer, pianist; Germany. B. 1812; d. 1879.

Scharwenka, Philipp (*shar-ven'-ka*). Pianist, composer; Polish Prussia. B. 1847.

Scharwenka, Xaver. Polish Prussia. B. 1850.

Schauroth, Adolphine von (*show-rote*). Pianist; Germany. B. 1814.

Schikaneder, J. E. Basso; Germany. B. 1751; d. 1812.

Schilling, Gustav. Writer; Germany. B. 1805; d. 1880.

Schindler, Anton (*shint'-ler*). Germany. B. 1796; d. 1864.

Schmidt, Aloys. Composer, pianist; Germany. B. 1789; d. 1866.

Schneider, Fr. J. C. Composer, organist, writer; Germany. B. 1786; d. 1853.

Schneider, J. G. Composer, organist; Germany. B. 1789; d. 1864.

Schneider, Wilhelm. Composer, organist; Germany. B. 1783; d. 1843.

Schnyder von Wartensee, Xaver. Composer, writer; Switzerland. B. 1786; d. 1868.

Schoberlechner (*sho'-ber-lech-ner*). Composer, pianist; Austria. B. 1797; d. 1843.

Schröder-Devrient, Wilhelmina. Soprano; Germany. B. 1804; d. 1860.

Schubert, Franz Peter. Composer; Austria. B. 1797; d. 1828.

Schuberth, Carl. Composer, 'cellist; Germany. B. 1811; d. 1863.

Schulhoff, Julius (*shool'-hof*). Composer, pianist; Bohemia. B. 1825; d. 1898.

Schumann, Robt. A. Composer, pianist; Germany. B. 1810; d. 1856.

Schumann, Clara (Wieck) (wife of Robt.). Pianist; Germany. B. 1819; d. 1896.

Schusterfleck (Ger.). See *Rosalia*.
Schwach (Ger.). Weak, soft.
Schwärmer (Ger.). See *Rauscher*.
Schwebung (Ger.) (*shveh'-boonk*). A beat. (Acoustic,) *i. e.*, produced by the simultaneous vibration of two sounds, especially prominent in unisons and octaves when not in tune.
Schweigezeichen (Ger.) (*schwei-geh tseich-en*). Lit., "silence sign." A rest.
Schwellen or **Anschwellen** (Ger.). To swell the tone.
Schweller (Ger.). The swell organ.
Schwellton (Ger.). See *Messa di Voce*.
Schwellwerk (Ger.). See *Schweller*.
Schwer (Ger.). Heavy; difficult.
Schwermütig (Ger.) (*schvehr'-mee-tig*). Sad; pensive.
Schwindend (Ger.). See *Morendo*.
Schwungvoll (Ger.) (*schvoong'-foll*). With elevated passion.
Scintillante (It.) (*shin-til-lan'-teh*), **Scintillante** (Fr.) (*sin-tee-yong*). Scintillating; brilliant; sparkling.
Sciolto (It.) (*shol'-to*), **Scioltezza** (*shol-tet'-za*), con, **Scioltamente** (*shol-tah-men'-teh*). Freedom; fluency; with freedom; freely.
Score. See *Partitur*.
Scoring. See *Instrumentation*.
Scorrendo (It.) (*skor-ren'-do*), **Scorrevole** (*skor-reh'-vo-leh*). Gliding; glissando.
Scotch Snap. A short note followed by a longer one; thus ♪♩ borrowed from Hungarian gypsy music.
Scozzese (It.) (*skotz-zeh'-seh*), alla. In Scotch style.
Scroll. The head of the violin, etc.
Sdegno (It.) (*sdehn'-yo*). Scorn; disdain.
Sdegnosamente (It.) (*sdehn'-yo-sa-men'-teh*) Scornfully.
Sdegnoso (It.) (*sdehn-yo'-so*). Scornful.
Sdrucciolando (It.) (*sdroot-sho-lan'-do*). See *Glissando*.
Se (It.) (*seh*). As if.
Sec (Fr.), **Secco** (It.). Dry. See *Recitative*.

Schuppanzigh, Ignaz (*shup'-pan-tzigh*). Violinist; Austria. B. 1776; d. 1830.
Schütt, Ed. Pianist; Russia. B. 1856.
Sechter, S. Composer, organist; Germany. B. 1788; d. 1867.
Seeling, Hans. Pianist, composer; Bohemia. B. 1828; d. 1862.
Seguin, A. E. S. Basso; England. B. 1809; d. 1852.

Second. (1) An interval embracing adjacent letters. (2) The lower of two equal voices or instruments. (3) The alto in a vocal quartet or chorus.
Seconda Donna. Second lady; the next in rank after the prima donna.
Secondo (It.) (*seh-con'-do*). Second; the lower part in a duet for two voices or instruments; the lower part in a four-hand pianoforte composition.
Seele (Ger.) (*seh'-leh*), **Ame** (Fr.). Soul. The sound-post of the violin.
Seg (It.). Abbreviation of **Segue**, *q. v.*, and of **Segno**.
Segno (It.). See abbreviation *S*.
Segue (It.) (*sehg'-weh*). Follows. **Segue il coro**, the chorus follows.
Seguendo (It.) (*sehg-wen'-do*), **Seguente** (*sehg-wen'-teh*). Following. **Attacca il seguente**, attack what follows.
Seguidilla (Sp.) (*seh-gwee-deel'-ya*). A dance in ¾ time.
Sehnsucht (Ger.). Longing.
Sehnsüchtig (Ger.). Longingly.
Sehr (Ger.). Very.
Semi-breve. A whole note. 𝅝
Semi-chorus. Half the chorus; a small chorus.
Semi-grand. A small (half) grand pianoforte.
Semi-quaver. A sixteenth note. ♬
Semi-tone. A half tone. A chromatic semi-tone changes the pitch without changing the letter; as, C—C♯; a diatonic semi-tone changes both, as, C—D♭.
Semplice (It.) (*sem-plee'-cheh*). Simple.
Semplicimente (It.) (*sem-plee-chee-men'-teh*). Simply; unaffectedly.
Semplicita (It.) (*sem-plee'-chee-tah*), con. With simplicity.
Sempre (It.) (*sem'-preh*). Always.
Sensibile (It.) (*sen-see'-bee-leh*), **Sensible** (Fr.) (*song-seebl'*). **Nota sensibile**, the leading note. **Note sensible**, "sensitive" note.
Sensibilita (It.) (*sen-see-bee'-lee-tah*), con. With feeling.
Sentito (It.) (*sen-tee'-to*). **Sentimento** (*sen-tee-men'-to*), con. With feeling; with sentiment.

Seguin, Ann Childe (wife of A. E. S.). Soprano; England. B. 18—; d. 1888.
Seguin, W. H. (brother of A. E. S.). Basso; England. B. 1814; d. 1850.
Seidl, Anton. Conductor; Hungary. B. 1850; d. 1898.
Sembrich, Marzella. Soprano; Germany. B. 1858.

Senza (It.) (*sen-tza*). Without.

Septet, Septuor. A composition for seven solo voices or instruments.

Septole (Ger.). Septuplet; a group of seven.

Se piace (It.) (*seh pe-ah'-cheh*). "Please yourself." *Ad libitum.*

Sequence, Melodic. The repetition of a melodic phrase at regular intervals. **Harmonic Sequence**, the repetition of a harmonic progression at regular intervals. **Contrapuntal Sequence**, a succession of common chords with roots moving in a regular "pattern."

Melodic Sequence.

Harmonic Sequence.

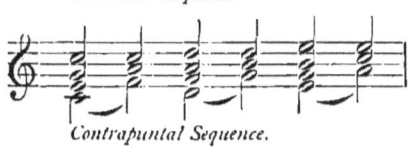
Contrapuntal Sequence.

Seraphine. A free-reed instrument that preceded the harmonium.

Serenade, Sérénade (Fr.), **Serenata** (It.), **Ständchen** (Ger.). Lit., an evening song. The Italian form, Serenata, is also applied to an instrumental symphonic composition, and by Händel to his cantata, "Acis and Galatea."

Sereno (It.) (*seh-reh'-no*). Serene; tranquil.

Serio (It.) (*seh-re-o*). Serious.

Serioso (It.). Gravely; seriously.

Serpent. A nearly obsolete instrument made of wood covered with leather, cup-shaped mouthpiece, finger-holes, and keys.

Service. A musical setting of the canticles, etc., of the Episcopal church.

Sesqui-altera. A mixture-stop in the organ. In ancient musical nomenclature the following compounds with Sesqui were used:—
Sesqui-nona, *i. e.*, the ratio of 9 to 10; minor whole tone.
Sesqui-octava, 8 to 9; major whole tone.
Sesqui-quinta, 5 to 6; minor third.

Servais, A. François (*ser-vay*). Composer, 'cellist; France. B. 1807; d. 1866.

Servais, Joseph (*ser-vay*). Composer, 'cellist; France. B. 1850; d. 1885.

Seyfried, J. X. Ritter von. Composer; Austria. B. 1776; d. 1841.

Sesqui-quarta, 4 to 5; major third.
Sesqui-tertia, 3 to 4; perfect fourth.
Sesqui-tone, a minor third.

Sestet. See *Sextet.*

Sestetto (It.). See *Sextet.*

Sestole. See *Sextuplet.*

Seule (Fr.) (*sool*). Alone.

Seventeenth. An organ-stop sounding the octave of the major 3d above the diapason; called also the tierce.

Seventh. An interval including seven letters. **Seventh Major**, seven letters and eleven half-tones, as C—B. **Seventh Minor**, seven letters and ten half-tones, as C—B♭. **Diminished Seventh**, seven letters and nine half-tones, as C♯—B♭.

Severamente (It.) (*seh-veh-rah-men'-teh*). Severely; strictly.

Severita (It.) (*seh-ver' ee-ta*), con. With severity; exactness.

Sextet, Sestet, Sestetto (It.), **Sextuor** (Fr.). A composition for six solo voices or instruments.

Sextuplet. A group of six notes occupying the time of four.

Sfogato (It.) (*sfo-gah'-to*) [from *sfogare*, to evaporate]. A soprano voice of thin, light quality and unusually high range is called a soprano sfogato.

Sforzando (It.) (*sfortz-an'-do*) or **Sforzato**, abbreviated **Sf.** or **Sfz.** "Forced." A strong accent immediately followed by piano.

Shake. See *Trill.*

Sharp. The sign, ♯, which raises the pitch of a letter a half tone. Sharp is sometimes used in the sense of augmented, as sharp 6th for augmented 6th; popular name for the black keys of pianoforte and organ.

Sharp Mixture. A mixture with shrill-voiced pipes.

Shawm. See *Chalameau.*

Shift. A change in the position of the left hand on the fingerboard of the violin; each shift is a fourth higher than the preceding one.

Si. (1) The note B in French, Italian, and Spanish. (2) The Italian impersonal pronoun, "one," or "they," as, *si piace*, "one" pleases, *i. e.*, as you please.

Siciliano (It.) (*see-cheel-ya'-no*), **Sicilienne** (Fr.) (*see-see-lee-en*). A pastoral dance in slow 6/8 time; slow movements, vocal or instrumental, are frequently called Sicilianas.

Sgambati, G. (*sgam-bah'-tee*). Composer, pianist; Italy. B. 1843.

Shakespeare, Wm. Tenor, teacher; England. B. 1849.

Sherrington, H. Lemmens. Soprano; England. B. 1834.

Side Drum. See *Drum.*

Siegeslied (Ger.) (*see'-ges leed*). Song of victory.

Signs. (Only the most important are here given. Complete information may be obtained by consulting the "Embellishments of Music," by Russell.)

Staccato. Spiccato.	Vibrato.	Pause.	Abbreviation, signifying the repetition of the preceding figure.
Segno.	Repeat.		Slur, when over or under sounds of different pitch, signifying legato. Tie, when the notes are on the same degree.
Sharp.	Double Sharp.	Flat.	Double Flat. Natural.
Crescendo.	Decrescendo.		Sforzando.
Arpeggio.	Brace.	Trill.	Turn. Mordent.
After Ped. means raise the foot from the pedal.	8va. Octave higher.	8va.Ba. Octave lower.	Heel and Toe; Organ music,— when above the notes, right foot; when below, left foot.

Signature, Signatur (Ger.), **Time.** The signs 𝄴 𝄵, etc. **Key Signature,** the sharps or flats marked at the beginning of a part or piece.

Simile (It.) (*see-mee-leh*). The same; in the same way.

Sinfonia (It.), **Sinfonie** (Ger.), **Symphonie** (Fr.), **Symphony** [from Gr., *sun; phoneo*, sounding together]. Originally had the same meaning that we attach to interval, *i. e.*, two simultaneous sounds. (1) By the early writers of Italian opera it was used in the modern sense of overture. (2) The introduction to a song is still called the symphony. (3) The adaptation of the large forms of composition (sonata and rondo) to the orchestra.

Sherwood. Wm. H. Composer, pianist; U. S. A. B. 1854.

Silbermann, Gottfried. Pianoforte maker; Germany. B. 1683; d. 1753.

Silcher, Fred. Composer, writer; Germany. B. 1789; d. 1860.

Singer, Otto. Composer, pianist; Germany. B. 1833; d. 1894.

Sivori, E. C. (*see'-vo-ree*). Violinist, composer; Italy. B. 1815; d. 1894.

Singend or **Singbar** (Ger.). Singing; cantabile.

Singhiozzando (It.) (*sin-ghee-otz-an'-do*). Sobbingly.

Singspiel (Ger.) (*sing-speel*). "Sing-play." Operetta; an opera without recitatives, the dialogue being spoken. "Der Freischütz," when first produced was of this character, which may be considered as one of Germany's contributions to the development of the opera, the Italian operas from the beginning being largely composed of recitative. The "Singspiel" form has found its most congenial home and its best exponents in France.

Sinistra (It.). Left.

Sino, Abbr., **Sin.** (It.) (*see'-no*). As far as; used after D. C., or al 𝄋; as al 𝄌. **Sin' al fine,** go to the sign, then as far as "fine." D. C. sin' al 𝄋, from the beginning as far as the sign.

Sixteenth Note. 𝅘𝅥𝅯

Sixth. An interval including six letters.

Sixth Major. Six letters, nine half-tones.

Sixth Minor. Six letters, eight half-tones. **Augmented Sixth,** six letters, ten half-tones. **Diminished Sixth,** six letters, seven half-tones.

Sixty-fourth Note. 𝅘𝅥𝅱

Slancio (It.) (*slan'-che-o*), con. With impetuosity.

Slargando (It.) (*slar-gan'-do*). Widening; growing slower.

Slargandosi (It.) (*slar-gan-do'-see*). Slower.

Slentando (It.) (*slen-tan'-do*). Gradually slower.

Slide. (1) The movable tube of the trombone. (2) See *Portamento.*

Slur. ⌢ Legato sign. In vocal music signifies that all the notes it includes are to be sung to one syllable.

Smanioso (It.) (*sma-ne-o'-so*). Frantic; raging.

Smaniante (It.) (*sma-ne-an'-teh*). Frantically.

Sminuendo (It.) (*smin-oo-en'-do*), **Sminuito** (*smin-oo-ee'-to*), **Smorendo** (*smo-ren'-do*). Same as *Diminuendo.*

Sloper, Lindsay E. H. Composer, pianist; England. B. 1826; d. 1887.

Smart, Sir G. T. Composer, organist; England. B. 1776; d. 1867.

Smart, Henry (brother of G.). Violinist; England. B. 1778; d. 1823.

Smart, Henry (son of H.). Composer, organist; England. B. 1813; d. 1879.

Smetana, Fr. (*smeh tah'-nah*). Composer' Bohemia. B. 1824; d. 1884.

Smorzando (It.) (*smor-tzan'-do*). Lit., "smothering;" morendo.
Snare Drum. See *Drum*.
Soave (It.) (*so-a'-veh*). Sweet.
Soavemente (It.) (*so-a-veh-men'-teh*). Sweetly.
Sogetto (It.). Subject; theme of a fugue.
Sognando (It.) (*sone-yan'-do*). Dreaming; dreamily.
Sol. The note G in Italian, French, and Spanish; fifth Aretinian syllable.
Solenne (It.) (*so-len'-neh*). Solemn.
Solennemente (It.) (*so-len-neh-men'-teh*). Solemnly.
Solennita (It.) (*so-len'-nee-ta*), con. With solemnity.
Sol-fa (verb). To sing with the syllables.
Solfeggio (It.) (*sol-fed-jo*). (1) A vocal exercise. (2) Used by Bach as a name for certain short instrumental pieces.
Solmization. A method of learning to sing by the application of syllables to the scale. The earliest invention of this method of fixing the succession of sounds forming the scale in the memory is attributed to Guido of Arezzo (*ah-rets-o*), who used for this purpose the syllables ut, re, mi, fa, sol, la, having chanced to observe that these syllables —the first in the successive lines of a Latin hymn — were sung to six successive notes which formed a hexachord scale : C, D, E, F, G, A. There were seven hexachord scales, as follows : First began on G, 1st line bass staff; this was called the hexachordum durum (hard hexachord). Second began on C, a 4th higher. Third began on F, another 4th higher; in this scale B was flat; it was called the hexachordum molle (soft hexachord). Fourth, fifth, and sixth were respectively an octave higher than the first, second, and third, and the seventh was two octaves higher than the first. The first note of every scale was called *ut* (afterward changed to *do*), therefore from its inception "do" was "movable." Various modifications of these syllables have at different times been used for solmization. One extensively used at one time was the practice of using only four of them, viz., mi, fa, sol, la. These were so arranged that *mi* always fell upon the third note in the tetrachord, for example, the scale of C was solfaed thus : —

Tetrachord.   Tetrachord.
C D E F | G A B C
sol la mi fa sol la mi fa

It was owing to the difficulty and, to ancient ears, harshness of the skip from the *fa* of the lower tetrachord to the *mi* of the upper that the expression, "mi contra fa," came to have a proverbial meaning. This interval, called the tritone (three tones), was by the ancient theorists stigmatized as "tritonus diabolus est." New syllables have at different times been proposed; one scheme of which the syllables were bo, ce, di, ga, lo, ma, ni, was called bocedization; another with da, me, ni, po, hi, la, be, was called damenization. The only modifications and additions to the syllables that have been permanently adopted are those used by the "Tonic Solfaists," *q. v.*

Solo (It.) (plural, **Soli**). Alone ; a composition in which the principal part is taken by one voice or instrument. **Solo Parts** are those sung or played by single performers as distinguished from chorus or tutti passages.

Somma (It.). Utmost; as **Con somma espressione**, with the utmost expression.

Sonabile (It.) (*so-nah'-bee-leh*), **Sonante** (*so-nan'-teh*). Resonant ; sounding ; sonorous.

Sonare (It.) (*so-nah'-reh*). To sound ; to play upon.

Sonata (It.) (*so-nah'-tah*). "Sound piece." (1) The highest development of musical form. (2) In modern use, an extended composition with several movements for pianoforte, or pianoforte in conjunction with one other instrument. A composition of this class for more than two instruments is called trio, quartet, etc.; for full orchestra, a symphony. The "form" of the sonata (see *Form*) has undergone many modifications since it was first adopted, about the beginning of the 17th century. At first it was applied indifferently to any instrumental piece, such, for example, as were commonly called "airs." Those written for the harpsichord or for viols were called "sonata da camera." Those for the organ (or frequently those for harpsichord or viols, if written in grave style), "sonata da chiesa" (church sonata). The distinguishing characteristic of the modern sonata form is the possession of two themes in different keys (see Scheme in article *Form*). The gradual growth of this binary development may be traced in the works of Kuhnau, Scarlatti, Alberti, Durante, and others. The binary form was first definitely settled by Ph. E. Bach. The only changes made since have been the immense development given to the form by Beethoven, and the adoption of other keys for the second theme.

Sonata di chiesa (It.) (*key-eh'-sa*). A church sonata ; organ sonata.

Södermann, J. A. (*sood'-er-man*). Composer ; Sweden. B. 1832; d. 1876.

Smith, Sidney. Composer, pianist ; England. B. 1839; d. 1889.

Sonatilla (It.) (*so-na-til'-la*), **Sonatina** (It.) (*so-na-tee'-na*), **Sonatine** (Fr.) (*so-na-teen*). A short, easy, undeveloped sonata.

Song, Gesang, Lied (Ger.), **Chant** (Fr.), **Canto** (It.). (1) Originally a poem. (2) A musical setting of a poem, especially for one voice. (3) Folk-song (Ger., *Volkslied*). A simple air containing but one member, the words lyrical or narrative (if the poem is a lengthy narrative it is generally called a ballad). (4) Art songs contain several members, and in many cases, as in the songs of Schubert, Franz, Schumann, and others, rise to the highest plane of art expression. The Germans have a word, *durchkomponiert*, which is applied to songs every stanza of which has a separate musical setting, so designed as to exalt and emphasize the expression of the words.

Songs without words, Lieder ohne Worte (Ger.), **Chants sans paroles** (Fr.). A title invented by Mendelssohn and given by him to a set of pianoforte compositions. Songs for several voices are called part songs, *q. v.*

Sonoramente (It.). Sonorously.

Sonore (It.), **Sonoro** [from Lat., *sonus*, sound]. Sonorous; sounding.

Sonorita (It.) (*so-no'-ree-ta*), con. With resonance.

Sopra (It.). On; above; upon.

Soprano (It.), **Sopran** (Ger.), **Dessus** (Fr.) (*des-soo*). The female or boy's voice of the highest range.

Soprano Clef. C clef on the 1st line.

Soprano Sfogato (*sfo-gah'-to*). An unusually high light soprano.

Sordamente (It.). Veiled, dampened, muffled tone.

Sordino (It.) (*sor-dee'-no*). A mute; small instruments of metal, wood, etc., put on the bridge of the violin, etc., to deaden the tone. Pear- or cylinder-shaped mutes of wood, cardboard, or leather are put in the bell of the horn or trumpet with the same object. The use of sordino is indicated by **Con S.**, their removal by **Senza S.**

Sordo (It.). Mute; muffled. **Clarinetto sordo**, muted clarionet.

Sortita (It.) (*sor-tee'-ta*). "Going out." Concluding voluntary; first appearance of any character in an operatic performance.

Sospirando (It.) (*sos-pee-ran'-do*), **Sospiroso** (*sos-pee-ro'-so*), **Sospirante** (*sos-pee-ran'-teh*), **Sospirevole** (*sos-pee-reh'-vo-leh*) [from *sospiro*, a sigh]. Sighing; sobbing; mournful.

Sonnleithner, Ch. (*son'-light-ner*). Composer; Austria. B. 1734; d. 1786.

Sostenuto (It.) (*sos-teh-noo'-to*), **Sostenendo** (*sos-teh-nen'-do*). Sustained; without haste.

Sotto (It.). Below. **Sotto voce**, in an undertone.

Soubasse (Fr.) (*soo-bass*). A 32-foot organ pedal-stop.

Soubrette (Fr.) (*soo-bret*). A waiting maid; a minor female rôle in comic or comedy opera.

Sound-board. A thin sheet of spruce pine, or fir, upon which the bridge that supports the strings of the pianoforte rests. The function of the sound-board is to increase the volume of the tone, which it does by taking up the vibration of the string. There are many unsolved problems in the relation which subsists between the string and the sound-board, as to the manner in which this amplification of the sound takes place. It is impossible to form a conception of the complications in the mode of vibration of the sound-board that must take place when, for example, a full chord is struck. Yet all these complications are not only simultaneous, but they obey the changing conditions of the most rapid execution with such swiftness and certainty that not a note is lost or a tone quality obscured.

Sound-box. The body of the violin, guitar, etc. The problems as to the function of the sound-box are even more complicated than those connected with the sound-board, as a sound-box is a combination of a sound-board and an enclosed mass of air the vibrations of which have an important bearing on the quality and intensity of the tone.

Sound-hole. The orifice or orifices in the upper part, called technically the " belly," of the violin, guitar, etc. In the violin family they are called F-holes, from their resemblance to the letter *f*.

Sound-post. A slender, cylindrical, wooden prop between the belly and the back in instruments of the violin family, placed under the foot of the bridge on the side of the highest string.

Sourdine (Fr.) (*soor-deen*). See *Sordino*.

Spaces. The intervals between the lines of the staff or between the leger lines.

Spalla (It.). The shoulder. Used in the sentence, **Viola da spalla**, one of the viols in a " chest."

Spanischer Reiter (Ger.). See *Spanisches Kreuz*.

Spanisches Kreuz (Ger.) (*spah-nish-es kroits*). Spanish cross; German name for double sharp ※.

Sontag, Henrietta G. W. Soprano; Germany. B. 1806; d. 1854.

Sparta (It.) (*spar-ta*), **Spartita** (*spar'-ti-ta*) [from *spartire*, to divide]. Hence, a score.

Spasshaft (Ger.). Jocose; merry; scherzando.

Spezzato (It.) (*spets-sa'-to*) [from *spezzare*, to break in pieces]. Divided; broken.

Spianato (It.) (*spe-a-nah'-to*). Leveled; tranquillo.

Spianto (It.) (*spe-an-to*). Level; smooth.

Spiccato (It.) (*spik-kah'-to*). Detached; pointed.

Spiel (Ger.) (*spcel*). Play.

Spielart. Style; touch.

Spielbar. Playable; well adapted to the instrument.

Spieloper. Operetta; comic opera.

Spieltenor. Light tenor; comic opera tenor.

Spinet. The predecessor of the harpsichord, called also couched harp.

Spirito (It.) (*spee-ree-to*), **con**, **Spiritoso** (*spee-ree-to'-so*), **Spiritosamente** (*spee-ree-to-sa-men'-teh*). With spirit; spirited; lively; animated.

Spitzflöte, **Spindelflöte** (Ger.). An organ-stop of reed-like quality, 8-, 4-, or 2-foot pitch.

Squilla (It.) (*squil'-la*). Little bell.

Squillante (It.) (*squil-lan'-teh*). Bell-like ringing.

Stabile (It.) (*stah-bee'-leh*). Firm; steady.

Stac. Abbreviation of Staccato.

Staccatissimo (It.) (*stac-cah-tis'-see-mo*). As detached as possible. The sign for staccatissimo is a pointed dot over the note ¦

Staccato (It.) (*stac-cah'-to*). Detached; cut off; separated.

Spagnoletti, P. (*span-yo-let'-tee*). 'Cellist; Italy. B. 1768; d. 1834.

Speidel, Wil. Composer, pianist; Germany. B. 1826; d. 1899.

Spindler, Fritz. Composer, pianist; Germany. B. 1817; d. 1905.

Spofforth, R. Composer; England. B. 1768; d. 1827.

Spohr, Louis. Violinist. composer; Germany. B. 1784; d. 1859.

Stainer, Sir John. Composer, organist; England. B. 1840; d. 1901.

Stanford, Ch. Villiers. Composer, organist; England. B. 1852.

Staudigl, Jos. (*stow'-digl*). Basso; Germany. B. 1807; d. 1861.

Staff or **Stave.** The five lines with their enclosed spaces. Gregorian music is written on a staff of four lines.

Standard Pitch. See *Pitch.*

Ständchen (Ger.). See *Serenade.*

Stark (Ger.). Loud; strong.

Stave. See *Staff.*

Stem, Hals (Ger.), **Queue** (Fr.), **Gambo** (It.). The part of a note consisting of a vertical line; also called tail.

Stentato (It.) (*sten-tah'-to*), **Stentando** (*sten-tan'-do*) [from *stentare*, to labor]. A heavy emphasis combined with a dragging of the time.

Step. From one letter to the next; a degree. **Whole Step**, a whole tone; **Half Step**, half tone; **Chromatic Step**, chromatic half tone.

Sterbend (Ger.) . (*stair-bent*). Dying; morendo.

Steso (It.) (*stay-so*). Extended. **Steso moto**, slow movement.

Stesso (It.) (*stes-so*). The same.

Sticcado (It.). Xylophone.

Stil (Ger.) (*steel*), **Stilo** (It.). Style; manner.

Stillgedacht (Ger.). Soft organ-stop with closed pipes; stopped diapason.

Stimmbildung. Voice formation; voice training.

Stimme (Ger) (*stim'-meh*). (1) Voice. (2) Part. (3) Sound-post. (4) Organ-stop.

Stimmen (verb). To tune.

Stimmung. Pitch, tuning.

Stimmungsbild. "Voicing picture," *i. e.*, a short composition designed to "voice" or express some given mood or emotion, *e.g.*, "Warum," by Schumann.

Staudigl, Jos. (*stow-digl*) (son of J.). Baritone. B. 1850.

Stavenhagen, B. Pianist; Reuss. B. 1862.

Steffani, A. (*stef-fah'-nee*). Composer; Italy. B. 1655; d. 1730.

Steggall, Ch. Composer, organist; England. B. 1826; d. 1905.

Stephens, Catherine. Soprano; England. B. 1791; d. 1882.

Steibelt, Dan. Composer, pianist; Germany. B. 1764; d. 1823.

Sterkel, J. F. X. Composer; Germany. B. 1750; d. 1817.

Sterling, Antoinette. Alto; U. S. A. B. 1850; d. 1904.

Sternberg, C. Composer, pianist; Russia. B. 1852.

Stinguendo (It.) (*stin-gwen'-do*) [from *stinguere*, to extinguish]. Fading away; becoming extinguished.

Stirato (It.) (*stee-rah'-to*), **Stiracchiato** (*stee-rak-ke-ah'-to*) [from *stirare*, to stretch]. Retarding the time.

Stop. (1) To press the finger on the string of violin, guitar, etc. **Double Stop**, pressing two strings at once. (2) (noun) A rank or set of organ-pipes. **Draw Stop**, the arrangement of levers by means of which the "wind" is admitted to the various ranks of pipes at will, called also register. **Foundation Stop**, one of 8-foot pitch. **Mutation Stop**, one sounding the major third or perfect fifth, or both, over the fundamental. **Solo Stop**, one with a tone quality suited to the rendition of melody.

Stracino (It.) (*strah-chee'-no*), **Stracicato** (*strah-chee-cah'-to*), **Stracicando** (*strah-chee-can'-do*), **Stracinando** (*strah-chee-nan'-do*). A drag, or slur; sliding from one note to another and at the same time slightly slackening the time.

Strain. Song, air, tune, or a part of one.

Strathspey. A Scotch dance in ¼ time.

Stravagante (It.) (*strah-vah-gan'-te*). Extravagant; fantastic.

Stravaganza (It.) (*strah-vah-gant'-sah*). A fantastic composition.

Streng (Ger.). Rigid; severe.

Strepito (It.) (*streh'-pee-to*), con. With noise; fury.

Strepitosamente (It.) (*streh-pee-to-sah-men'-teh*). Furiously.

Strepitoso (It.) (*streh-pee-to'-so*). Furious.

Stretta, Stretto (It.). "A throng." (1) Hurrying the time at the close. (2) In fugue, causing the voices to follow one another at less distance so that the subject and answer are brought closer together.

Stridente (It.) (*stree-den'-teh*). Strident; noisy; impetuous.

String. Abbreviation for Stringendo.

Stigelli, G. (*stee-jel'-lee*). Composer, tenor; Germany. B. 1819; d. 1868.

Stockhausen, M. Soprano; Germany. B. 1803; d. 1877.

Stradella, A. Composer; Italy. B. 1645; d. 1681.

Stradivari, A. (*strah-dee-vah-ree*). Violin maker; Italy. B. 1644; d. 1737.

Stradivari, F. Violin maker; Italy. B. 1670; d. 1743.

Stradivari, O. Violin maker; Italy. B. 1679; d. 1742.

Strakosch, Maurice. Pianist; Germany. B. 1825; d. 1887.

String. Cords made of wire, catgut, or silk, used for musical instruments.

String Band. The violins, violas, violoncellos, and double bass, also spoken of collectively as the "strings" or the string quartet.

String Instruments. Those in which the tone is produced by the vibration of strings. They are classified as follows: 1st, strings plucked by the fingers—harp, guitar, etc.; 2d, strings struck by plectra—mandolin, zither, etc.; 3d, strings vibrated by means of a bow—violin, etc.; 4th, strings struck with hammers—pianoforte, dulcimer, etc.

String Quartet. A composition for two violins, viola, and violoncello.

String Quintet, Sextet, Septet, Octet are formed by combining the string instruments in various proportions.

Stringendo (It.) (*strin-jen'-do*). Hurrying the time.

Strisciando (It.) (*strish-e-an'-do*). Creeping; gliding.

Stromentato (It.). Instrumented; scored; orchestrated.

Stromento (It.) (*stro-men'-to*). Instrument.

Stromento di corda. String instrument.

Stromento di fiato or di vento. Wind instrument.

Stück (Ger.) (*stick*). A piece. **Concertstück**, concert piece. **Salonstück**, parlor piece.

Study, Étude (Fr.), **Studio** (It.). (1) A composition designed to facilitate the acquirement of some special difficulty. (2) A name often given by modern writers to pieces analogous to the old toccata, *q. v*.

Stufe (Ger.) (*stoo'-feh*). A step; degree of the scale.

Stürmisch (Ger.). Stormy; furioso

Suave (It.) (*soo-a'-veh*). Sweet.

Suavemente (It.) (*soo-a-veh-men'-teh*). Sweetly.

Strauss, Ed. (son of following). Composer; Austria. B. 1835.

Strauss, John (father of following). Composer; Austria. B. 1804; d. 1849.

Strauss, John (brother of following). Composer; Austria. B. 1825; d. 1899.

Strauss, Jos. Composer; Austria. B. 1827; d. 1870.

Strauss, Ludwig. Violinist; Austria. B. 1835.

Streabog. Pseudonym of J. L. Gobbaerts.

Strelezki, A. Pianist, composer; pseudonym of an English writer. B. 1859; d. 1907

Suavita (It.) (*soo-ah'-vee-ta*), con. With sweetness.

Sub-bass. An organ pedal-stop of 16- or 32-foot tone.

Sub-dominant. The 4th degree of the scale; not called sub-dominant because it is below the dominant, but because it is the same distance below the tonic that the dominant is above.

Sub-mediant. The 6th of the scale.

1. Tonic. 2. Mediant, *i. e.*, half-way to dominant. 3. Dominant. 4. Sub-mediant, *i. e.*, half-way to sub-dominant. 5. Sub-dominant.

Sub-octave. A coupler on the organ that pulls down the keys an octave below those struck.

Sub-principal. Open organ-stop, 32- and 16-foot pitch.

Sub-tonic. The leading note, 7th of the scale.

Subito (It.) (*soo-bee'-to*), **Subitamente.** Quickly. **Volti subito,** abbreviated **V. S.,** turn over quickly.

Subject. The theme of a fugue; any one of the themes of a sonata, rondo, etc.

Subordinate Chords. Those on the 2d, 3d, and 6th of the scale.

Suite (Fr.) (*sweet*). A set or series of movements. The suite originally consisted solely of dance tunes to which "airs" or movements, designated by the tempo terms, allegro, etc., were added. The classical suite contained: 1st, allemand; 2d, coranto; 3d, saraband; 4th, gigue, preceded by a prelude. Occasionally the gavotte, pavan, loure, minuet, etc., may be found with or in place of some of the above dances. According to the rule of the suite, all the movements had to be in the same key.

Suivez (Fr.) (*swee-vey*). Follow; a direction for the accompanist to follow the soloist.

Sujet (Fr.) (*soo-zhay*). Subject.

Sullivan, Sir A. S. Composer; England. B. 1842; d. 1900.

Suppe, F. von (*soop'-peh*). Composer; Austria. B. 1820; d. 1895.

Sussmayer, F. X. Composer; Austria. B. 1766; d. 1803.

Sul, Sull, Sulla (It.). Upon; on; by; in violin music a passage to be played on a certain string is marked Sul E, or A, or D, or G, as the case may be.

Sul ponticello (It.). By the bridge; in violin playing, a direction to play with the bow close to the bridge.

Suonata. See *Sonata*.

Superfluous. Same as *Augmented*.

Super-octave. (1) An organ-stop of 2 foot pitch, same as fifteenth. (2) A coupler in the organ that pulls down the keys one octave above those struck.

Super-tonic. The 2d degree of the scale.

Super-dominant. The 6th degree of the scale.

Supplichevole (It.) (*sup-plee-kay'-vo-leh*), **Supplichevolmente** (*sup-plee-kay-vol-men'-teh*). Pleading; supplicating.

Suspension. Tying or prolonging a note from one chord into the following. See *Retardation*.

Süss (Ger.) (*sees*). Sweet.

Sussurando (It.) (*soos-soo-ran'-do*). Murmuring.

Sussurante (It.) (*soos-soo-ran'-teh*). Whisperingly.

Svegliato (It.) (*svehl-ya'-to*). Brisk; lively.

Svelto (It.) (*svel'-to*). Swift; quick; easy.

Swell Organ. A part of the organ enclosed within a box provided with shutters, which are opened and closed by a lever, called the swell-pedal, worked by the foot.

Symphony. See *Sinfonia*.

Symphonic. In the manner of a symphony.

Symphonic Ode. A combination of symphony and chorus, as Beethoven's Ninth Symphony, or Mendelssohn's Lobgesang.

Symphonic Poem. A modern name for an orchestral composition supposed to illustrate a poem or story.

Syncopation. A shifting of the accent, caused by tying a weak beat to a strong beat.

Syren. (1) An acoustical apparatus for determining the vibrational rates of sounds. (2) A species of foghorn.

Syrinx. See *Pandean Pipe*.

Svendsen, J. S. Composer, violinist, conductor; Sweden. B. 1840.

Svendsen, Oluf. Flutist; Sweden. B. 1832; d. 1888.

Sweelenck (*sveh'-link*). Composer, organist; Holland. B. 1562; d. 1621.

T

T. Abbreviation of Tasto, Tenor, Tempo, Tutti, Toe (in organ music).

Taballo (It.). Kettle-drum.

Tablature (Fr.) (*tab-lah-toor*), **Intavolatura** (It.), **Tablatur** (Ger.). An obsolete system of notation used for the lute principally; another form was used for the organ, harpsichord, etc.

Table (Fr.) (*tahbl*). The belly or soundboard.

Table Music. (1) Music intended to be sung by several people sitting around a table. (2) Music appropriate for entertainment during the pauses in the "serious" work of eating and drinking.

Tabor, Tabret, Taboret. A small drum, like a tambourine without the "jingles." It hung in front of the performer, who beat it with one hand and played a "pipe" or flageolet with the other.

Tacet (Lat.), **Tace** (It.) (*tah'-cheh*). Be silent, or "is silent;" signifies that the instrument thus marked is silent during the phrase or movement; as **Andante tromboni tacet**, during the "andante" the trombones are silent.

Tafelclavier (Ger.). Square pianoforte.

Tafelmusik. Table music.

Tail. (1) Stem of a note. (2) The piece of wood to which the strings of the violin, etc., are attached at the base of the instrument.

Taille (Fr.) (*tah-ee*). The tenor voice or part.

Takt (Ger.). Time, as **Im Takt**, a tempo; measure, as **Ein Takt**, one measure (or bar); beat, as **Auftakt**, up beat.

Taktmässig. In time.

Taktstrich. A bar (line, not measure).

Talon (Fr.). The "frog" or heel of the bow.

Tambour (Fr.). (1) A drum. (2) A drummer.

Tambour de basque. Tambourine.

Tamboura, Tambura (also Pandora). An Eastern species of the lute.

Tambourin (Fr.) (*tam-boo-rang*). (1) A tabor. (2) A French rustic dance.

Tadolini, G. (*tah-do-lee'-nee*). Composer; Italy. B. 1793; d. 1872.

Talexy, A. (*tah'-lex-ee*). Composer, pianist; France. B. 1820; d. 1881.

Tamberlik, Enrico. Tenor; Italy. B. 1820; d. 1889.

Tambourine. A small variety of drum consisting of a hoop of wood or metal about two inches in depth, with a head of parchment. Small circular plates of metal called jingles are inserted in pairs in holes in the hoop, strung loosely on wires. The tambourine is held in the left hand and struck with the fingers or palm of the right hand; used to accompany dancing in Spain, Italy, and southern France; occasionally used in the orchestra in ballet music. The "roll" is indicated thus ⸘ The "jingle" ⸘

Tamburo (It.). Drum; side drum.

Tamburone (It.) (*tam-boo-ro'-neh*). The great drum.

Tam-tam. Gong.

Tändelnd (Ger.) (*tehn-delnd*). Playful.

Tangent. The brass pin in the action of the clavichord that was forced against the string when the key was struck.

Tantino (*tan-tee-no*), very little.

Tanto (It.). So much; too much. **Allegro non tanto**, not so fast; lit., "fast, not too much."

Tanz (Ger.) (*tants*). Dance.

Tanzlieder. Songs to accompany dancing. See *Ballad*.

Tanzstücke. Dancing pieces.

Tanzweisen. Dancing tunes.

Tarantella (It.), **Tarantelle** (Fr.). A rapid dance in ⁶⁄₈ time; the name is derived from *tarantula* (the poisonous spider). The dance is popularly believed to be a remedy for the bite of this insect.

Tardamente. (It.) (*tar-dah-men'-teh*). Slowly.

Tardando (It.) (*tar-dan'-do*). Slowing; retarding.

Tardato (It.) (*tar-dah'-to*). Made slower.

Tardo (It.) (*tar'-do*). Slow; dragging.

Tartini Tone. An undertone produced by the simultaneous vibration of two strings, etc., first observed by Tartini, the violinist. Called also a differential tone.

Tastatur (Ger.) (*tas-tah-toor*). **Tastatura** (It.) (*tas-tah-too'-ra*). Keyboard.

Tamburini, A. (*tam-boo-ree'-nee*). Baritone; Italy. B. 1800; d. 1876.

Tansur, Will. Composer, organist; England. B. 1706. d. 1783.

Tartini, G. (*tar-tee'-nee*). Violinist, composer; Italy. B. 1692; d. 1770.

Taste (Ger.) (*tas'-teh*). A pianoforte or organ key; pedal key.

Tastenbrett (Ger.), **Tastenleiter.** Keyboard.

Tastiera (It.) (*tas-tee-eh'-ra*). Fingerboard of violin, guitar, etc. **Sulla Tastiera**, a direction in violin music to play with the bow near the fingerboard,—the opposite of *Sul ponticello*, q. v.

Tasto (It.) A "touch." (1) A key. (2) A fret. (3) Touch. (4) Fingerboard. The preceding words from *Tastatur* are all derived from *Tasto*.

Tasto Solo. Literally, "key alone," *i. e.*, one key or note at a time. A direction in figured bass that the notes are to be played without chords, *i. e.*, unison or octaves.

Tattoo or **Taptoo.** The drumbeat ordering soldiers to retire for the night.

Technic, Technik (Ger.), **Technique** (Fr.). The purely mechanical part of playing or singing.

Technicon. A mechanism for strengthening the fingers and increasing their flexibility.

Techniphone. See *Virgil Clavier*.

Tedesco or **Tedesca, alla** (It.). In German style.

Tema (It.) (*teh'-mah*). Theme; subject; melody.

Temperament. The division of the octave. **Equal Temperament.** The modern system of tuning divides the octave into twelve equal parts, called semitones. **Unequal Temperament** (which was formerly used for all keyed instruments, and retained until quite recently for the organ) tuned the natural notes true, and distributed the superfluous interval among the "black" keys. The discovery of the art of equally tempering the scale lies at the foundation of modern music. Without it, the sudden excursions into remote keys would be impossible. Although we have lost something in purity of intonation, the loss is more than made up in the gain of twelve keys, all equally well in tune. Some enthusiasts, generally acousticians, express great dissatisfaction with our modern scale. A sufficient reply is, that the scale that satisfied the ears of, and made possible the music of the great writers from Bach to Beethoven, must of necessity be the best musical scale.

Tempestosamente (It.) (*tem-pes-to'-sa-men'-teh*). Impetuously.

Tempestoso (It.) (*tem-pes-to'-so*). Tempestuous.

Tempête (Fr.) (*tam-peht*). Tempest. A French dance—formerly fashionable—resembling a quadrille.

Taubert, Carl G. W. Composer; Germany. B. 1811; d. 1891.

Tempo (It.). Time. "Tempo" is universally used to signify "rate of movement."

Tempo Indications—

Slow { Largo, Grave, Lento, Adagio. }   Moderate { Andante, Moderato, Commodo. }

Fast { Allegro, Presto. }

Words used to modify the above: *Poco*, a little. Before a word meaning *slow*, signifies an *increase* of speed, as *poco lento*, a little slow; before a word meaning *fast*, it signifies a *decrease* of speed, as *poco allegro*, a little fast. *Piu*, more. Before a word meaning *slow*, signifies a *decrease* of speed, as *piu lento*, slower; before a word meaning *fast*, it signifies an *increase* of speed, as *piu allegro*, faster. *Assai*, very. After a word meaning *slow*, decreases the speed, as *adagio assai*, very slow; after a word meaning *fast*, increases the speed, as *allegro assai*. *Molto*, much; has the same meaning as *assai*.

THE DIMINUTIVE *Etto*.

Slow { Larghetto, a little faster than Largo. Adagietta, a little faster than [Adagio.

Fast, Allegretto, a little slower than [Allegro.

THE SUPERLATIVE *Issimo*.

Slow { Larghissimo, Lentissimo, Adagissimo, } As slow as possible.

Fast { Allegrissimo, Prestissimo, } Fast as possible.

THE DIMINUTIVE *Ino*.

Slow, Andantino, faster than Andante.

Andante means "going" [from *andare*, to go], therefore Andantino means "going a little." A large number of words are used in conjunction with the tempo indications that refer more to the manner or style of the performance than to the speed, as Appassionata, with passion; Vivace, with life. The majority of these words are preceded by con, with; as—

Con brio, ... with vigor,
Con calore, . . . with warmth,
Con fuoco, . . . with fire,
Con moto, etc., with motion,
} After words meaning fast.

Con espressione with expression,
Con dolcezza, . with sweetness,
Con dolore, . . . with sadness,
Con tristezza, . with sorrow,
} After words meaning slow.

Tempo commodo. Convenient; easy movement.

Tempo di ballo. Dance time.

Tempo giusto. Strict; exact time.

Tempo marcia. March time.

Tausig, Carl. Composer, pianist; Poland. B. 1841; d. 1871.

Tempo ordinario. Ordinary; usual.
Tempo primo. First time, used after a ritard. or accel. to indicate a return to the original time.
Tempo rubato. See *Rubato*.
Tempo wie vorher (Ger.). Same as *Tempo primo*.
Temps (Fr.) (*tam*). (1) Time. (2) Beat.
Temps faible or levé. Weak beat; up beat.
Temps fort or frappé. Strong beat; down beat.
Tendrement (Fr.) (*tondr-mong*). Tenderly.
Tenendo il canto (It.). Sustaining the melody.
Teneramente (It.) (*teh-neh-ra-men'-teh*). Tenderly; delicately.
Tenerezza (It.) (*teh-neh-ret'-za*), con. With tenderness, delicacy.
Tenero (It.) (*teh'-neh-ro*). Tender: delicate.
Tenor, Tenore (It.), **Taille or Ténor** (Fr.).
(1) The highest natural male voice. (2) In the old system of music, the cantus or plain song. (3) A common name for the viola. The word tenor is supposed to be derived from Lat., *teneo*, to hold, as it *held* the melody.
Tenor Clef. C clef on 4th line.
Tenor Violin. Viola.
Tenore buffo. A comic tenor singer.
Tenore di grazia. A "smooth-singing" tenor singer.
Tenore leggiero. A light tenor singer.
Tenore robusto. A vigorous, strong tenor singer.
Tenorino (It.) (*ten-o-ree'-no*). "Little tenor." Falsetto tenor.
Tenorist. A tenor singer; also viola player.
Tenoroon. (1) See *Oboe di caccia*. (2) Any organ-stop of 8-foot tone that does not go below middle C.
Tenuto (It.) (*teh-noo'-to*). Abbreviated **Ten.** Hold; a direction to sustain the notes for their full value. Sign 𝄐.
Tepidita (It.) (*teh-pee'-dee-ta*), con. With indifference.
Tepiditamente (It.) (*teh-pee-dee-ta-men'-teh*). Coldly; lukewarmly.
Tercet. (Fr.) (*tehr-say*). A triplet.
Ternary Form. Rondo with three themes.
Ternary Measure. Simple triple time.
Tertian. A two-rank stop, sounding the major 3d and 5th in the third octave above the fundamental.
Telemann, G. P. (*teh'-leh-man*). Composer, organist; Germany. B. 1681; d. 1767.

Terz (Ger.) (*terts*), (It.) **Terza.** Third.
Terzetto (It.) (*tert-set'-to*). A vocal trio.
Terzflöte (Ger.). (1) A flute sounding a 3d above the written notes. (2) An organ stop sounding the major 3d in third octave.
Tessitura (It.) (*tes-see-tu'-rah*). Texture. The general range of the voice included in a given song, etc.
Testo (It.) (*tehs'-to*). Text. (1) The "words" of any vocal composition. (2) The theme or subject.
Tetrachord [from Gr., *tetra*, *chordon*]. Four strings; hence, a succession of four sounds. The tetrachord always consists of two whole tones and one half-tone. These intervals may be arranged in three ways. The oldest arrangement, called the Pythagorean tetrachord, began with the half-tone, thus : —

It is generally supposed that the original four-string lyre (called the tetrachordon) was tuned to these sounds. The addition of another tetrachord, beginning with the highest note of this one, gives the scale of the heptachord, or seven-string lyre, thus : —

This is called the scale of conjunct tetrachords, the A being the note common to both. The addition of a note *below* this scale, thus : —

gives the original octave scale of the lyre. This scale is the normal Greek scale, called the Dorian. It is doubtless the origin of the modern minor scale. The tetrachord known as Hucbald's had the half-tone in the middle, thus: D E F G.

The *Hexachord scales* (*q. v.*) were formed from this tetrachord by adding one letter above and one below, thus :—

C D E F G A.

In the modern major scale the half-tone lies between the third and fourth letters of the tetrachord, thus : C D E F, and the scale consists of two of these tetrachords separated by a whole tone.

Terschak, Ad. Composer, flutist; Germany. B. 1832; d. 1907.

Tetrachordal System. The original name of the *Tonic Sol Fa, q. v.*.

Theil or **Teil** (Ger.). A part (portion, not "voice").

Theme, Thème (Fr.) (*tchm*), **Thema** (Ger.) (*teh-ma*). The subject of a fugue; one of the subjects of a sonata or rondo. The subject of a set of variations. The "cantus" to which counterpoint is added.

Theorbo, Théorbe (Fr.). A large variety of lute.

Third. An interval including three letters, and, if major, two whole tones; if minor, three half tones; if diminished, two half-tones:—

T.irty-second Note ♪.

Thorough Bass, Figured Bass, Continued Bass. A system of musical shorthand originally; now used as a means of teaching harmony.

Threnody [Gr. *threnos*]. A song of mourning; dirge.

Thumb Position. Violoncello music; sign ↓, the thumb is laid across the strings, making a temporary bridge.

Tibia (Lat.). The "shinbone." Latin name for the flute, which was originally made from the bone, the name of which it bears.

Tibia Utricularis. Bagpipe.

Tibicen (Lat.). A flute player.

Tie, Fascia (It.), **Bindebogen** (Ger.), **Liaison** (Fr.). A curved line joining two notes on the same degree. The first note is sounded, the second is "held." In old editions, in place of the tie, it was customary to write a single note on the bar-line, equal in value to the two notes that in modern practice are tied. Thus:—

Any number of notes may be tied. The

Thalberg, S (*tal-berg*). Composer, pianist; Switzerland. B. 1812; d. 1871.
Thayer, A. W. Writer; U. S. A. B. 1817; d. 1897.
Thayer, Eugene. Organist, composer; U. S. A. B. 1838; d. 1889.
Thomas, C. Ambroise (*to-mah, am-bro-az*). Composer; France. B. 1811; d. 1896.
Thomas, Theo. Violinist, conductor; Germany. B. 1835; d. 1905.

sign must be repeated for each one, thus:—

The first note is struck, but the sound is prolonged until the time value of all has expired.

Tief (Ger.). Deep; low.

Tierce. (1) A third. (2) An organ stop. See *Terz*.

Tierce de picardie (Fr.). The major 3d in place of the minor in the final chord of a piece in the minor key. At one time this manner of ending was the rule.

Tierce Position. A common chord with root in bass and third at top.

Timbale (Fr.), **Timballo** (It.). Kettledrum.

Timbre, (Fr.) (*tambr*). Quality of tone. In German *Klangfarbe*, for which *Clangtint* has been proposed as an English equivalent.

Timbrel. Tambourine.

Time. (1) The division of music into portions marked by the regular return of an accent. All varieties of time are founded on two units—the Binary = 1 2, and Ternary = 1 2 3. Time signatures for the most part are formed from figures written like fractions, the upper figure giving the rhythmic units and the number of times the value of the note indicated by the lower figure occurs in the measure. Time is Simple Binary when the upper figure is 2; Simple Ternary, when the upper figure is 3. Compound times are formed by adding together two or more of the time units. When the number of accents resulting from this combination are *even*, it is called Compound Common time; when they are odd, Compound Triple time. Simple Duple time is indicated by this sign ₵. As now used, it always means the value of a whole note in the measure, and is called Alla Capella time. Like all duple times, it must have but one accent in the measure, no matter how the time value of the measure may be divided. The first compound of Duple time, viz., 4/4 time, is often marked **C** and is called Common time, under the impression that the sign is the letter C, whereas it is

Thomé, F. L. J. (*toh-meh*). Composer; Mauritius. B. 1850; d. 1910.
Thunder, Henry. Organist, composer; Ireland. B. 1832; d. 1881.
Thursby, Emma. Soprano; U. S. A. B. 1857.
Titjens, T. C. J. (*tee-tcel-ens*). Soprano; Germany. B. 1831; d. 1877.

the old sign for Imperfect time, viz., a broken circle, and originally meant two beats in the measure. Three beats was called Perfect time; the sign was ◯. With the exception of the times with 4 for the upper figure, all the compound times are multiples of the ternary unit, as $\frac{6}{2}, \frac{6}{4}, \frac{6}{8}-\frac{12}{4}, \frac{12}{8}, \frac{12}{16}$, etc., Compound Common; $\frac{9}{4}, \frac{9}{8}, \frac{9}{16}$, Compound Triple. The accents in compound times are determined by the number of units in the measure. The first is the strongest, third next, the second is weak, the fourth weaker.

[musical notation examples]

In Compound Triple, the second and third are both weak.

[musical notation example]

Timidezza (It.) (*tee-mee-det'-za*), con. With timidity.
Timorosamente (It.) (*tee-mo-ro-sa-men'-teh*). Timorously.
Timoroso (It.) (*tee-mo-ro'-so*). Timorous; hesitating.
Timpani (It.) (*tim'-pa-nee*). Kettle-drums. Abbreviated **Timp.**
Timpanista (It.). Player on the kettle-drums.
Tirade (Fr.) (*tee-rad*). A rapid run or scale passage.
Tirasse (Fr.) (*tee-rass*). A pedal keyboard that "draws down" the manual keys.
Tirata (It.) (*tee-rah'-tah*). See *Tirade.*
Tirato (It.), **Tiré** (Fr.) (*tee-reh*). "Drawn" bow, *i. e.*, down bow.
Toccata (It.) (*tok-kah'-tah*) [touched, from *toccare*, to touch]. (1) A prelude or overture. (2) A brilliant composition resembling somewhat the modern "Étude" for piano or organ.
Toccatina (It.) (*tok-kah-tee'-nah*). A little toccata.
Toccato (It.). A bass trumpet part.
Todtenmarsch (Ger.) (*tote'-ten marsh*). Funeral march.
Ton (Ger.), **Ton** (Fr.). Tone; sound; pitch; key; scale.
Tonal Fugue. A fugue in which the answer is slightly changed to avoid modulation.
Tomaschek, W. Composer, pianist; Bohemia. B. 1774; d. 1850.

Tonality. Pertaining to the key.
Tonart. Key.
Tonbildung. Tone production.
Tondichter. Tone poet.
Tondichtung. Tone poem.
Tone. (1) Sound. (2) Quality of sound. (3) Interval of major second. (4) A Gregorian chant.
Tongue. (1) See *Reed.* (2) (verb) To interrupt the sound of a wind instrument by raising and lowering the tip of the tongue, as in the act of pronouncing the letter T. **Double-tonguing** is produced by a like action of the tip and the middle of the tongue; **Triple-tonguing**, by the tip, the middle, and the tip.
Tonkunst. Tone art; music.
Tonkünstler. Composer; artist in tone.
Tonic. The keynote of a scale, whether major or minor.
Tonic Chord. The common chord of which the tonic is the root.
Tonic Section. That part of the sonata or rondo that is the principal key; the first theme.
Tonic Sol Fa. A system of musical notation in which the syllables doh, ray, me, fah, soh, lah, te, with certain modifications, are used in place of notes, staff, clefs, and all the ordinary characters of musical notation. The Tonic Sol Fa is based on the assumption, amply proved by experience, that the mental association between a succession of sounds and a succession of syllables helps materially to fix the former in the memory (see *Hexachord*). The principle of the Tonic Sol Fa system is as old as the time of Guido; the modern development of it originated with Miss Sarah Ann Glover, of Norwich, England, in 1812, and was perfected by the Rev. John Curwen about thirty years later.
Tonleiter. Tone ladder; scale.
Tonsetzer. Composer; tone setter.
Tonstück. Tone piece; composition.
Tonstufe. Tone step; a degree in the scale.
Tostamente (It.) (*tos-tah-men'-teh*). Quickly.
Tostissimo (It.) (*tos-tis'-see-mo*), **Tostissamamente** (*tos-tis-sah-mah-men'-teh*). Fast as possible.
Tosto (It.). Quick. **Piu tosto,** faster.
Touch. (1) The resistance of the keys of the pianoforte or organ. (2) The manner in which a player strikes the keys.
Touche (Fr.) (*toosh*). Digital; key; fret; fingerboard.
Tosti, F. P. (*tos-tee*). Composer; Italy. B. 1846.

Toucher (Fr.) (*too-shay*). To "touch;" play the pianoforte.

Toujours (Fr.) (*too-zhoor*). Always; as, Toujours piano, always soft.

Tradotto (It.) (*trah-dot'-to*). Transcribed; arranged.

Tragen der Stimme (Ger.). Carrying of the voice. See *Portamento*.

Trainé (Fr.) (*tray nay*). Slurred; legato.

Trait (Fr.) (*tray*). A run; passage; sequence.

Tranquillamente (It.). Quietly; composedly.

Tranquillita, con (It.). With tranquility.

Tranquillo (It.). Tranquil; quiet.

Transcription. The arrangement of a vocal composition for an instrument, or of a composition for some instrument for another.

Transient Modulation. A short excursion into a non-related key.

Transition. (1) An abrupt modulation. (2) The connecting passages between the themes of a rondo or sonata.

Transpose. To change the key of a composition to one higher or lower.

Transposing Instruments. Instruments whose sounds do not correspond with the written notes; as horns, clarionets, trumpets, etc.

Transverse Flute. See *Flute*.

Trascinando (It.) (*trah-shee-nan'-do*). Dragging; retarding.

Trattenuto (It.) (*trat-teh-noo'-to*). Held back; retarded.

Trauermarsch (Ger.). Funeral march.

Traurig (Ger.) (*trou'rig*). Mournful; sad.

Traversflöte (Ger.). See *Flute*.

Tre (It.) (*tray*). Three.

Tre corde. Three strings, used in pianoforte music to signify a release of the una-corda pedal.

Treble. (1) The highest part in vocal music for mixed or female voices. (2) The G clef on second line. (3) The first violin in quartet, and the flute, oboe, and clarionet in the orchestra generally.

Treibend (Ger.). Hastening; accelerando.

Tremando (It.) (*treh-man'-do*), **Tremolando** (It.) (*treh-mo-lan'-do*), **Tremolo** (It.) (*treh'-mo-lo*). Abbreviation **Trem.** The rapid reiteration of a note or chord. In music for string instruments written thus:—

In pianoforte music:—

Tremoloso (It.) (*treh-mo-lo'-so*). Tremulously.

Tremulant, Tremolante (It.), **Tremblant** (Fr.) (*trom-blont*). A mechanism in the organ that causes the sound to waver.

Tremulieren (Ger.). To trill or to sing. *Vibrato, q. v.*

Trenchmore. An old English dance in $\frac{6}{8}$ time.

Trenise (Fr.). A figure in the quadrille.

Très (Fr.) (*tray*). Very; as, Très vite, very fast.

Triad. A chord of three sounds; a common chord, consisting of root, 3d major or minor, and 5th. If the 5th is diminished, it is called a diminished triad; if augmented, an augmented triad.

Maj.   *Min.*   *Dim.*   *Aug.*

Triangle. A pulsatile instrument, consisting of a steel rod bent into an equilateral triangle. Struck with a small steel rod, it gives a very clear penetrating sound.

Trill, Trillo (It.), **Trille** (Fr.), **Triller** (Ger.). The rapid iteration of the written note and the note above, indicated by the sign, *tr*~~~~. The trill continues to the end of the waved line. The following exhaustive account of the trill is abridged from Russell's "Embellishments of Music":—

The oldest form of trillo was a mere repetition of a tone; thus:—

The gruppo of the Italians approaches nearer the modern trill:—

Tourjee, Eben. Writer; U. S. A. B. 1834; d. 1891.

Tours, Berthold. Composer, violinist; Holland. B. 1838; d. 1897.

Tourte, F. (*toort*). Violin-bow maker; France. B. 1747; d. 1835.

Another old form of embellishing a tone was called the ribattuta, thus:—

The oldest form of the modern shake was held to be derived from appoggiaturas and their resolutions.

Marpurg, Em. Bach, and Türk, all claim the shake to be a rapid succession of appoggiaturas. (Vorschläge von oben.)

There is no doubt, however, that the shake came quite directly from the gruppo, as explained by Caccini (1600), and the attempt to square its delivery with the appoggiatura quite overlooked the real character of the embellishment, which differed essentially from the harmonic grace.

Until the time of Beethoven, the trill beginning with upper auxiliary note was most generally used.

However, the present method of beginning with the principal tone was gradually gaining the attention of writers, even Marpurg sounding a note of warning (1755) against the "vicious innovations" of some who began the pralltriller with the principal tone. The trill is generally finished with a turn.

The after-turn is usually written out at the close of the trill, but whether or not this be so, the trill is not complete without this closing beat:—

To make the trill symmetrical with an after-turn, an additional tone is inserted, just before the close, otherwise there will be a break between the last and the next to the last beats; thus:—

This gap between D and B is filled by the insertion of an additional principal tone, which will make the next to the last beat contain three tones (a triplet); thus:—

This makes a satisfactory close to a trill, the two beats (five notes) making a complete turn of quintuplet form.

Many writers call this (quintuplet) the turn of the trill, but properly speaking the after-turn of the trill is only the last beat, the triplet preceding being a real part of the trill.

From this it will be seen that the beats of a trill may be either twofold or threefold, and the smallest complete trill, according with the modern acceptation of the correct form of the embellishment, would be with two beats, five notes; thus:—

However, in Bach, and even later—in Mozart—trills are sometimes quite consistent with correct performance which have *two beats of two notes;* thus:—

In more modern music, however, this would scarcely be justified, unless marked with an appoggiatura upon the upper degree (as per rule quoted).

The rapidity of a trill is reckoned by the number of beats, not by the number of tones, sounded within a given note's time. The trill upon a long note has no positive number of beats, this being decided, in case there is no particular accompanying figure, by the character of the composition and also measurably by the ability of the interpreter. The after-turn, however, should always be played in the same time as the trill, regardless of the size of note used for its representation in the notation. *If these notes be of regular size, forming part of the measure, they will be a guide as to the rapidity of the trill,* the after-turn of which will constitute *one beat*.

Execution:—

The inverted trill (*i. e.*, beginning with upper tone) completes itself *without the triplet before the after-turn;* thus:—

The incomplete trill has no after-turn, being the simple alternation of the principal tone with its auxiliary.

When followed by an unaccented note, the trill may be incomplete, but must not end with the auxiliary tone, for *all trills must close with the principal tone;* thus:—

In this case the *last beat* of the trill contains three tones, thus bringing a triplet at the end of the ornament.

This is always the case with incomplete trills beginning on principal tone, therefore the smallest possible trill in modern music contains a single beat of three tones,—principal, auxiliary, principal :—

The trill of one beat can only occur on very short notes, as the pralltriller explained in previous paragraph.

In the old form, beginning on upper auxiliary, the smallest actual trill possible would be of four notes (two beats), since the single twofold beat is but an appoggiatura.

Accompanied trills require a strict rhythmic conformity with the accompaniment.

If the trill be accompanied by a single note, the number of beats is somewhat optional, yet they should be in some direct ratio with the rhythm of the piece.

In duple or quadruple time, the beats should be two, four, or eight in number, on an eighth or fourth note, while on a dotted note in triple measure three beats will be found symmetrical in effect.

If the trill be accompanied by groups of notes, the number of beats must be more strictly determined. Thus, a trilled note, with four accompanying tones, will require either two, four, or eight beats, according to the duration of the note :—

If the trill be accompanied by three notes, there will be either three or six beats.

When the tempo is very rapid, making it impracticable to play a trill of four beats to the group, and yet too slow for two beats only (practically making the trill, note for note, with the accompanying figure), the trill may be made with one threefold beat, followed by a fourfold turn, as follows :—

The same arrangement of the trill may be used with two beats, one of three notes and one of two notes, in case of a rapid accompaniment of three tones, thus :—

The five notes are played as a quintuplet (equal in length), against the triplet in the accompaniment.

In the older classics, a trill upon a dotted note is played according to the rule for a turn similarly placed, *i. e.*, the last tone falls upon the time of the dot.

This is much used in classic cadences, with anticipated final note.

If the following note be above the trilled tone, the turn is required, but if it be below, the turn is not necessary, the trill ending with principal tone upon the dot.

First :—

Execution :—

Second :—

Execution :—

While the turn is not essential in the second example above, yet it could readily be used, and to insure a more accurate ensemble, in case of more than one performer, the phrase would better be closed with a turn after the trill.

The more modern method of treatment of trills on dotted notes would be to trill the entire length of the tone (with dot), and consider the short tone following of the same length as the notes of the trill.

The same rules, however, regarding the after-tone will apply here as in the older rendering.

The trill upon a tied note or on a note followed by another on same degree (without trill) requires a single lower auxiliary to form a turn immediately before the second note.

This note may be *written in, or not*, but is always required.

Execution :—

A brilliant modern device in trilled passages is the gradual quickening of the frequency of the beats, from a simple beat to a double, triple, etc.

This, with combined *crescendo* and *diminuendo*, produces an effect somewhat similar to the ancient ribattuta. Some composers have indicated such methods of trilling in full, thus :—

Execution :—

The chain of trills [Ger., *Trillerketten;* It., *catena di trilli*] is a succession of trilled tones ascending or descending by degrees or by skips.

If the notes be very short and in quick succession, not more than the simplest form of threefold beat can be played.

Execution :—

The after-turn need not always be used, if not written in the phrase. This will be decided largely by the rapidity of the passage.

More elaborate and less rapid chains of trills require a complete trill upon every tone, and frequently the notes are of sufficient length to allow a trill of several beats, thus:—

Allegro.

A chain of trills without after-tones, as follows, is also authorized by such authorities as Türk, Bach, etc.

This manner of performance gives the accent to the upper auxiliary tone.

In extremely rapid tempo, a very effective trill chain may be used with but four tones, beginning upon the upper auxiliary and closing with a twofold after-turn.

Instead of the following more modern manner:—

This short form has been called the half trill, and is only used with beginning on upper auxiliary tone.

Instead of the conventional after-turn of two notes, frequent use is made (especially by modern composers) of an elaborate closing figure as a "tirata":—

The four notes here will constitute two beats of the same rapidity as the beats of the trill.

The various beginnings of a trill may be applied to the modern manner of performance or the older way, *i. e.*, with accent upon the principal tone or the upper auxiliary.

In the performance of a classic work the player or singer is allowed the privilege of discrimination in choice, but it may be generally stated that the modern ear will less likely be offended by the accenting of the principal tone than of the auxiliary.

But if one desires to give an exact classic rendering of Bach, or even so recent a composer as Mozart, the embellishments throughout must be consistent in their delivery and not mixed, the trills especially being made either *all* of modern or older pattern. In the latter case, the quaintness of some of the ancient embellishments produces very charming effects, and no amount of objecting criticism can avail against the performance as a true classic rendering.

In modern music especially there will be found various approaches to the trill, thus, each indicating the same effect:—

Written.

or,

Older manner.

Wagner (*Musikalische Ornamentik*) gives a strong and rapid introductory beat to longer trills, which may often be used with good effect; thus:—

This immediately throws the accent of the trill upon the upper auxiliary, although it begins with the principal tone, thus seemingly fulfilling the requirements of both the older and the modern rules. Ludwig Klee also uses this form of the introductory beat, but with the difference that the first beat forms a triplet:—

This ingenious delivery of the trill is not frequently seen, but will certainly bear careful study, and is especially helpful in cases of doubt as to which of the methods of delivery to use (the old or modern).

In the case of tied notes, when the second note is a shorter one and not to be trilled, as:—

the former way of delivery used no after-turn, and consequently the only proper beginning of the trill was on the principal tone, as the trill from the upper auxiliary made a weak close.

not

There were many similar disadvantages attending the old manner of trilling, yet withal much of artistic force often follows its use.

The rules given should be carefully applied in all cases of doubt, when the composer has not indicated by a small note the tone upon which the trill enters.

It will be well for the student to bear in mind that the greater weight of opinion among classic reviewers and editors rests with the *older method* of trill delivery (from upper tone), and most editions of Beethoven, Mozart, Haydn, etc., having annotations, give this manner of performance as correct. It is to be remarked, however, that modern performers (virtuosi), who really create the style and through whom we expect the better elements of traditions to be conserved, do not, as a rule, testify in their performances to the absolute truth of this manner of trilling.

More modern composers (Chopin, Schumann, etc.) have so positively written their trills, with the accent upon the principal tone, as to have cultivated almost beyond recall, even in the greater virtuosi, the feeling for such a manner of performance rather than with the accented upper auxiliary.

Examples.—The Trill.

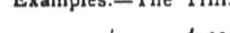

From above (inverted), in strictly classic readings.

TRILL 104 TRILL

With Appoggiatura or slurred note.

Unusual prefixes and closes. (Double After-beat, etc.)

TRILL

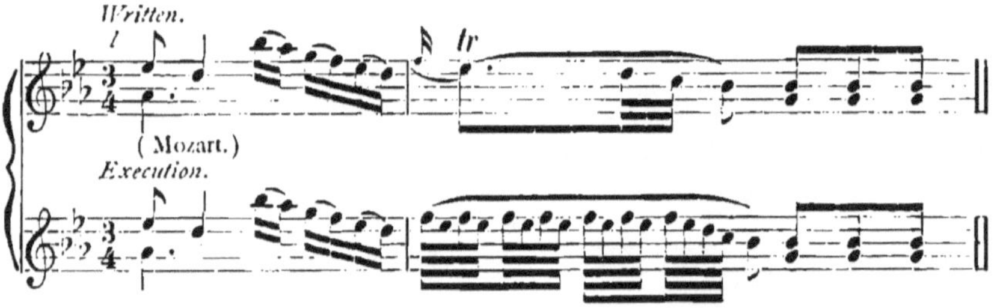

Trinklied (Ger.). Drinking song.

Trio (It.) (*tree-o*). (1) A composition for three voices or instruments. (2) One of the parts of a minuet or march, etc. The origin of its application is very uncertain.

Triole (Ger.), **Triolet** (Fr.). A triplet.

Triomphale (*tree-om-fal*), **Triomphant** (Fr.) (*tri-om-font*), **Trionfale** (*tree-on-fah'-leh*), **Trionfante** (It.) (*tree-on-fan'-teh*). Triumphant; triumphal.

Triple Counterpoint. One so contrived that the three parts may change places, each one serving as bass, middle, or upper part.

Triplet, Triole (Ger.), **Triolet** (Fr.), **Tripla** (It.) or **Tripola.** Three notes played in the time of two of the same value.

Triple Time. See *Time*.

Tristezza (It.) (*tris-tet'-za*), con. With sadness; sadly.

Tritone [Lat., *tritonus*, three tones], **Triton** (Fr.), **Tritono** (It.). The interval of the augmented 4th, as—

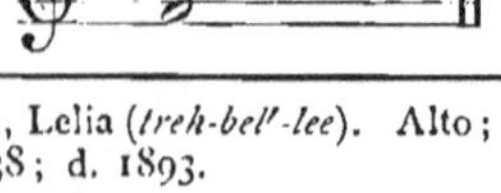

Trebelli, Lelia (*treh-bel'-lee*). Alto; France. B. 1838; d. 1893.

Trois (Fr.) (*tro-a*). Three.

Trois temps. Triple time.

Troll [from Ger., *trollen*, to roll about]. (1) (verb) To sing a catch or round. (2) (noun) A catch or round.

Tromba (It.). Trumpet; a brass instrument of piercing, brilliant tone quality.

Tromba marina (It.). See *Nonnengeige*.

Trombetta (It.). A small trumpet.

Trombone, Posaune (Ger.). (1) A brass instrument with a sliding tube, by means of which the pitch may be varied. Three trombones are used in the modern orchestra, viz., alto, tenor, and bass. A smaller trombone formerly used was called the Descant Trombone. (2) A reed stop of 8-, 16-, or 32-foot pitch in the organ.

Trommel (Ger.). Drum.

Trompe (Fr.). Hunting horn.

Trompe de bearn. Jews-harp.

Trompette (Fr.). Trumpet.

Troppo (It.). Too much. **Allegro non troppo,** "Allegro," not too much.

Tschaikowsky, P. I. (*chi-kow'-skee*). Composer; Poland. B. 1840; d. 1893.

Troubadour, Trouvère (Fr.), **Trovatore** (It.). The poet musicians of the eleventh century, in southern France, Italy, and Spain. The troubadours originated in Provençe. From thence their "gentle art," or "gay science," as it was called, spread over Europe.

Troveur, Trouverre (Fr.). A writer of romances, fabliaux, etc.; also a troubadour.

Trübe (Ger.) (*tree'-beh*). Gloomy; dismal.

Trumpet. See *Tromba*.

Tuba (Lat.). (1) Trumpet. (2) A bass instrument of the saxhorn family, frequently used with, or in place of, the bass trombone.

Tuba mirabiles (Lat.). Tuba "wonderful." A reed-stop in the organ with heavy wind pressure, 8- or 16-foot tone.

Tumultuoso (It.) (*too-mul-too-o'-so*). Agitated; tumultuous.

Tune. (1) Air; melody. (2) Just intonation.

Tuner. One who adjusts the sounds of an instrument to the standard and relative pitch.

Tuono (It.). (1) Sound. (2) Mode.

Turca, alla (It.). In the Turkish manner.

Turkish Music or **Jannisary Music.** Drums, cymbals, gongs, etc., to produce noise.

Turn. (Abridged from Russell's "Embellishments of Music.")

The Turn partakes in its delivery somewhat of the character of the composition in which it appears, and should be played (or sung) according to Louis Koehler, broad in slow tempo, light and flowing in brighter movements, and always legato. It may be broadly divided into four classes:—

1. The symbol ∾ placed over the note (♩), or the note preceded by the embellishment written in full.

2. A turn between two notes on different degrees (or four small notes between).

3. A turn between two notes of similar pitch.

4. The turn after a dotted note. The delivery of this turn is the same as the third class in its effect, since the dot is simply another way of writing a second similar note.

An exception to this fourth rule is made if the dotted note with turn directly precedes a close (possibly forming part of the cadence) and is followed by two notes of equal value leading up or down to the closing notes of the phrase.

Tuckerman, S. P. Composer, organist; U. S. A. B. 1819; d. 1890.

Turini, Fr. (*too-ree'-nee*). Composer; Bohemia. B. 1590; d. 1656.

Tutta (It.). All. **Con tutta forza.** With full power.
Tutti (It.) (*too-tee*). In scores, a notification to all the performers and singers to take part.
Tuyau (Fr.) Pipe.
Tuyau d' orgue. Organ pipe.
Tuyau à anche. Reed pipe.
Tuyau à bouche. Flue pipe.
Twelfth. An organ stop sounding the 12th above the diapason.
Tympani. See *Timpani*.
Tyrolienne (Fr.) (*tee-rol-yen*). (1) A Tyrolese song for dancing. (2) Tyrolese song with jodel.

U

U. C. Abbreviation of Una corda, one string.
Uebergang (Ger.) (*e'-ber-gangk*). Passage; transition; modulation.
Uebung (Ger.) (*e'-boonk*). Exercise; study; practice.
Uguale (It.) (*oo-gwah'-leh*). Equal.
Ugualmente (It.) (*oo-gwahl-men'-teh*). Equally; evenly.
Umfang (Ger.) (*vom-fangk*). Compass.
Umore (It.) (*oo-mo'-reh*), con. With humor.
Umstimmung (Ger.)(*oom-stim-moonk*). The change of the pitch of a brass instrument by the addition or change of " crooks; " the change of the pitch of kettle-drums.
Un (It.) (*oon*), **Una** (*oo'-nah*), **Uno** (*oo'-no*). One; as, **Una voce,** one voice.
Un or **Une** (Fr.) (*ong, oon*). One.
Unda maris (Lat.). " Wave of the sea." The vox celestis, an organ stop, 8-foot pitch, with a tremulous tone.
Unessential Dissonances. Those that occur by suspension, the essential dissonances being the 7th and 9th, and, according to some authorities, the 11th and 13th over the dominant.

Unessential Notes. Passing and changing notes.
Ungarisch (Ger.). Hungarian.
Ungeduldig (Ger.). Impatiently.
Ungestüm (Ger.). Impetuous; con impeto.
Unison. Sounds consisting of the same number of vibrations per second. The term " unison passage " is applied to vocal or instrumental parts in the octave also.
Unisono (It.) (*oo-nee-so-no*). Unison.
Unisson (Fr.) (*oo-nis-song*). Unison.
Un poco (It.). A little.
Un pochino (It.) (*po-kee'-no*), **Un pochettino** (*po-ket-tee'-no*). A very little.
Unruhig (Ger.) (*oon-roo'-ig*). Restless.
Unschuldig (Ger.) (*oon-shool-dig*). Innocent.
Up-bow. In violin playing the motion of the bow from the point to the nut. The sign is ∨; the down-bow ⊔ .
Ut (Fr.) (*oot*). The note C; the first of the Aretinian syllables, changed in Italy to *do*, a better vowel sound for solfeggio.
Ut (Lat.). As; like. **Ut supra,** as before.

Ulrich, Hugo. Composer; Silesia. B. 1827; d. 1872.
Urspruch, Anton. Pianist, composer. B. 1850; d. 1907.

V

V. Abbreviation of Violino, Voce, Volta.
V-cello. Abbreviation of Violoncello.
Vla. Abbreviation of Viola.
Va (It.). Go; as, **Va crescendo,** go on getting louder.
Vacillando (It.) (*vat-chil-lan'-do*). " Vacillating." A direction to play without strict regard to time.
Vago (It.). Vague; dreamy.
Valce (It.) (*val-cheh*), **Valse** (Fr.) (*vals*). Waltz; a dance of German origin in ¾ time.

Valse à deux temps (Fr.) (*doo tomp*). A species of waltz with two steps to each measure.
Value. The value of a note or rest is its relative duration, the standard being the whole note or rest, which may be divided into half, quarter, eighth, sixteenth, thirty-second notes, etc. The value of a note is increased one-half by placing a dot after it; a second dot adds to its value an amount equal to half that of the first. The absolute value of a note depends upon the tempo, *i. e.,* rate of movement of the piece in which it occurs.

Vaccaj, N. (*vak-kah'-ee*). Composer; Italy. B. 1790; d. 1848.
Verdi, G. (*vehr'-dee*). Composer; Italy. B. 1813; d. 1901.

Valve. See *Piston.*

Variante (Fr.) (*vah-ree-ongt*). A variant; other reading.

Variations, Variationen (Ger.) (*fah-ree-a-tse-o'-nen*), **Variazioni** (It.) (*va-ree-at-zee-o'-nee*). Melodic, rhythmic, and harmonic modifications of a simple theme, each one more elaborate than the last.

Varie (Fr.) (*vah-ree*), **Variato** (It.) (*var-ya'-to*). Varied; with variations.

Varsovienne (Fr.) (*var-so-vee-en*), **Varsovianna** (It.) (*var-so-vee-an'-na*). A dance in ¾ time resembling the mazurka, invented in France.

Vaudeville (Fr.) (*vode-veel*). A light operetta consisting of dialogue interspersed with songs; the name is said to come from Vaux de Vire in Normandy.

Veemente (It.) (*veh-eh-men'-teh*). Vehement; forceful.

Veemenza (It.) (*veh-eh-men'-tsa*), con. With vehemence.

Velato (It.) (*veh-lah'-to*), **Voce velato,** a veiled voice, *i. e.*, lacking in clearness and resonance.

Vellutata (It.) (*vel-loo-tah'-tah*). Velvety; smooth.

Veloce (It.) (*veh-lo'-cheh*). Rapid; swift.

Velocissimamente (It.) (*veh-lo-chis-see-ma-men'-teh*). Very swiftly.

Velocissimente (It.) (*veh-lo-chis-see-men'-teh*). Swiftly.

Velocita (It.) (*veh-lo'-chee-tah*), con. With rapidity.

Ventage. The holes in the tubes of wind instruments, the opening or closing of which by the finger-tip or by valves worked by keys alters the pitch by varying the sounding length of the tube.

Ventil. (1) Valve; piston. (2) In the organ a contrivance for cutting off the wind from a part of the organ.

Venusto (It.) (*veh-noos'-to*). Graceful; fine.

Veränderungen (Ger.) (*fer-an'-de-roong-en*). Variations.

Vergnügt (Ger.) (*fehr-gneegt'*). Pleasant; cheerful.

Verhallend (Ger.). See *Morendo.*

Verlöschend (Ger.) (*fehr-lesh'-end*). See *Morendo.*

Vermittelungsatz (Ger.) (*fehr-mit'-tel-oonk-sotz*). A subsidiary part; episode in sonata, etc.

Verschiebung (Ger.) (*fehr-shee'-boonk*), mit. Use "soft pedal."

Verschwindend (Ger.) (*fehr-shwin'-dend*). Dying away.

Versetzung (Ger.) (*fehr-set'-soonk*). Transposition.

Verspätung (Ger.) (*fehr-spay'-toonk*), **Verweilend** (*fehr-wei'-lent*), **Verzögernd** (*fehr-tseh'-gernt*). Delaying; retarding.

Verve (Fr.) (*vehrv*). Spirit. Avec verve, with spirit.

Verzweiflungsvoll (Ger.) (*fehr-tsvy'-floonks-foll*). Lit., full of desperation. Despairingly.

Vezzoso (It.) (*vets-so'-so*), **Vezzosamente** (*vets-so-sa-men'-teh*). Beautiful; graceful; gracefully.

Vibration. The rapid motion to and fro that produces the phenomena of sound by setting up a wave-motion in the air.

Vibrato (It.) (*vee-brah'-to*), **Vibrante** (*vee-bran'-teh*). "Vibrating" with strong, "intense" tone; vocal music, heavy accent in piano playing.

Viel (Ger.) (*feel*). Much; many.

Vielle (Fr.) (*vee-el'*). Rote; hurdy-gurdy.

Vier (Ger.) (*feer*). Four.

Vierstimmig. Four-voiced. **Vierfach,** fourfold.

Vif (Fr.). Lively.

Vigorosamente (It.) (*vee-go-ro-sa-men'-teh*). Vigorously; boldly.

Vigoroso (It.) (*vee-go-ro'-so*). Vigor; force.

Villancico (Sp.) (*veel-lan'-thee-co*). Originally a species of song or madrigal, later a motet sung in church at certain services.

Villanella (It.). An ancient Italian folk-song.

Viol. The precursor of the violin. Viols were made in sets of six called a "chest of viols;" the smallest was about the size of the modern viola, and all were provided with frets.

Vestris, L. E. Alto; England. B. 1797; d. 1856.

Viadana, L. (*vee-ah-dah'-nah*). Composer; Italy. B. 1565; d. 164–.

Viardot-Garcia, M. F. P. (*vee-ar'-do-gar-she-a*). Composer, soprano. B. 1821; d. 1910.

Vieuxtemps, H. (*vee-oo-tom*). Composer, violinist; France. B. 1820; d. 1881.

Vilbac, A. C. R. Composer, pianist; France. B. 1829; d. 1884.

Villaume, J. B. (*vee-yome*). Violin maker; France. B. 1798; d. 1875.

Villaume, N. (nephew of J. B.). Violin maker; France. B. 1800; d. 1871.

Villaume, N. F. (nephew of J. B.). Violin maker; France. B. 1812; d. 1876.

Villaume, S. (nephew of J. B.). Violin maker; France. B. 1835; d. 1875.

Viotti, G. B. (*vee-ot'-tee*). Composer, violinist; Italy. B. 1753; d. 1824.

Viola. The alto violin, generally called the tenor. The viola is slightly larger than the violin, and has four strings tuned as follows:—

Music for it is written with the C clef on the third line.

Viola da braccia (arm viola), **Viola da gamba** (leg viola), **Viola da spalla** (shoulder viola), **Viola pomposa.** Obsolete varieties of the viola family. The last was the invention of Sebastian Bach.

Viole (Fr.). Viola.

Viole d'amour (Fr.) (*d'ah-moor*), **Viola d'amore** (It.) (*d'ah-mo-reh*). A variety of the viola with wire sympathetic strings in addition to the usual gut strings.

Violin, Violon (Fr.), **Violino** (It.), **Fiddle, Geige** (Ger.). The words "violin" and "fiddle" both come from the Latin *vitula* or *fitula*, a mediæval form of string instrument played with a bow. The violin has four strings, tuned as follows:—

The strings are of gut, the lowest, or G string, covered with thin wire.

Violin Clef. The G clef on the second line.

Violina. A 4-foot organ-stop with string-like tone.

Violino principale (It.) (*prin-chee-pah'-leh*). The solo violin, or leader of the violins.

Violino ripieno. A violin part only used to fill up the tutti.

Violoncello (It.). The "little violone." The violoncello has four strings of gut, tuned an octave below the viola:—

The C and G strings are covered with wire.

Violonar (Fr.). Double bass.
Violonaro (Fr.). See *Octo Bass.*
Violone (It.). The double bass, *q. v.*
Virgil Clavier. A soundless keyboard for practice.
Virginal. A small instrument of the harpsichord family.

Vivier, E. L. (*vee-vee-eh*). Horn player; Corsica. B. 1821.
Vogl, Heinrich Tenor; Bavaria. B. 1845; d. 1900.
Vogl, Theresa (wife of H.). Soprano. B. 1846.

Virtuoso (masc.) (It.) (*vir-too-o'-so*), **Virtuosa** (fem.) (*vir-too-o'-sah*). An eminent skilled singer or player. The word was formerly used in the same sense as "amateur."

Virtuos (Ger.), **Virtuosin** (fem.) (Ger.), **Virtuose** (Fr.). Virtuoso.

Vista (It.). Sight. **A prima vista,** at first sight.

Vistamente (It.) (*vis-tah-men'-teh*), **Vitamente** (It.) (*vee-tah-men'-teh*), **Vive** (Fr.) (*veev*), **Vivente** (It.) (*vee-ven'-teh*), **Vivido** (It.) (*veel-vee-do*), **Vivezza** (*vee-vet-za*), con. Lively; briskly; with animation; vividly.

Vivace (It.) (*vee-vah'-cheh*), **Vivacemente** (*vee-vah-cheh-men'-teh*), **Vivacita** (*vee-vah'-chee-tah*), con, **Vivacezza** (*vee-vah-chet'-zah*). Lively; rapid; with animation; with vivacity.

Vivacissimo (*vee-vah-chis'-see-mo*). Very lively and fast.

Vivo (It.) (*vee-vo*). Alive; brisk.

Vocal. Belonging to the voice; music meant to be sung or well designed for singing.

Vocalion. A variety of reed organ in which the quality and power of the tone is much modified by resonators.

Vocalise (Fr.) (*vo-cal-ees*), **Vocalizzi** (It.) (*vo-cah-lit'-zee*). Vocal exercises.

Vocalization. (1) The manner of singing. (2) The singing of studies—solfeggio—to one or more vowel sounds.

Voce (It.) (*vo-cheh*). The voice.

Voice. (1) The sound produced by the human organs of speech. (2) A part in a polyphonic composition. There are three well-marked varieties of the male and female voice. Male voices are divided into bass, baritone, and tenor; the analogues in the female voice are alto, mezzo-soprano, and soprano.

Voicing. Regulating the quality and power of the tone of organ-pipes.

Voix (Fr.) (*vo-a*). Voice.

Voix celeste (Fr.). Vox angelica.

Volante (It.) (*vo-lan'-teh*). "Flying." The rapid, light execution of a series of notes.

Volkslied (Ger.) (*folks-leed*). Popular song.

Voll (Ger.) (*foll*). Full.

Volonté (Fr.) (*vo-lon-teh*), **A volonté.** At will; a piacere.

Volta (It.). Turn. **Una volta,** first turn or first time.

Vogl, J. M. Baritone. B. 1768; d. 1840.
Volckmar, Wil. (*folk'-mar*). Composer, organist; Germany. B. 1812; d. 1887.
Volkmann, F. R. (*folk'-man*). Composer; Bohemia. B. 1815; d. 1883.

Volti (It.) (*vol-tee*) (verb). Turn. **Volti subito**, abbreviated V. S., turn over (the page) rapidly.
Voluntary. An organ solo before, during, or after church service, frequently extempore.
Vordersatz (Ger.) (*for'-der-sots*). Principal theme; sonata.
Vorspiel (Ger.) (*for-speel*). Prelude; overture; introduction.

Vogler, Abbé G. J. Composer, organist, writer; Germany. B. 1749; d. 1814.

Vox (Lat.). Voice.
Vox celestis, Vox angelica. See *Unda maris*.
Vox humana. An organ-stop imitating the human voice. (Fr., *Voix humaine*).
Vuide (Fr.) (*voo-eed*), **Vuoto** (It.) (*voo-o-to*). Open. **Corde vuide, Corda vuide**, open string, *i. e.*, a string of instruments of violin family sounded without being touched by the finger.

Voss, Carl. Pianist; Poland. B. 1815; d. 1882.

W

Waits, Waytes, Waightes. Watchmen who "piped the hours" at night on a species of hautboy called a wait, or shawm. In modern times "Christmas waits" are parties of singers who go from house to house collecting pennies on Christmas Eve.
Waldflöte (Ger.) (*volt-flay-teh*). Forest flute; a 4-foot open organ-stop. **Waldquinte** is a 12th with the same tone quality.
Waldhorn (Ger.). Forest horn; hunting horn; the French horn without valves.
Waltz. See *Valse*.
Walze (Ger.) (*vol'-tseh*). A run, alternately ascending and descending; a "roller."
Wankend (Ger.). Hesitating.
Wärme (Ger.) (*vehr'-meh*). Ardor; warmth.
Wehmut (Ger.) (*veh'-moot*). Sadness.
Wehmütig (Ger.). Sad; melancholy.
Weich (Ger.). Weak; soft; minor.
Weinend (Ger.). Weeping; lamenting.

Wachtel, Theodor. Tenor; Germany. B. 1823; d. 1895.
Wagenseil, G. C. (*vah'-gen-sile*). Composer, pianist. Austria. B. 1715; d. 1777.
Wagner, W. Richard. Composer; Germany. B. 1813; d. 1883.
Wagner, Johanna (niece of R.). Soprano; Germany. B. 1828; d. 1894.
Wallace, Wm. V. Composer, pianist; Ireland. B. 1814; d. 1865.
Warren, S. P. Composer, organist, pianist; Canada. B. 1841.
Webbe, Sam. Composer, organist; Minorca. B. 1740; d. 1816.
Webbe, Sam (son of first). Composer, organist; England. B. 1770; d. 1843.
Weber, Aloysia (*reh-ber*). Soprano; Germany. B. 1750; d. 1839.
Weber, Carl M. von. Composer; Germany. B. 1786; d. 1826.
Weber, Gottfried. Theorist; Germany. B. 1779; d. 1839.

Well-tempered (Wohltemperiertes) Clavier (Ger.). A title given by Bach to a set of preludes and fugues in all the keys. See *Temperament*.
Wenig (Ger.). Little; un poco.
Whistle. A small flue-pipe or flageolet; the first step in advance of the pandean pipe, *i. e.*, a tube blown across the top.
Whole Note ø.
Whole Step. A whole tone.
Wie (Ger.). As; the same. **Wie vorher**, as before.
Wiederholung (Ger.) (*wee-dehr-ho'-loonk*). Repetition.
Wiegenlied (Ger.) (*wee'-gen-leed*). Cradle song; berceuse.
Wind Band. (1) The wind instruments in the orchestra. (2) A band composed of wind instruments only, called also a harmony band.

Wehle, Carl (*veh'-leh*). Pianist; Bohemia. B. 1825; d. 1887.
Weigl, Joseph. Composer; Austria. B. 1766; d. 1846.
Weigl, Thad. (brother of J.). Composer; Germany. B. 1777; d. 182–.
Weitzmann, C. F. (*vites'-man*). Theorist; Germany. B. 1808; d. 1880.
Wesley, S. S. Composer, organist; England. B. 1810; d. 1876.
Whiting, Geo. E. Composer, organist; U. S. A. B. 1842.
Widor, Ch. M. (*vee-dor*). Composer, organist; France. B. 1844.
Wieck, Fred. Pianist, writer; Germany. B. 1785; d. 1875.
Wieniawski, H. (*vee-nee-av'-skee*). Violinist, composer; Poland. B. 1835; d. 1880.
Wilhelmj, A. E. D. F. V. (*vil-hel'-mee*). Violinist; Germany. B 1845; d. 1908.
Willaert, Adrien. Composer; Belgium. B. 1490; d. 1562.

Wolf. (1) The dissonant effect of certain chords on the organ or pianoforte tuned in unequal temperament. See *Temperament*. (2) Certain notes on the violin or other bow instruments that do not produce a steady, pure tone.

Wood-stops. Organ-stops with wooden pipes.

Wood-wind. The flute, oboe, clarionet, and fagotto in the orchestra.

Wuchtig (Ger.). Weighty; emphatic.

Würde (Ger.). Dignity. **Mit Einfalt und Würde**, with simplicity and dignity.

Wütend (Ger.). Raging; furioso.

Willmers, H. Rudolf. Composer, pianist; Germany. B. 1821; d. 1878.

Woelfl, Jos. (*velfl*). Pianist, composer; Austria. B. 1772; d. 1814.

Wollenhaupt, H. A. (*vol' - len - howpt*). Composer, pianist; Germany. B. 1827; d. 1863.

Wraniczky, Paul (*rah-nit'- skee*). Composer; Moravia. B. 1756; d. 1808.

X Y Z

Xylophone, Strohfiedel (Ger.), **Claquebois** (Fr.), **Gigelira** (It.). An instrument consisting of strips of wood graduated to produce the diatonic scale. They are supported on ropes of straw, etc., and are struck by hammers held one in each hand. An ingenious form of the xylophone is found in Africa, called the marimba. From Africa it was brought to South America, where it has been greatly enlarged by the Negroes of Guatemala.

Yodel. See *Jodel*.

Zampogna (It.) (*zam-pone'-ya*). A bagpipe; also a harsh-toned species of hautboy.

Zapateado (Sp.) (*tha - pah - te - a' - do*). "Stamping." A Spanish dance in which the rhythm is marked by stamping.

Zarabanda (Sp.) (*tha-ra - ban'-da*). See *Saraband*.

Zart, Zärtlich (Ger.). Tender; tenderly; suave.

Zartflöte (Ger.). A soft-toned flute in the organ.

Zeitmass (Ger.). Tempo.

Zelo (It.) (*zeh'-lo*). Zeal; earnestness.

Zelosamente (It.) (*zeh-lo - sah - men'- teh*). Earnestly.

Zeloso (It.) (*zeh-lo'-so*). Zealous; energetic.

Ziemlich (Ger.) (*tseem'-lich*). Moderately. **Ziemlich langsam**, moderately slow.

Ziganka. A Russian peasant dance in ⅔ time.

Yriarte, S. (*e-ree-ar'-teh*). Writer; Teneriffe. B. 1750; d. 1791.

Ysaye, E. (*e-sah'-ee*). Violinist; Belgium. B. 1858.

Zachau, F. W. (*tsah-cow*). Composer, organist; Germany. B. 1663; d. 1717.

Zandt, Marie van. Soprano; U. S. A. B. 1861.

Zarlino, G. (*zar-lee'-no*). Composer, theorist; Italy. B. 1517; d. 1590.

Zelter, Carl F. Composer, writer; Germany. B. 1758; d. 1832.

Zimbalon, Cymbal, Czimbal. The Hungarian dulcimer.

Zingaresca (It.) (*zin-gah-res'-ca*), **Zigeunerartig** (Ger.) (*tsee-goy'-ner-ar-tig*). In Gypsy style.

Zinke (Ger.). Cornet; an obsolete variety of hautboy.

Zither (Ger.) (*tsit'-ter*). A string instrument consisting of a shallow box over which pass two sets of strings,—one set of gut for the accompaniment, the other, of steel and brass, pass over a fretted fingerboard; on these the melody is played. The notes are stopped by the left hand, and the melody strings are struck by a plectrum attached to a ring on the thumb of the right hand; the accompaniment is played by the first, second, and third fingers of the right hand.

Zitternd (Ger.). Trembling.

Zögernd (Ger.). Hesitating; retarding.

Zoppo (It.). Lame. **Alla zoppo**, halting; limping; syncopated.

Zukunftsmusik (Ger.). Music of the future. The music of Wagner and his disciples is thus called by both friend and enemy, but with different meanings.

Zunehmend (Ger.). Crescendo.

Zurückhaltend (Ger.) (*tsoo-reck'-hal-tend*). Retarding.

Zwischensatz (Ger.). An episode.

Zwischenspiel (Ger.). "Between play;" interlude.

Zerrahn, Carl. Conductor; Germany. B. 1826.

Zeuner, Ch. (*tsoy'-ner*). Organist; Germany. B. 1797; d. 1857.

Zimmermann, Agnes. Composer, pianist; Germany. B. 1847.

Zingarelli, N. A. (*zing-ah-rel'-lee*). Composer; Italy. B. 1752; d. 1837.

Zumsteeg, J. R. Composer, 'cellist; Germany. B. 1760; d. 1802.

Zundel, Johann. Composer, organist; Germany. B. 1815; d. 1882.

ENGLISH WORDS IN CONSTANT USE, WITH THEIR EQUIVALENTS IN ITALIAN, FRENCH, AND GERMAN.

A

A. La (Fr. and It.). A (Ger.).
A Flat. La bémol (Fr.). La bemolle (It.).
  As (Ger.).
A Sharp. La dièse (Fr.). La diesis (It.).
  Ais (Ger.).
A Major. La majeur (Fr.). La maggiore
  (It.). A dur (Ger.).
A Minor. La mineur (Fr.). La minore (It.).
  A moll (Ger.).
Accelerate. See *Growing Faster.*
Accidental.
  Accidente (It.).
  Accident (Fr.).
  Zufälliges Zeichen (Ger.).
Accented.
  Marcato; Ben marcato (It.).
  Marqué, Bien marque (Fr.).
  Betont; Markiert (Ger.).
Accompaniment.
  Accompagnimento (It.).
  Accompagnement (Fr.).
  Begleitung (Ger.).
Affectionately. See *Tender.*
Again.
  Ancora; Ancor (It.).
  Encore (Fr.).
  Wieder (Ger.).
Agility.
  Agilita; Velocita (It.); (used with con =
  with).
  Hurtigkeit, (mit) (Ger.).
Agitated.
  Agitato (It.).
  Agité (Fr.).
  Bewegt; Aufgeregt (Ger.).
Agreeable.
  Piacevole (It.).
  Agréable (Fr.).
  Angenehm (Ger.).
Air.
  Canto; Aria (It.).
  Chant; Air; Mélodie (Fr.).
  Weise; Lied (Ger.).
A Little Faster.
  Poco piu mosso (It.).
  Un peu plus vite (Fr.).
  Ein wenig schneller (Ger.).
A Little Slower.'
  Poco meno mosso (It.).
  Un peu plus lent (Fr.).
  Ein wenig langsamer (Ger.).
All Together.
  Tutti (It.).

Always.
  Sempre (It.).
  Toujours (Fr.).
  Immer (Ger.).
Always Loud.
  Sempre forte (It.).
  Toujours fort (Fr.).
  Immer stark (Ger.).
And.
  E (before a consonant); ed (before a
  vowel) (It.).
  Et (Fr.).
  Und (Ger.).
Animated.
  Animato; Vivo; Con anima; Svegliato;
  Resvigliato (It.).
  Animé (Fr.).
  Belebt; Aufgeweckt (Ger.).
Answer (in fugue).
  Riposta; Consequente (It.).
  Comes (Lat.).
  Réponse; Réplique (Fr.).
  Antwort; Gefährte (Ger.).
As.
  Come (It.).
  Comme (Fr.).
  Wie (Ger.).
At Pleasure.
  A Piacere; A bene placito (It.).
  Ad libitum (Lat.).
  A volonté (Fr.).
  Nach Belieben (Ger.).

B

B. Si (Fr. and It.). H (Ger.).
B Flat. Si bémol (Fr.). Si bemolle (It.).
  B (Ger.).
B Sharp. Si dièse (Fr.). Si diesis (It.).
  His (Ger.).
B Major. Si majeur (Fr.). Si maggiore
  (It.). H dur (Ger.).
B Minor. Si mineur (Fr.). Si minore (It.).
  H moll (Ger.).
Bagpipe.
  Cornemusa; Sampogna (It.).
  Cornemuse (Fr.).
  Sackpfeife; Dudelsack (Ger.).
Ballad.
  Ballata (It.).
  Ballade (Fr.).
  Ballade (Ger.).
Bar.
  Linea; Barra (It.).
  Barre (Fr.).
  Taktstrich (Ger.)

Beat.
    Battuta (It.).
    Battement de mesure, or de temps (Fr.).
    Taktschlag (Ger.).
Beginning.
    Capo; Principio (It.).
    Anfang (Ger.).
Belly (of violin, etc.).
    Tavola; Pancia (It.).
    Table (Fr.).
    Decke (Ger.).
Boat Song.
    Barcaruolla; Gondoliera (It.).
    Barcarolle (Fr.).
    Gondellied (Ger.).
Bold.
    Fiero; Ardito (It.).
    Fier (Fr.).
    Heftig (Ger.).
Book (number or volume).
    Libro (It.).
    Cahier (Fr.).
    Heft (Ger.).
Book (containing words of opera, etc.).
    Libretto (It.).
Bow.
    Arco (It.).
    Archet (Fr.).
    Bogen (Ger.).
Bound.
    Legato (It.).
    Lié (Fr.).
    Gebunden (Ger.).
Bridge.
    Ponticello (It.).
    Chevalet (Fr.).
    Steg (Ger.).
By Degrees.
    Poco a poco (It.).
    Peu à peu (Fr.).
    Nach und nach; Allmählich (Ger.).

C

C. Ut (Fr.). Do (It.). C (Ger.).
C Flat. Ut bémol (Fr.). Do bemolle (It.).
    Ces (Ger.).
C Sharp. Ut dièse (Fr.). Do diesis (It.).
    Cis (Ger.).
C Major. Ut majeur (Fr.). Do maggiore (It.). Cis dur (Ger.).
C Minor. Ut mineur (Fr.). Do minore (It.). Cis moll (Ger.).
Calm.
    Calmato; Tranquillo (It.).
    Ruhig (Ger.).
Caprice.
    Capriccio (It.).
    Caprice (Fr.).
    Grille (Ger.).
Coquettishly
    Con civetteria (It.)

Cradle Song.
    Ninnerella (It.).
    Berceuse (Fr.).
    Wiegenlied (Ger.).

D

D. Re (It.). Ré (Fr.). D (Ger.).
D Flat. Re bemolle (It.). Ré bémol (Fr.). Des (Ger.).
D Sharp. Re diesis (It.). Ré dièse (Fr.). Dis (Ger.).
D Major. Re maggiore (It.). Ré majeur (Fr.). D dur (Ger.).
D Minor. Re minore (It.). Ré mineur (Fr.). D moll (Ger.).
Decided.
    Deciso; Risoluto (It.).
    Avec decision (Fr.).
    Bestimmt; Entschlossen (Ger.).
Decreasing (in movement). See *Growing Slower*.
Decreasing (in loudness). See *Growing Softer*.
Decreasing (in movement and loudness). See *Growing Softer and Slower*.
Detached.
    Staccato; Spiccato (It.).
    Détaché (Fr.).
    Abgestossen (Ger.).
Distinctly. See *Accented*.
Divided.
    Divisi (It.).
    Divisé (Fr.).
Doleful.
    Con dolore; Tristamente; Mesto (It.).
Dying Away.
    Morendo; Espirando; Estinguendo;
    Sminuendo; Smorendo; Smorzando;
    Mancando; Diminuendo (It.).
    Schwindend; Sterbend; Verhallend;
    Verlöschend; Verschwindend (Ger.).

E

E. Mi (It.). Mi (Fr.). E (Ger.).
E Flat. Mi bemolle (It.). Mi bémol (Fr.).
    Es (Ger.).
E Sharp. Mi diesis (It.). Mi dièse (Fr.).
    Eis (Ger.).
E Major. Mi maggiore (It.). Mi majeur (Fr.). E dur (Ger.).
E Minor. Mi minore (It.). Mi mineur (Fr.). E moll.
Easy.
    Facile (It.).
    Facile (Fr.).
    Leicht (Ger.).
Emphatic.
    Marcato; Sforzato (It.).
    Bien marqué; Bien rhythmé (Fr.).
    Betont (Ger.).

End.
  Fine (It.).
  Fin (Fr.).
  Schluss (Ger.).
Equal.
  Eguale ; Spianato.
Even, Evenly. See *Equal.*
Emotion.
  Emozione (It.).
  Empfindung; Ergriffenheit; Gefühl; Innigkeit (Ger.).
Exercise.
  Exercizio (It.).
  Exercice (Fr.).
  Uebung (Ger.).
Expression.
  Espressione (It.) (con = with).
  Expression (Fr.) (avec = with).
  Ausdruck (Ger.) (mit = with).
Extreme, Extremely.
  Molto ; Di molto (It.).
  Très (Fr.).
  Sehr ; Ausserst (Ger.).

F

F. Fa (It.). Fa (Fr.). F (Ger.).
F Flat. Fa bemolle (It.). Fa bémol (Fr.). Fes (Ger.).
F Sharp. Fa diesis (It.). Fa diése (Fr.). Fis (Ger.).
F Major. Fa maggiore (It.). Fa majeur (Fr.). F dur (Ger.).
F Minor. Fa minore (It.). Fa mineur (Fr.). F moll (Ger.).
Fading Away. See *Growing Softer and Slower.*
Fast.
  Allegro; Vivace ; Vivo ; Presto (It.).
  Vif (Fr.).
  Rasch ; Schnell ; Geschwind ; Hurtig (Ger.).
Faster.
  The words above with Piu before them :
  Piu mosso (It.).
  Plus vif (Fr.).
  Schneller ; Rascher (Ger.).
Faster by Degrees. See *Growing Faster.*
Faster and Louder.
  Stringendo ; Affrettando ; Incalzando (It.).
  Stärker und schneller (Ger.).
Festive.
  Festivo (It.)
  Feierlich (Ger.).
Fiery.
  Con fuoco ; Con calore (It.).
  Avec ardeur (Fr.).
  Feuerig (Ger.).
First Part or Voice.
  Primo (It.).
  Premier (Fr.).
  Erste (Ger.).

Flowing.
  Scorrendo (It.).
Forcibly.
  Con forza (It.).
  Avec force (Fr.).
  Mit Kraft ; Kräftig (Ger.).
Forcing.
  Forzando ; Sforzando ; Sforzato (It.).
From.
  Da (It.).
From the Beginning.
  Da capo (It.).
  Vom Anfang (Ger.).
From the Sign.
  Dal segno (It.).
From the Beginning to the Sign.
  Da capo al segno (It.)
From the Beginning to the End.
  Da capo al fine (It.).
Furious.
  Furioso ; Con furia (It.).
  Wütend (Ger.).

G

G. Sol (It.). Sol (Fr.). G (Ger.).
G Flat. Sol bemolle (It.). Sol bémol (Fr.). Ges (Ger.).
G Sharp. Sol diesis (It.). Sol diése (Fr.). Gis (Ger.).
G Major. Sol maggiore (It.). Sol majeur (Fr.). G dur (Ger.).
G Minor. Sol minore (It.). Sol mineur (Fr.). G moll (Ger.).
Gay.
  Giojoso (It.).
  Gai (Fr.).
  Fröhlich ; Heiter ; Munter (Ger.).
Gondola Song.
  Gondoliera (It.).
  Gondellied (Ger.).
" Going."
  Andante (It.).
  Gehend (Ger.).
Graceful.
  Grazioso ; Con grazia (It.).
  Avec grace (Fr.).
  Lieblich (Ger.).
Gradual. See *By Degrees.*
Grand.
  Grandioso ; Nobile (It.).
  Grand (Fr.).
  Erhaben (Ger.).
Growing Faster.
  Accelerando ; Calcando ; Pressante ; Pressando il tempo ; Ravvivando il tempo (It.).
  En serrant ; Pressez (Fr.).
  Belebend ; Eilend ; Drängend ; Treibend (Ger.).

Growing Louder.
Crescendo; Piu forte (It.).
Anwachsend; Gesteigert; Zunehmend (Ger.).

Growing Softer.
Decrescendo; Diminuendo; Diluendo; Perdendo; Perdendosi (It.).
Abnehmend; Abschwellend (Ger.).

Growing Slower.
Rallentando; Ritenuto; Ritardando; Relasciando; Rimettendo; Ritenendo; Slargando; Slentando; Stiracchiato; Stirato; Trattenuto (It.).
Schleppend; Verweilend; Zögernd; Zurückhaltend (Ger.).

Growing Slower and Softer. See *Dying Away*.

Growing Louder and Faster.
Stringendo; Incalzando (It.).

H

Half.
Mezzo (It.).
Demi (Fr.).
Halb (Ger.).

Hastening. See *Growing Faster*.

Heartfelt.
Affetuoso; Con affetto (It.).
Herzlich; Innig (Ger.).

Held Back.
Ritenuto (It.).
Retenu (Fr.).
Zurückhaltend (Ger.).

Held, Held Down.
Tenuto (It.).

Hurrying. See *Growing Faster*.

I

Impetuous.
Impetuoso; Con impeto; Con slancio; Smanioso; Smaniante (It.).
Ungestüm (Ger.).

In Haste.
Con fretta (It.).

In the Same Manner.
Simile (It.).

In the Same Time.
L'istesso tempo (It.).
Au même temps (Fr.).
Dasselbe Zeitmass (Ger.).

In Time.
A tempo (It.).

In the Previous Time.
A tempo primo (It.).
In vorigem Zeitmass (Ger.).

Increasing. See *Growing Faster; Growing Louder; Growing Softer; Growing Slower*.

J

Jestingly.
Scherzando (It.).
Launig (Ger.).

Joyously, Jubilant.
Giojoso; Giubiloso (It.).
Fröhlich; Freudenvoll; Jubelnd (Ger.).

L

Lamenting.
Piangendo; Lamentoso (It.)

Left Hand.
Mano sinistra (It.).
Main gauche (Fr.).
Linke Hand (Ger.).

Less.
Meno (It.).

Lightly.
Leggiero; Con legerezza (It.)

Little by Little. See *By Degrees*.

Lively. See *Animated*.

Longing.
Desiderio (con) (It.).
Sehnsucht (mit) (Ger.).

Loud.
Forte (It.).
Fort (Fr.).
Stark (Ger.).

Louder.
Piu forte (It.).
Plus fort (Fr.).
Stärker (Ger.).

Loud, Always.
Sempre forte (It.).
Toujours fort (Fr.).
Immer stark (Ger.).

Loud as Possible.
Forte possibile; Con tutta forza (It.).
Avec toute force (Fr.).
Stark wie möglich (Ger.).

Lullaby. See *Cradle Song*.

M

Majestic.
Maestoso; Pomposo (It.).
Majestique (Fr.).
Majestätisch (Ger.).

Many-voiced.
Mehrstimmig (Ger.).

Marked. See *Accented*.

Mark (Accent) the Melody.
Ben marcato la melodia, or il canto (It.)

March.
Marcia (It.).
Marche (Fr.).
Marsch (Ger.).

Melody.
Melodia; Canto (It.).
Mélodie; Chant (Fr.).
Melodie (Ger.).

Moderate (in tempo).
Moderato (It.).
Mässig; Gemässigt (Ger.).

More.
  Più (It.).
  Plus (Fr.).
  Mehr (Ger.).
Motion, Faster.
  Plus vite (Fr.).
Motion, More.
  Più moto (It.).
Much.
  Molto (It.).
  Bien (Fr.).
  Viel (Ger.).

N
Night-piece.
  Notturno (It.).
  Nocturne (Fr.).
  Nachtstück (Ger.).
Not so Fast.
  Meno mosso (It.).
  Nicht so schnell (Ger.).
Not too Fast.
  Non troppo allegro, or Presto ma non tanto (It.).
  Nicht zu schnell (Ger.).

O
Obliged, Indispensable.
  Obbligato (It.).
  Obligé (Fr.).
Of.
  Di (It.).
  De (Fr.).
  Von (Ger.).
Or, Otherwise.
  Ossia; Oppure; Ovvero (It.).

P
Passionate.
  Passionato; Appassionato (It.).
  Passioné (Fr.).
  Leidenschaftlich (Ger.).
Pastoral.
  Pastorale (It.).
  Pastoral (Fr.).
  Pastoral (Ger.).
Pathetic.
  Patetico (It.).
  Pathetique (Fr.).
  Pathetisch (Ger.).
Piece.
  Pezzo (It.).
  Morceau (Fr.).
  Stück (Ger.).
Placid.
  Placido (It.).
  Tranquille (Fr.).
  Ruhig (Ger.).
Plaintive.
  Lamentando; Dolendo; Dolente; Doloroso; Con dolore; Flebile; Piangendo (It.).
  Avec doleur; Plaintif (Fr.).
  Klagend; Traurig (Ger.).

Playful.
  Giocoso; Scherzoso; Scherzando (It.).
  Plaisant; Avec plaisanterie (Fr.).
  Spielend; Scherzhaft; Leichtfertig (Ger.).
Possible.
  Possibile (It.).
  Possible (Fr.).
  Möglich (Ger.).
Prayer.
  Preghiera (It.).
  Prière (Fr.).
  Gebet (Ger.).
Pressing (the tempo). See *Growing Faster.*
Pronounced.
  Ben pronunciato; Ben marcato (It.).
  Bien prononcé; Bien marqué (Fr.).
  Sehr markiert (Ger.).
Psalm.
  Salmo (It.).
  Psaume (Fr.).
  Psalm (Ger.).

Q
Quiet. See *Placid.*

R
Rapid.
  Rapido; Celere; Veloce (It.).
  Rapide; Avec célérité; Vite (Fr.).
  Schnell; Geschwind; Rasch (Ger.).
Rather.
  Quasi (It.).
  Etwas (Ger.).
Rather Fast.
  Quasi presto (It.).
  Etwas rasch (Ger.).
Religious.
  Religioso; Devoto (It.).
  Dévot (Fr.).
  Religiös (Ger.).
Right Hand.
  Mano destra (It.).
  Main droite (Fr.).
  Rechte Hand (Ger.).

S
Sad. See *Plaintive.*
Second.
  Secondo (It.).
  Second (Fr.).
  Zweite (Ger.).
Singing.
  Cantando; Cantabile (It.).
  Chantant (Fr.).
  Singend (Ger.).
Slow.
  Lento; Adagio (It.).
  Lent (Fr.).
  Langsam (Ger.).
Slower.
  Più lento; Meno mosso (It.).
  Plus lent (Fr.).
  Langsamer (Ger.).

Slurred, Smooth.
　Legato; Portamento (It.).
　Lié (Fr.).
　Gebunden (Ger.)
Soft.
　Piano; Dolce (It.).
　Doux (Fr.).
　Leise; Schwach (Ger.).
Softer.
　Meno forte; Piu piano (It.).
　Plus doux (Fr.).
　Schwächer (Ger.).
Solemn.
　Solenne (It.).
　Solemnel (Fr.).
　Feierlich (Ger.).
Somewhat. See *Rather.*
Song
　Canto (It.).
　Chant (Fr.).
　Gesang; Lied (Ger.).
Sorrowful. See *Plaintive.*
Sparkling.
　Brillante; Scintillante (It.).
　Brillant; Scintillant (Fr.).
　Funkelnd (Ger.).
Spirit, Spirited.
　Con spirito; Con brio (It).
　Avec âme (Fr.).
　Mit Geist; Geistlich (Ger.).
Still, Yet.
　Ancora (It.).
　Encore (Fr.).
　Noch (Ger.).
Still Faster.
　Ancor piu mosso (It.).
　Encore plus vite (Fr.).
　Noch geschwinder (Ger.).
Sustained.
　Sostenuto (It.).
　Soutenu (Fr.).
　Getragen (Ger.).
Sweet.
　Dolce; Amabile (It.).
　Doux (Fr.).
　Süss; Lieblich (Ger.).
Swift. See *Rapid.*

T
Taste.
　Con gusto; Gustoso (It.).
　Avec goût (Fr.).
　Mit Geschmack (Ger.).
Tearfully.
　Lagrimando (It.). See *Plaintive.*
Tenderly.
　Tenerosa; Con affetto (It.).
　Tendre (Fr.).
　Zärtlich (Ger.).
Thoughtful.
　Pensieroso (It.).
　Pensif (Fr.).
　Tiefsinnig (Ger.).

To.
　A; Ad (It.).
To the.
　Al; Alla (It.).
Too.
　Troppo (It.).
　Trop (Fr.).
　Zu (Ger.).
Too Slow, Not.
　Non troppo lento (It.).
　Pas trop lent (Fr.).
　Nicht zu langsam (Ger.).
Tranquil. See *Placid.*
Trembling.
　Tremolo; Tremolando (It.).
　Tremblement; Balancement (Fr.).
　Bebung; Zitternd (Ger.).
Tune. See *Song.*
Twice as Fast.
　Doppio movimento (It.).

U
Undulating.
　Ondeggiante (It.). See *Tremolo.*

V
Very.
　Molto; Assai (It.).
　Très (Fr.).
　Sehr (Ger.).
Very Fast.
　Allegro assai (It.).
　Très vite (Fr.).
　Sehr rasch (Ger.).
Vivacious. See *Animated.*
Voice.
　Voce (It.).
　Voix (Fr.).
　Stimme (Ger.).

W
Wailing. See *Plaintive.*
Warmly.
　Con calore (It.).
　Avec chaleur (Fr.).
　Feurig (Ger.).
Wavering. See *Trembling.*
Well.
　Ben; Bene (It.).
　Bien (Fr.).
　Wohl; Gut (Ger.).
Whim.
　Ghiribizzo; Capriccio (It.).
　Caprice (Fr.).
　Grille (Ger.).
With.
　Con; Col; Colla (It.).
　Avec (Fr.).
　Mit (Ger.).
Without Growing Slower.
　Senza rallentare (It.).
　Sans ralentir (Fr.).
　Ohne Zurückhaltung (Ger.).

ALPHABETICAL LIST OF THE MOST CELEBRATED OPERA COMPOSERS, WITH THE TITLES OF THEIR BEST-KNOWN WORKS.

Many names of operas will be found that are almost unknown in America, but are still performed in Europe. Some are given because they have a historical interest. Complete lists are not given, except in the case of the great masters; in other cases only those works that still keep the stage are given.

Adam.
Postillon de Longjumeau (*pos-tee-yon de long-zhu-mo*).
Le Chalet.
Le Brasseur de Preston.
Roi d'Yvetot.
Cagliostro.
Giselle.

Auber.
Le Maçon.
La Muette de Portici (Massaniello) (*la muette de por-tee-chee*).
Fra Diavolo.
Le Domino Noir (The Black Domino).
Lestocq.
Les Diamants de la Couronne (Crown Diamonds).
Le Cheval de Bronze (The Bronze Horse).

Balfe.
Bohemian Girl (La Zingara).
Satanella (Power of Love).
Rose of Castile.
Siege of Rochelle.
Puritan's Daughter.
The Talisman.

Barnett, John.
The Mountain Sylph.

Beethoven.
Fidelio (first called Leonora). The original German title is Fidelio oder die eheliche Liebe (Fidelio or Conjugal Love).

Bellini.
Norma.
Capuletti e Montecchi.
La Sonnambula.
I Puritani.
Il Pirata.
Beatrice di Tenda.
La Straniera.

Benedict.
Gypsies' Warning.
Brides of Venice.
Crusaders.
Lily of Killarney.

Berlioz.
Benvenuto Cellini (*ben-veh-noo'-to chel-lec'-nee*).
Béatrice et Bénédict.

Bishop, H. R.
Knight of Snowdon.
Guy Mannering.
Clari. The song, "Home, Sweet Home," is from this opera.

Bizet.
Carmen.
Pearl Fishers.
Vasco di Gama.
Fair Maid of Perth.

Boieldieu.
La Dame Blanche (The White Lady). The story is taken from Sir Walter Scott's novel, "The Monastery."
Chaperon Rouge (Red Riding Hood).
Calif of Bagdad.

Boito.
Mefistofele.
Boito is better known as the author of the librettos of several of Verdi's later operas.

Caccini.
Daphne (the first opera composed).
Euridice (*eu-ree-dee-cheh*). These operas were produced in Florence at the beginning of the 17th century.

Cherubini.
Lodoiska.
Les Deux Journées (*leh doo zhour-neh*) (The Two Days).
Wasserträger (The Water-carriers).
Faniska.

Cimarosa.
Il Matrimonio Segreto. The only one of his seventy-six operas remembered.

Clay, F.
Princess Toto.
Don Quixote.

Dalayrac.
Le Corsaire.
Fanchette.
Nina.
Azémia.

Damrosch, W.
The Scarlet Letter.

David, F.
La Perle du Brésil.
Lalla Rookh.
Le Saphir.

Delibes.
    Jean de Nivelle.
    Lakmé.
Donizetti.
    Anna Bolena.
    Lucia di Lammermoor (*loo-che-a*).
    La Favorita.
    Figlia del Regimento (Daughter of the Regiment).
    Lucrezia Borgia.
    Linda di Chamounix (*sha'-moo-nee*).
    Don Pasquale.
    L'Elisire d'Amore (*eh-lee-see-reh d'ah-mo-reh*) (The Elixir of Love).
Dvorak.
    Manda.
    Dimitrij (*dee-mee-tree'*).
    Der Bauer ein Schelm.
    Der König und der Köhler.
    Die Dickschädel.
Flotow.
    Martha.
    Stradella.
    Indra.
    L'Ombre.
Gevaert.
    Georgette.
    Le Billet de Marguerite.
    Quentin Durward.
    Château Trompette.
    Le Capitaine Henriot.
Glinka.
    La Vie Pour le Tzar (Life for the Czar).
    Russlau et Ludmilla.
Gluck.
    Orpheus.
    Alcestis.
    Iphigénie en Tauride (*if-ee-zheh-nee ong taw-reed*).
    Antigone.
Goldmark.
    La Reine de Saba (*la rane de saba*).
Gossec.
    Les Pêcheurs (*leh peh-shoor*).
Gounod.
    Faust.
    Mereille.
    Cinq Mars.
    Romeo et Juliette.
    Polyeucte.
    La Reine de Saba (Queen of Sheba).
Gretry.
    Richard. The only one now performed of the fifty he wrote.
Gyrowetz.
    Agnes Sorel.
    Die Prüfung (The Trial).
    Der Augenarzt (The Oculist).
Halévy.
    La Juive.
    L'Éclair.
    La Reine de Chypre (*la rane de keepr*).

Händel.
    Rinaldo.
    Radamisto.
    Rodelinda, etc. Never performed now; chiefly remembered as the source of many beautiful songs.
Hérold.
    Zampa.
    Pré aux Clercs.
Humperdinck.
    Hänsel und Gretel.
    Children of the King.
Joncières.
    Dimitri.
Kreutzer, C.
    Das Nachtlager in Granada (Siege of Granada).
Kücken.
    Die Flucht nach der Schweiz (Flight into Switzerland).
    Der Prätendent (The Pretender).
Lassen.
    Le Roi Edgard ⎫
    Frauenlob   ⎬ Produced in Weimar under Liszt's direction.
    Der Gefangene ⎭
Lecocq.
    Fleur de Thé.
    Fille de Madame Angot.
    Giroflé Girofla.
Leoncavallo.
    I Pagliacci (*e pal-yatch'-ee*) (The Mountebanks).
Lortzing.
    Czar und Zimmermann.
    Der Waffenschmidt (*waffen-schmit*).
    Undine.
Macfarren, G. A.
    Don Quixote.
    Robin Hood.
    Helvellyn.
Marschner.
    The Vampyre.
    Hans Heiling.
    Ivanhoe (The Templar and the Jewess).
Mascagni.
    Cavalleria Rusticana (*cah-vah-leh-ree'-a rus-tee-cah'-nah*) (Rustic Chivalry).
Massé.
    Galathée (*gah-lah-teh*).
    Les Noces de Jeannette (*leh noce de zhan-net*) (Jeannette's Marriage).
    Paul et Virginie.
Massenet.
    Roi de Lahore.
    Manon.
    Le Cid (*le thid*).
    Don César de Bazan.
Mehul.
    Two Blind Men of Toledo.
    Joseph.
    Le Jeune Henri.

Mendelssohn.
Lorelei (unfinished).
Camacho's Wedding.
Heimkehr aus der Fremde. Known as Son and Stranger in English.

Mercadante.
Il Giuramento (*eel ju-rah-mento*).
Elisa e Claudio.

Meyerbeer.
Les Huguenots.
L'Africaine.
L'Etoile du Nord (Star of the North).
Le Prophète.
Dinorah.
Robert le Diable.

Monteverdi.
Arianna. Monteverdi was the second in the succession of opera composers, and the father of the Italian school of opera.

Mozart.
Don Giovanni, or Il Dissoluto Punito.
Le Nozze di Figaro (*leh not-zeh dee fig'-ah-ro*) (The Marriage of Figaro).
Idomeneo (*e-do-meh-neh'-o*).
Die Entführung aus dem Serail (*dee entfeer-unk ous dehm seh-rahl*) (The Escape from the Seraglio).
Cosi fan Tutti (German title, Weibertreue).
Il Flauto Magico (German title, Zauberflöte). Mozart was the author of a large number of operas and operettas, but this list includes all that are now performed.

Nicolai.
The Merry Wives of Windsor.
The Templar.

Offenbach.
Barbe Bleue.
La Belle Hélène.
Genevieve de Brabant.
Grande Duchesse de Gérolstein.
Perichole. And about seventy others. The above list gives the titles of those that were most popular—a popularity that is now rapidly on the wane, and deservedly so.

Pacini, G.
Medea.
Saffo.

Paisiello.
La Molinara.

Paladilhe.
Suzanne.

Piccinni.
Dido.
Atys.

Pepusch.
Beggar's Opera. Libretto by the poet Gay, written as a travesty of the Italian opera of the 18th century.

Ponchielli.
La Gioconda (*jo-con'-dah*).
Marion Delorme.
Promessi Sposi (*promes-see spo-see*).

Planquette.
Les Cloches de Corneville (Chimes of Normandy).

Ricci.
Crispino e la Comare (*cris-pee'-no eh lah co-mah'-reh*) (The Cobbler and the Fairy).

Rossini.
Barbier de Seville.
Cenerentola (*cheh-neh-ren'-to-lah*) (Cinderella).
La Gazza Ladra (*gatza lah-dra*) (Maid and Magpie).
Guillaume Tell.
Semiramide (*seh-mee-rah'-mee-deh*). Of his large number of operas these are the only ones that have kept the stage; especially is this true of William Tell, Barber of Seville, and Semiramide.

Rousseau.
Le Devin du Village (The Village Priest).

Rubinstein.
The Demon.
Nero.
Tower of Babel.
Paradise Lost.

Salieri.
Tarare (*tah-rah'-reh*).

Saint-Saëns.
Samson and Delilah.
Etienne Marcel.

Schubert.
Rosamund.
Teufelslustschloss (Devil's Country Seat).
Alfonso and Estrella.
Fierabras (*fee-eh-rah-bras*). In addition to these, Schubert left many operas in a partly finished state.

Schumann.
Genoveva (*geh-no-veh-vah*).

Spohr.
Faust.
Jessonda.
Zemira ed Azor.

Spontini.
Olympia.
Vestale.
Fernando Cortez.

Sullivan, A. S.
Mikado.
Pinafore.
Patience.
Pirates of Penzance.
Sorcerer.
Iolanthe.

Suppe, F. von.
  Fatinitza.
  Boccaccio (*bok-katch'-ee-o*).

Thalberg.
  Christina ⎫ Both failures.
  Florinda ⎭

Thomas, Ambroise.
  Mignon.
  Hamlet.
  Francesca de' Rimini (*fran-ches'-ka deh ree'-mee-nee*).

Tschaikowsky.
  Mazeppa.
  Maid of Orleans.

Verdi.
  Ernani.
  Rigoletto.
  Trovatore (*tro-vah-to'-reh*).
  Un Ballo in Maschera (*mas-keh'-rah*) (Masked Ball).
  Don Carlos.
  Sicilian Vespers.
  Aida (*ah-ee'-dah*).
  Otello.
  Falstaff.

Wagner.
  Rienzi (*ree-ent'-see*) (The Last of the Tribunes).
  Der fliegende (*flee'-gen-deh*) Holländer (Flying Dutchman).

Wagner (*continued*).
  Tannhäuser und der Sängerkrieg auf der Wartburg (The Singers' Contest on the Wartburg).
  Lohengrin.
  The Nibelungen (*nee'-beh-lung-en*) Ring Series:
    Part I. Das Rheingold.
    Part II. Die Walküre (*val-kee-reh*).
    Part III. Siegfried.
    Part IV. Die Götterdämmerung.
  Tristan und Isolde.
  Die Meistersinger von Nürnberg.
  Parsifal, ein Bühnenweihfestspiel (Stage-consecrating Festival-play).

Wallace.
  Maritana.
  Lurline.

Weber.
  Der Freischütz (*dare frigh-sheetz*).
  Euryanthe (*u-ree-an'-the*).
  Oberon.
  Several fragments of other operas, and pianoforte scores of two — Silvana and Abu Hassan—are in existence.

Winter.
  Maria von Montalban.
  Das unterbrochene Opferfest (Interrupted Sacrifice).

APPENDIX.
ADDITIONAL PROPER NAMES.

Adamowski, Timothee (*a-dam-ŏv-skee*). Violinist; Poland. B. 1858.
Allegri, Gregario (*al-leh-gree*). Composer; Italy. B. 1584; d. 1602.
Allitsen, Frances (*allit-sen*). Composer; England.
Arenski, A. S. (*ah-ren-skee*). Composer; Russia. B. 1862; d. 1906.
Badarczewska, Thekla (*ba-dark-zef-ska*). Composer; Poland. B. 1838; d. 1862.
Banister, H. C. Pedagog; England. B. 1831; d. 1897.
Bantock, Granville. Composer; England. B. 1868.
Beach, Mrs. H. H. A. (Amy M. Cheney). Composer; U. S. A. B. 1867.
Buxtehude, Dietrich (*bux-těh-hov-dah*). Organist; Denmark. B. 1639; d. 1707.
Calvé, Emma (*cal-veh*). Soprano; France. B. 1864 (?).
Campanari, Giuseppe (*cam-pa-näh-ree*). Baritone; Italy. B. 1860.
Caruso, Enrico (*en-ree-ko ca-rōo-so*). Tenor; Italy. B. 1873.
Cavalieri, Emilio del (*cah-vah-lee-ĕh-ree*). Composer; Italy. B. 1550; d. 1599.
Chabrier, Alexis E. (*sha-bree-eh*). Composer; France. B. 1842.
Charpentier, Gustave (*shar-pon-tu-eh*). Composer; France. B. 1860.
Coleridge-Taylor, Samuel. Anglo-African composer; England. B. 1875.
Cornelius, Peter. Composer; Germany. B. 1824.
Czibulka, Alphons (*chee-bŭl-ka*). Composer; Hungary. B. 1844; d. 1894.
Damrosch, Frank. German-American Teacher; Germany. B. 1859.
Debussy, Achille Claude (*deh-boŭs-see*). Composer; France. B. 1862.
Delius, Frederick. Composer; England. B. 1863.
Denza, Luigi (*dent-sa*). Composer; Italy. B. 1846.
Deppe, Ludwig (*dep-pah*). Pedagog; Germany. B. 1828; d. 1890.
Dunstable, John of. Composer; England. B. 1380 (?); d. 1453.
Elgar, Sir Edward William. Composer; England. B. 1857.

Elman, Mischa. Violinist; Russia. B. 1891.
Engelmann, Hans. Composer; Germany. B. 1872.
Fielitz, Alex. von. Composer; Germany. B. 1860.
Franck, Cesar. Composer; Belgium. B. 1822; d. 1890.
Gabrilowitsch, Ossip (*ga-bree-lo-vĭtch*). Pianist; Russia. B. 1878.
Gadski, Johanna E. A. (*gádskee*). Soprano; Germany. B. 1871.
Geibel, Adam. Composer; Germany. B. 1855.
German, Edward. Composer; England. B. 1862.
Glazounow, Alexander (*gla-zov-nov*). Composer; Russia. B. 1865.
Godowsky, Leopold (*go-dŏw-skee*). Pianist and composer. B. 1870.
Guido d'Arezzo (*gwee-dod'ah-ritz-so*). Theorist; Italy. B. 995 (?); d. 1050 (?).
Hadley, Henry K. Composer; U. S. A. B. 1871.
Herbert, Victor. Composer; Ireland. B. 1859.
Holbrook, Joseph C. Composer; England. B. 1878.
Holmes, Augusta Mary. Composer; France. B. 1847; d. 1903.
Humperdinck, Engelbert (*hum-per-dink*). Composer; Germany. B. 1854.
Kubelik, Johann (*koo-beh-lik*). Violinist; Bohemia. B. 1880.
Lack, Theodore. Composer; France. B. 1846.
Lehmann, Lilli (*leh-man*). Soprano; Germany. B. 1848.
Lehmann, Liza. Composer; England. B. 1858.
Lemare, Edwin H. Organist; England. B. 1865.
Leoncavallo, Ruggiero (*leh-on-ca-vallo*). Composer; Italy. B. 1858.
Mascagni, Pietro (*mas-cán-yee*). Composer; Italy. B. 1863.
Melba, Nellie. Soprano; Australia. B. 1859.
Nevin, Ethelbert. Composer; U. S. A. B. 1862; d. 1901.

APPENDIX (*Continued*).

Nikisch, Arthur. Conductor; Hungary. B. 1855.
Norris, Homer A. Composer; U. S. A. B. 1860.
Perosi, Don Lorenzo (*peh-ro-see*). Composer; Italy. B. 1872.
Powell, Maud. Violinist; U. S. A. B. 1868.
Puccini, Giacomo (*put-chee-nee jah-co-mo*). Composer; Italy. B. 1858.
Rachmaninoff, Sergei. Composer; Russia. B. 1873.
Reger, Max (*reh-gehr*). Composer; Germany. B. 1873.
Rimski-Korsakoff, Nikolas A. (*rimskee-kòr-sa-koff*). Composer; Russia. B. 1844.
Safonoff, Wassili. Conductor; Russia. B. 1852.
Sauer, Emil. Pianist; Germany. B. 1862.
Schradieck, Henry (*shrah-deck*). Violinist; Germany. B. 1846.
Schumann-Heink, Ernestine. Contralto; Germany. B. 1861.

Schytte, Ludwig T. (*skit-teh*). Pianist and composer; Denmark. B. 1850.
Scriabine, Alexander (*skree-a-bee-neh*). Pianist; Russia. B. 1872.
Sgambati, Giovanni (*sgam-bàh-tee*). Pianist; B. 1843.
Sibelius, Jean (*see-bèe-lee-us*). Composer; Finland. B. 1865.
Sinding, Christian. Composer; Norway. B. 1856.
Smith, Wilson G. Composer; U. S. A. B. 1855.
Sousa, John Philip. Composer; U. S. A. B. 1854.
Strauss, Richard (*strows*). Composer; Germany. B. 1864.
Szumowska, Antoinette (Szumowska-Adamowski) (*shoo-mor-ska*). Pianist; Poland. B. 1868.
Tetrazzini, Luisa (*te-traht-zèe-nee*). Soprano; Italy. B. 1874.
Van der Stucken, Frank. Composer; U. S. A. B. 1858.

www.ingramcontent.com/pod-product-compliance
Lightning Source LLC
Chambersburg PA
CBHW022140160426
43197CB00009B/1367